M000275573

Thomas Jefferson's Military Academy

Jeffersonian America

Jan Ellen Lewis, Peter S. Onuf, and James Horn, Editors

THOMAS JEFFERSON'S MILITARY ACADEMY

Founding West Point

EDITED BY

Robert M. S. McDonald

University of Virginia Press ■ *Charlottesville and London*

University of Virginia Press

Printed in the United States of America on acid-free paper
First published 2004

1 3 5 7 9 8 6 4 2

LIBRARY OF CONGRESS CATALOGING-IN-PUBLICATION DATA
Thomas Jefferson's military academy : founding West Point / edited by Robert M.S. McDonald.
p. cm. — (Jeffersonian America)
Includes bibliographical references and index.
ISBN 0-8139-2298-4 (cloth : acid-free paper)
1. United States Military Academy—History—19th century. 2. Jefferson, Thomas, 1743–1826—Contributions in military education. I. McDonald, Robert M. S., 1970– II. Series.
U410.L1T49 2004
355'.0071'173—dc22

2004008745

Detail from *View of West Point Looking South* by George Catlin, oil on canvas, circa 1828. (WEST POINT MUSEUM ART COLLECTION)

For the Corps

Whatever enables us to go to war, secures our peace.

—Thomas Jefferson to James Monroe, 11 July 1790

Contents

List of Abbreviations

AHP — Harold C. Syrett and Jacob E. Cooke, eds. *The Papers of Alexander Hamilton.* 27 vols. New York, 1961–87.

AJL — Lester J. Cappon, ed. *The Adams-Jefferson Letters: The Complete Correspondence between Thomas Jefferson and Abigail and John Adams.* Chapel Hill, N.C., 1959.

Ford — Paul Leicester Ford, ed. *The Writings of Thomas Jefferson.* 10 vols. New York, 1892–99.

JER — *Journal of the Early Republic*

L&B — Andrew A. Lipscomb and Albert Ellery Bergh, eds. *The Writings of Thomas Jefferson.* 20 vols. Washington, D.C., 1903–4.

Lib. Cong. — Library of Congress, Washington, D.C.

Malone — Dumas Malone. *Jefferson and His Time.* 6 vols. Boston, 1948–81.

TJ — Thomas Jefferson

TJP — Julian P. Boyd et al., eds. *The Papers of Thomas Jefferson.* 30 vols. to date. Princeton, N.J., 1950–.

TJW — Merrill D. Peterson, ed. *Thomas Jefferson: Writings.* New York, 1984.

USMA Lib. — United States Military Academy Library, West Point, N.Y.

WJA — Charles Francis Adams, ed. *The Works of John Adams.* 10 vols. Boston, 1850–56.

WMQ — *William and Mary Quarterly*

Preface

James Fenimore Cooper was raised to despise Thomas Jefferson, but his 1823 visit to the United States Military Academy nearly changed his mind. Soon after his arrival at West Point, the novelist wrote, he encountered "two or three of the intelligent men" who inhabited the place. They insisted that he follow them to the library to view Thomas Sully's new portrait of Jefferson, commissioned two years earlier by faculty and cadets to honor the founder of their institution. Although Cooper "would have gone twice as far to see the picture of almost any other man," he complied.

He was stunned. The portrait possessed "a dignity, a repose," and "a loveliness" that, even though he had viewed "hundreds of celebrated ones both here and in Europe," he had never before witnessed. Sully's depiction hinted at none of the radicalism and "political heresy" that Cooper had ascribed to the third president. "I saw nothing but Jefferson, standing before me," Cooper recalled, and not, as he had imagined, in "slovenly attire" but as "a gentleman, appearing in all republican simplicity, with a grace and ease on the canvas, that to me seemed unrivalled." Art so compelling, he thought, could not be artifice: "It has really shaken my opinion of Jefferson."[1]

The discontinuity between Cooper's expectations and observations echoed the surprise sometimes registered by individuals—friends and foes alike—who encountered Jefferson himself. When, while suffering from one of his chronic headaches, Secretary of State Jefferson testified before a congressional committee, Pennsylvania senator William Maclay, who tended to share his political views, expressed disappointment that he displayed a "laxity of Manner" and "rambling Vacant look" contradicting the "firm collected deportment which I expected." Washington socialite Margaret Bayard Smith, when first introduced to Jefferson in 1800, possessed "previously conceived ideas of the coarseness and vulgarity of his appearance and manners and was therefore equally awed and surprised" to encounter a man "whose deportment was so dignified and gentlemanly, whose language was so refined, whose voice was so gentle, and whose countenance was so benignant." Jefferson, she re-

WEST POINT MUSEUM ART COLLECTION

Thomas Jefferson by Thomas Sully, oil on canvas, 1822.

called, "at once unlocked my heart." A Federalist newspaper, however, in 1802 reported that visitors to the Executive Mansion often encountered a shabby man who appeared to be a gardener or coachman. To their "astonishment" he would then introduce himself as the president.[2]

To these moments of dissonance—these instances when observers of Jefferson expected more (or less) than met their eyes—we can add his creation, through the 1802 Military Peace Establishment Act, of the United States Military Academy. Few could have anticipated such a move. In 1793 Jefferson had opposed a Federalist proposal to create a national military school and as recently as 1799 had registered his preference "for relying, for internal defense," not on a professional army during times of peace but "on our militia solely, till actual invasion." Even his 1802 law suggests a paradox, for in it he not only founded the academy but also reduced the size of the army.[3] For decades the small number of historians who glanced at his establishment of West Point described it as "ironical," given his reluctance to go to war and his penchant for an army on the cheap, as a "Hamiltonian institution" that contradicted his commitment to states' rights (as well as state militias) and the strict construction of the Constitution, which said nothing of such a school. Most recently, Karl-Friedrich Walling, a scholar of Alexander Hamilton's hawkish advocacy of American military prowess, noted that "after 1800 Hamilton and Jefferson slowly and reluctantly switched roles." Hamilton, suddenly an outsider, began to call for safeguards against potential engines of political tyranny, while Jefferson, who now embraced a "more responsible" defense program, "in 1802 . . . signed into law a bill establishing an American military academy."[4]

Did Jefferson's establishment at West Point of a school for soldiers really signal a shift in his views? In 1803 he continued to maintain that "peace is our passion." Yet a dozen years earlier—when by some accounts he stood most inclined to turn the other cheek—he asserted that "whatever enables us to go to war, secures our peace."[5] A constant for Jefferson appears to have been a disdain for military entanglements. James Madison, his closest friend and lifelong political collaborator, explained that "of all the enemies to public liberty war is, perhaps, the most to be dreaded, because it comprises and develops the germ of every other." International strife, after all, was "the parent of armies," the costly institutions that spawned "debts and taxes" and throughout history had served as "the known instruments for bringing the many under the few."[6]

Expensive wars, as Madison suggested, could lead to oppressive armies.

But perhaps Jefferson's sponsorship of West Point did less to signal a departure from this fear than to affirm a faith that an effective military establishment, properly led by enlightened, liberty-loving officers, could help to deter threats against America's government and—if this first mission failed—rebuff attacks on Americans' freedoms. Was Jefferson's academy somehow analogous to his controversial gunboats, the defensive craft for which the president who otherwise trimmed the navy's budget appropriated thousands of dollars in the belief that the citizen-sailors who piloted them would better repel—and less likely invite—foreign attacks than the large, professionally crewed, oceangoing navy envisioned by the Adams administration?[7] That is, did Jefferson, through the academy, somehow hope to reconcile republicanism and republican thrift with the costs of liberty's defense? Maybe, but the essays contained within this volume constitute an account of the academy's founding that goes beyond issues of military readiness and economy to consider the broader contexts within which the academy emerged and from which it developed.

The need for such a collection is apparent. A glance at Frank Shuffelton's meticulous and comprehensive annotated bibliography, now available on the Web, of the 4,000 books and articles (scholarly and otherwise) about Jefferson published between his 1826 death and 1997 points readers to only three works concerning West Point. The subject has attracted no more attention from writers than Jefferson and prairie dogs (also three entries), Jefferson and clocks (five entries), and Jefferson and wine (thirty-nine entries). Writers consider Jefferson and the University of Virginia, the other school he founded, in 135 essays and monographs.[8] If, in the relatively expansive world of Jefferson scholarship, this phenomenon suggests a somewhat surprising omission, then in the much more modest body of work on the history of West Point, it constitutes a gaping hole. The result is the sort of confusion exemplified by the recent assertion of former secretary of state Alexander M. Haig Jr., a member of West Point's class of 1947, that the famed superintendent Sylvanus Thayer—appointed as a cadet by Jefferson several years after the academy's founding—is "the Academy's founder."[9]

The longstanding inattention to Jefferson's role underscores the importance of Theodore Crackel's groundbreaking work on West Point's establishment as an institution for the education of officers. In the three studies cataloged by Shuffelton—a 1981 journal article as well as a 1985 dissertation that was revised and published in 1987 as *Mr. Jefferson's Army*—Crackel argues that, despite a long line of scholars claiming otherwise, "it was not armies *per se*" that Jefferson and other Republicans feared "but an army loyal to incorrect political principles." Jefferson envisioned the academy as one of several mechanisms through which he could transform the Federalist-leaning officer corps into a thoroughly republicanized (and Republicanized) cadre of men dedicated to the defense of the nation's Revolutionary ideals. He worked hard, Crackel contends, to appoint as cadets at West Point individuals who shared his political views. By the end of his presidency, Jefferson had not only republicanized but also expanded the army—and his eagerness to accomplish the second task suggests much about his success in accomplishing the first.[10]

These insights make way for a new set of questions about the Jeffersonian origins of the academy—questions the authors of the essays contained within this volume raise and to which they respond. Since Peter Onuf offers a powerfully synthetic summary of their work, only a brief synopsis is necessary. Between Onuf's introduction and Jean Yarbrough's wonderfully provocative afterword appear seven essays arranged in a rough chronology around three themes: first, the contexts that surrounded the emergence of Jefferson's academy; then, its possible (and possibly multiple) purposes; and, finally, its legacies.

Don Higginbotham, David Mayer, and Elizabeth Samet remind us just how bold the idea of a military academy must have seemed in 1802. As Higginbotham demonstrates in his study of "Military Education before West Point," the United States Military Academy possessed the potential to become a place of pedagogical innovation. Certainly it constituted a marked departure from the time-worn pattern established in Great Britain, where, despite advances on the European continent toward the development of formal institutions of military schooling, aspiring officers apprenticed themselves to experienced elders or engaged in the independent study of field manuals and other books relating to the art of war. If, however, in the Anglo-American context, West Point stood out as a significant development in the history of military education, in Europe it must have raised few eyebrows. There the sort of school called for by George Washington, intended to cement officers' loyalty to the national regime, or in 1802 approved by Jefferson—ostensibly as a training center for artillerists and engineers—had several counterparts.

Yet, as Mayer's essay points out, the fact that the academy's missions seemed so conventional allowed Jefferson to view it as a "Necessary and Proper" outgrowth of the national government's power to "raise and support Armies." Mayer contends that Jefferson's earlier opposition, on what he claimed were constitutional grounds, to Federalist plans for a military academy cannot be taken at face value: although oftentimes caricatured as a "strict constructionist," Jefferson stood willing to grant the national government expansive powers within its narrowly circumscribed purview. Since this clearly included the training of army officers, what explains his decision in 1793 to raise a constitutional roadblock? Put simply, Jefferson regarded a military academy as too important—and potentially too influential over the character of the nation's future military leaders—to be entrusted to his enemies.

In addition, the idea of such an institution struck many as out of step with the ideological imperatives of the American Revolution. Samet's essay describes the real suspicion with which thoughtful citizens well into the nineteenth century regarded would-be "Great Men and Embryo-Caesars." At a time when Jeffersonians claimed to exalt measures over men, the academy emerged as a foundry for the very sort of men most likely to earn hero status and therefore most capable of using their democratic fame for despotic purposes. Thus John Adams joined Jefferson in casting wary glances toward—and ultimately attempting to republicanize—the figures in arms who not only defended liberty but also loomed as its greatest potential enemies.

This suspicion, of course, had always been a component of the traditional republican critique of military establishments—as Crackel's earlier writings make clear. In this volume, however, Crackel's contention that Jefferson's creation of the academy should be read as an effort to republicanize the officer corps is reinforced by his essay exposing a parallel campaign directed toward the national government's Federalist-leaning civilian bureaucracy. Crackel points out that President Jefferson ignored neither the threats posed by renegade postmasters, judges, and other officeholders nor the positive roles to be played by faithful federal appointees, stationed in cities and towns throughout the Union, in securing his empire of liberty.

But Jefferson was fond of reminding correspondents that "light and liberty go together."[11] And Jennings Wagoner and Christine Coalwell McDonald make a powerful case that when the third president established the academy, he had more than narrowly political intentions. Their educational interpretation of the institution's purpose seeks to supplement but not to supplant Crackel's reading of available evidence. Jefferson, they note, selected cadets and faculty members not only on the basis of partisan loyalty but also for intellectual attainment and potential. He served as the perpetual patron of the United States Military Philosophical Society, a scientific group first convened by Jonathan Williams, a moderate Federalist whom he appointed as the academy's first superintendent. He even made suggestions about the composition of the library. He established the academy at a time when he found himself flush with ideas about education, including a proposal—which he championed—to establish a national university. Might the academy, which—as Mayer contends—was authorized by the Constitution, serve as the nucleus for such an institution, which Jefferson believed required the sanction of a constitutional amendment? The benefit of hindsight makes clear that if Jefferson ever harbored these hopes, he set himself up for disappointment. Wagoner and McDonald explain that his plans to establish a national university in the capital city, the place to which he also proposed to move the academy, went nowhere. Not until his twilight years, when he turned his attention toward the creation of the University of Virginia, did he succeed in establishing a school "on a plan so broad & liberal & *modern*."[12]

Meanwhile, according to Samuel Watson's account, such visions of grandeur limited Jefferson's legacy at West Point by fueling personal ambitions that impeded significant progress. Bad enough that Williams and Joseph Gardner Swift, the second superintendent, spent more time attempting to relocate the academy than they did improving its actual operations; even worse, Alden Partridge, Swift's successor, commenced a campaign to transform the institution through micromanagement. These men had all the best intentions for the academy, but what troubles Watson is that their actions hinged on egocentric notions of honor that flew in the face of the republican precept of selfless service.

Superintendent Thayer, who led the academy from 1817 to 1833, was altogether different. He worked to instill in the Corps of Cadets the same professional ethos that his own career exemplified—a guiding belief that truly honorable individuals stood willing to sacrifice their own interests to those of the nation. Watson, who borrows the words of Revolutionary patriot Benjamin Rush when he describes Thayer's project as an attempt to reconstruct as "Republican Machines" America's young military men, is well aware that Thayer challenged the Revolutionary—and Jeffersonian—concept of the citizen-soldier. Instead of upholding the traditional belief that those who serve in the army should view themselves merely as civilians in uniform, with civilian rights and interests, Thayer insisted that they see themselves as uniformed professionals who protected citizens' rights and projected their interests. Thanks to Thayer, members of the standing army that Jefferson sanctioned would render themselves safe for the Republic by sublimating their own Jeffersonian aspirations to those of their civilian counterparts.

The wedge that this drove between soldiers and citizens, I suggest in my own essay, contributed to the estrangement of Jefferson from the academy that he created. Unlike General Washington, the father of the country, and Colonel Thayer, who gained renown as the father of the academy, Citizen Jefferson was no military man. The third president seemed less than ideal as an institutional hero for this and for other reasons. His name was appropriated by Jacksonian Democrats, who many West Pointers resented, and southern secessionists, from whom West Point's leaders struggled to distance their institution. In addition, men such as Robert E. Lee, Winfield Scott, Elihu Root, and Theodore Roosevelt—all of whom had powerful West Point connections—held him up as an example of civilian foolishness. Only in the past fifty years has Jefferson begun to receive credit for creating the academy, and only in the past several years has that credit been substantial.

While my essay points toward several factors contributing to the reemergence of the academy's "Lost Founder," Jean Yarbrough's afterword hints at another. The values that Jefferson espoused and the virtues that he exemplified now resonate among members of the army officer corps at least as well as they do among civilian elites—if not more strongly. After all, as Yarbrough asserts, the nation's well-born—the people who comprise its unnatural aristocracy—in Jefferson's day dominated positions of military leadership but currently have little contact with West Point and Reserve Officers' Training Corps (ROTC) programs or the sacrifices demanded of military leaders. Some readers may disagree with elements of her argument and so may some of the contributors to this volume. Independence of mind has always animated the Jeffersonian spirit. Yet so has the idea that certain causes demand self-sacrifice. This is the point emphasized by Yarbrough, who agrees that Jefferson founded the academy to make the army more like America but contends that today he might wish to make America more like West Point.

If the tensions suggested by these essays discomfit modern-day Jeffersonians or those with more "military" mind-sets—groups drawn to this volume, perhaps, in search of more tidy explanations of the academy's origins—then the authors' interpretations have been true to life. After all, the qualities most essential to a "military academy"—especially a Jeffersonian one—are so oppositional that the concept can be said to constitute an oxymoron. While military training conditions young men (and now also young women) to obey authority, academic education provokes them to question it. The tensions between obedience and vigilance—or fidelity and skepticism—or selflessness and self-assertion—are at least as old as the Republic itself, and for two centuries the United States Military Academy has embraced them. It has continued to recognize—and its graduates have continued to embody—the imperative of self-discipline, a concept described more gently but more profoundly when, in the very last of his myriad letters, Jefferson prophesied that someday free and responsible individuals throughout the world would accept "the blessings and security of self-government."[13]

The authors of these essays first presented their research at a November 2001 conference on "Thomas Jefferson's Military Academy." Although it was organized by West Point's Department of History, each of the contributors—and most especially the ones on the faculty of the United States Military Academy—declares his or her scholarly independence in the production of this volume and joins in issuing the customary caveat that the opinions it expresses do not necessarily represent the views of the academy, the army, the Department of Defense, or the United States government. This fact makes all the more remarkable the tremendous support volunteered by the fine professionals who serve these instruments of the American people.

The conference was convened to help commemorate the bicentennial of Jefferson's 1802 establishment of the institution that has become something like the nation's alma mater—a school that helped to educate Nicholas P. Trist, Jefferson Davis, Edgar Allan Poe, Robert E. Lee, William Tecumseh Sherman, U. S. Grant, Philip Sheridan, John J. Pershing, Douglas MacArthur, George Patton, Dwight Eisenhower, Omar Bradley, Maxwell Taylor, William Westmoreland, and H. Norman Schwarzkopf. As such, the conference was an appropriately large enterprise, one that involved too many dedicated individuals to acknowledge in the book that their hard work helped to make possible.

Yet a few stand out. Colonel Robert Doughty, head of the United States Military Academy's Department of History, from the start gave this project his unwavering and enthusiastic support. So did Colonel (Retired) Judith Luckett and Colonel Gary Tocchet, who led the especially talented team of American historians who took charge of the planning and execution of the conference. Beatriz Villa, their remarkably proactive administrative assistant, and Major Kevin Murphy, the department's able executive officer, tamed paperwork, took care of important details, and finessed their way around potential crises great and small. As fonts of historical wisdom, West Point's Alan Aimone, Suzanne Christoff, and Steve Grove proved invaluable. Mike Moss and David Reel of the West Point Museum performed many favors, including the granting of permission to reproduce as cover art and illustrations works in the possession of the West Point Museum Art Collection of the United States Military Academy. Former cadets who now serve as army officers, such as Jefferson Bunce, Gina Fox, Andy Gordon, Phil Hensel, Aimee Ruscio, Andrew Salmo, and Ken Wainwright—and especially Caleb Cage, Adrienne Harrison, Brendan McShea, and Bill Rausch—provided cheerful assistance in numerous and important ways. Colonel Lance Betros and Lieutenant Colonel Dana Mangham made the most of opportunities to sustain the scholarly environment within which this collection took shape and moved forward toward publication.

Far from West Point, the wonderfully cooperative professionals associated with the University of Virginia Press rendered almost seamless the transition from manuscript to book. Richard Holway, who offered his help and sage advice throughout the process, deserves special mention. So do our anonymous reviewers, who provided thoughtful recommendations and careful critiques.

Of the individuals whose efforts made possible this volume, the contributions of one proved particularly invaluable. A. Ross Wollen, a member of West Point's class of 1965, helped to conceive this project and then through his creative input and generous patronage helped to nurture it and bring it to fruition. Were it not for his modesty, it would not be inappropriate to dedicate to him this collection of essays, which instead the authors have written for the past, present, and future members of a group first assembled by Thomas Jefferson—the United States Corps of Cadets. Each year it augments the lengthening line of soldier-scholars who live and sometimes die for the very best Jeffersonian principles.

Notes

1. James Fenimore Cooper to Charles Kitchel Gardner (24 April–17 June [?] 1823), in James Franklin Beard, ed., *The Letters and Journals of James Fenimore Cooper*, 6 vols. (Cambridge, Mass., 1960–68), 1:95–96.

2. Transcription from Maclay's diary manuscript, 24 May 1790, *TJP* 16:381n; Margaret Bayard Smith, *The First Forty Years of Washington Society*, ed. Gaillard Hunt (1906; New York, 1965), 5–8; "Lavater's Aphorisms," *New-York Evening Post*, 20 April 1802.

3. TJ, Notes of a Cabinet Meeting on the President's Address to Congress, 23 November 1793, *TJP* 26:428; TJ to Elbridge Gerry, 26 January 1799, *TJW*, 1056–57.

4. Malone, 4:510; Russell F. Weigley, *Towards an American Army: Military Thought from Washington to Marshall* (New York, 1962), 28; Karl-Friedrich Walling, *Republican Empire: Alexander Hamilton on War and Free Government* (Lawrence, Kans., 1999), 286.

5. TJ to Sir John Sinclair, 30 June 1803, *TJW*, 1133; TJ to James Monroe, 11 July 1790, *TJP* 17:25.

6. James Madison, *Political Observations*, 20 Apr. 1795, in William T. Hutchinson, et al., eds., *The Papers of James Madison: Congressional Series*, 17 vols. (Chicago and Charlottesville, Va., 1962–91), 15:518.

7. See Spencer Tucker, *The Jeffersonian Gunboat Navy* (Columbia, S.C., 1993) and Gene A. Smith, *For the Purposes of Defense: The Politics of the Jeffersonian Gunboat Program* (Newark, Del., 1995).

8. Shuffelton's *Thomas Jefferson: A Comprehensive, Annotated Bibliography of Writings about Him, 1826–1997*, is available on the Web at http://etext.virginia.edu/jefferson/bibliog/. Two of the best appraisals of Jefferson's role in the founding of the University of Virginia are too recent for inclusion in Shuffelton's bibliography. See Garry Wills, *Mr. Jefferson's University* (Washington, D.C., 2002) and Cameron Addis, *Jefferson's Vision for Education, 1760–1845* (New York, 2003).

9. Alexander M. Haig Jr., "Foreword," in *The Campus Guide: West Point: U.S. Military Academy* by Rod Miller (New York, 2002), xvi.

10. Theodore J. Crackel, "The Founding of West Point: Jefferson and the Politics of Security," *Armed Forces and Society* 7 (Summer 1981): 529–43; Crackel, "Mr. Jefferson's Army: Political Reform of the Military Establishment, 1801–1809" (Ph.D. diss., Rutgers University, 1985); Crackel, *Mr. Jefferson's Army: Political and Social Reform of the Military Establishment, 1801–1809* (New York, 1987), 3 (quotation). See also Crackel's *West Point: A Bicentennial History* (Lawrence, Kans., 2002), 43–51.

11. TJ to Tench Coxe, 1 June 1795, *TJP* 28:373. See also TJ to Jean Nicolas Demeunier, (26 June 1786,) ibid., 10:63; TJ to Bishop James Madison, 31 January 1800, *TJW*, 1077; TJ to the Citizens of Washington, 4 March 1809, in L&B, 16:334; TJ to John Adams, 12 September 1821, *AJL*, 575.

12. TJ to Joseph Priestley, 18 January 1800, *TJW*, 1070.

13. TJ to Roger C. Weightman, 24 June 1826, ibid., 1517.

Thomas Jefferson's Military Academy

Introduction

PETER S. ONUF

As draftsman of the Declaration of Independence, Thomas Jefferson helped define the meaning of America. Unlike George Washington, the "father of his country," the civilian Jefferson was not an "indispensable" military man; nor was he a great lawgiver, like James Madison, author of the federal Constitution, or a great state builder, like his brilliant adversary, Secretary of the Treasury Alexander Hamilton. Jefferson is instead remembered for the memorable language of the second paragraph of the Declaration—"all men are created equal . . . endowed by their creator with certain inalienable rights," including "life, liberty, and the pursuit of happiness." His exalted status as democratic icon reflects the democratizing implications of a declaration that enables Americans to see themselves as their own founders.[1]

To an envious and skeptical John Adams, who took pride in his own heroic contributions to American independence, Jefferson's felicitous phrases—glittering generalities recycling the conventional, "self-evident" wisdom—seemed a slender foundation for his colleague's immortal reputation. What, after all, do they really mean? And what, after all, did Jefferson really contribute to the American founding? These questions have, throughout American history, shadowed Jefferson's bright image. Fervent believers in the ideals set forth in the Declaration have never tired—and will never tire—of charging Jefferson (and America) with failing to live up to its inspiring precepts. Meanwhile, hardheaded "realists" warn that blind adherence to exalted principles too often leads to imprudent interventions in a dangerous and unpredictable "real" world.[2]

Not surprisingly, the realist tradition has flourished in military circles, where Jefferson's stock has historically been low. Yet Jefferson's image has never been fixed or static, and there are signs that even his severest critics are already taking a new look at their old nemesis. The bicentennial of the United States Military Academy is a good time to assess Jefferson's role as its founder—or at least as the president who sponsored and signed the legislation establishing the institution. A reconsideration of the academy's history also yields a fresh perspective on Jefferson's role as one of the nation's founders. His legacy, this volume demonstrates, cannot be reduced to a few disconnected words or phrases.

As Robert McDonald shows, Jefferson historically inspired little enthusiasm in a military establishment that was much more eager to assert the paternity of George Washington or to celebrate Superintendent Sylvanus Thayer as its true founder. Yet the traditional bias against Jefferson is dissipating. Jefferson's hostility to "big government" has been ideologically resonant in a conservative military culture traditionally suspicious of civilian elites—and despite its own leading role in the vast expansion of the federal state during the twentieth century. The ratio of self-identified Republicans to Democrats among up-and-coming army officers is now eight to one (64 percent to 8 percent), reversing, though certainly exaggerating, partisan preferences at elite colleges and universities preparing future civilian leaders. This ideological polarization, McDonald concludes, "probably constitutes good news for Jefferson's reputation within the army."[3] At the very least, custodians of institutional memory will no longer feel compelled to overlook Jefferson's crucial role in West Point's founding. But it remains to be seen if West Point will embrace him as a true founder, rendering him the same respect and reverence now given to Washington and Thayer.

Why does this matter? Americans have always had mixed feelings about the role of "great men," and particularly of military heroes. Jefferson and Adams, Elizabeth Samet suggests, were acutely self-conscious about the danger of exalting one great man, or an "aristocratic" elite, above the multitude, even in the case of Washington, the self-abnegating American Cincinnatus. Yet they also cherished their own reputations as founders of the Republic, fearful that Americans might forget why the revolutionaries had made such great sacrifices and what they hoped their bold experiment in republican self-government would achieve. They worried about how *we* would remember *them,* about the historical memory and civic consciousness of subsequent generations. In warning against the idolatrous apotheosis of founders, they hoped to keep alive a vital sense of a founding that must be constantly remembered and renewed.[4]

Of course, Jefferson did not worry specifically about his standing at West Point. If partisan and ideological enemies have conspired to obliterate his actual role in the academy's founding, it must be said that Jefferson himself contributed to this obliteration by saying so little on the subject. He was, as the inscription he ordered for his tombstone proudly recorded, "Father of the University of Virginia," but he made no corresponding claim for West Point.[5] But Jefferson would agree with McDonald that the real question has always been "not whether Jefferson made West Point, but what West Point makes of Jefferson."[6] This is simply a local specification of a larger question: What do Americans now make of Jefferson and the founding generation generally? West Point's answer to McDonald must also take into account—and, finally, must be shaped by—that larger question. The military has always to some extent—sometimes more, sometimes less—defined itself *against* the larger society, and particularly the civilian political establishment. But it has also defined itself in *subordination* to civil society, sublimating the ambivalence that fosters its corporate identity in unquestioning subscription to the values of "Duty, Honor, Country."

Rethinking the founding of West Point requires rethinking the nation's founding as well. Conditions in the military may now be propitious for a more favorable view of Jefferson. But to embrace him as the founder—or one of the founders—of the academy means to reconsider the army's historic aversion to this quintessential civilian and to ask what role the military should now play in republican society. His ideological appeal to contemporary Republicans is understandable. Yet the historical Jefferson cannot be reduced to the conservative—or, more accurately, classically liberal—precepts that make him so attractive to so many military people today. In fact, it is precisely because Jefferson's legacy is so complex, because he forces Americans to think about their history and about their present purposes, that he serves the American people so well as a "founder." Jefferson could be this kind of founder for West Point.

The civilian Jefferson played no direct personal role in winning the Revolution. Not surprisingly, in his celebration of the mass popular movement to overthrow British tyranny, he emphasized the patriotism of citizen-soldiers, not the skills of a professional military. Unlike Colonel Hamilton, who recklessly threw himself into the breach at Yorktown, Governor Jefferson kept himself out of harm's way, fleeing to safety when Benedict Arnold invaded Virginia. But if Jefferson was himself no hero, he was, in characteristic civilian fashion, eager enough that others should die. "The tree of liberty must be refreshed from time to time with the blood of patriots and tyrants," he told William Stephens Smith in 1787. In a letter to William Short six years later, he did not blink at mass slaughter: "I would have seen half the earth desolated" in the name of republican revolution. "Were there but an Adam and an Eve left in every country, and left free, it would be better than as it now is."[7] Here, for skeptical military men, were the classic symptoms of civilian bloodthirstiness, justifying itself by appeal to the most exalted ideological principles.

Yet, if republican ideology authorized massive sacrifices for the public good, it also encouraged vigilant civilians to keep professional soldiers on a short leash. For the British Real Whig thinkers whose radical ideas inspired Jefferson, a professional "standing army" was the most dangerous tool of despotic power. He juxtaposed the republican ideal of the good citizen who, in time of crisis, "would fly to the standard of the law, and would meet invasions of the public order as his own personal concern," to the abject servility of the professional soldier who would obey any master.[8] But he most distrusted the officer corps, would-be aristocrats who commanded the troops and set themselves above the civilian population. Here was a class of courtiers without a king—though Washington might provide a plausible equivalent—anxious to advance its corporate and personal interests at the people's expense. Because war offered the greatest opportunity to fulfill these aristocratic ambitions, a professional army had an interest in fostering a never-ending cycle of conflicts. Not coincidentally, a state of war constituted the greatest threat to the survival of republican government, exaggerating the claims of arbitrary executive power and jeopardizing the lives, liberties, and property of taxpayers.

Jefferson expressed a pervasive Revolutionary ambivalence about war making. The determination of contemporaries—and most modern historians—to dissociate the "Revolution" from the war reflects this ambivalence. Adams's assertion that "the Revolution was in the Minds of the People, and this was effected, from 1760 to 1775, in the course of fifteen Years before a drop of blood was drawn at Lexington" is the most famous and influential expression of this ambivalence.[9] Of course, this displacement of the actual war in accounts of the Revolution foregrounded the contributions of republican statesmen and ideologues who took a leading role in the imperial crisis and in the subsequent history of state making and constitution writing. But it also reflected a genuine conundrum. If patriotic revolutionaries rose up in resistance to the increasingly expansive pretensions of despotic imperial government, how could they avoid recreating among themselves—by imposing unprecedented levels of taxation and concentrating power in strong governments—the very thing they meant to destroy? How could good republicans govern themselves effectively enough to win the war and secure the subsequent peace without jeopardizing their liberties? How could the army, the key institution of the old regime, be made safe for the new republic?

The role of the military in American republican society remained a flash point for ideological and partisan conflict in the post-Revolutionary period. In these debates, Jefferson often took the role of civilian critic, warning against the concentration of power in an overly energetic federal government too eager to resort to military force. As leader of the emergent Republican opposition, Jefferson decried the militarism of Hamiltonian High Federalists as they prepared for war against revolutionary France—the new nation's erstwhile "sister republic"—and, still more ominously, against their domestic enemies. Ideological polarization in the late 1790s thus reinforced the anti-Jeffersonian bias of military leaders, overwhelmingly Federalist appointees who became increasingly skeptical about Republican good faith and patriotism. Yet again, they charged, Republican ideologues were carried away by blind adherence to so-called "principles," thus supporting a morally bankrupt French regime and risking the very survival of the Republic by resisting preparedness measures and fomenting disunion.[10]

During the Quasi-War with France (1797–1800), Federalists had no doubt that the willingness to prepare for war was the true test for republican patriots. Preserving independence was the sine qua non of self-government, making Republican appeals to antistatist, libertarian sentiment profoundly dangerous. Jefferson's reputation in military circles thus sank to its all-time low as Republicans mobilized anti-administration forces in a great campaign to purge the Republic of "monocrats" and "aristocrats." In Republican rhetoric, the mythic "citizen-soldier" was now recast as the patriotic partisan—real soldiers simply served as tools of a corrupt administration preparing to meet nonexistent external threats. Historians have been hard-pressed to take such "hysterical" rhetoric seriously, but it is clear that Jefferson and his allies were convinced that the future of the republican experiment was at stake in the war crisis.[11] They were also convinced that their High Federalist opponents meant to exploit the crisis to subvert states' rights and individual liberties. The Federalist administration could not be trusted to sustain civilian supremacy over the military. To the contrary, Republicans were convinced that the administration was powerless to control a move for military supremacy that masqueraded as preparedness and was masterminded by Hamilton and his allies.

Army leaders have always felt misunderstood. Indeed, a sense of alienation from an ungrateful and uncomprehending society is an essential prop to the military's corporate identity.[12] The Revolution itself provided the paradigm case of civilian obliviousness to the real costs of independence, and the same themes were rehearsed in the Republican campaign against the military in the late 1790s. From these experiences, the army developed a narrative of its own history, predicated on its quasi-adversarial role with the public and pivoting on its own patriotic dedication to sustaining the Republic and submitting to civilian rule, however foolish and misguided it might be. Instead of setting themselves up as a distinct, privileged class, army officers struggled to develop an ethos of professionalism or "regularity" that would demonstrate their unwavering fealty to republican principles. Far from seeking to promote counterrevolution and a monarchical revival, these self-sacrificing public servants would always exercise a conservative, moderating force, checking rather than abetting a bloodthirsty popular will.

The peaceful transition of power in 1801 shows that Republican fears of a counterrevolutionary coup were vastly exaggerated.[13] Instead, it was the Republican governors of Pennsylvania and Virginia who took steps to mobilize military force against the possibility of a "stolen election." Federalists flirted with Aaron Burr, negotiating a deal with Jefferson's putative running mate that would *not* have violated any provision of the federal Constitution, but they never considered a military coup. However alienated from Jefferson they might be, army leaders could not imagine betraying their historic role as patriotic defenders of the Republic—nor, to be practical, could they imagine that the tiny number of troops at their disposal could be put to any good use. Indeed, the image of Jefferson as pacifist and Francophile "philosopher" that emerged out of the partisan polemics of the late 1790s served to reinforce by juxtaposition the ethos of moderation in the military. In opposition to civilian "idealism," army leaders fostered a culture of "realism." They would always be prepared to make the necessary sacrifices to preserve American independence, and they understood that any challenge to civilian supremacy would inevitably subvert the republican regime.

Jefferson played at best a minimal, even a negative, role in the army's narrative of its history and developing collective identity. He was the very embodiment of civilian foolishness, heedless about threats of war—even as his own policies threatened to bring it on—too sanguine about the possibilities of commercial diplomacy, unwilling to invest in defensive measures that might have reduced the danger of conflict. There is much to be said for this narrative, most notably in the way it inculcates the fundamental premise of civilian supremacy, resolving the tension between army and society through the precepts of professionalism. Because Jefferson served as a foil for this emerging ethos, it is hardly surprising that he would be West Point's "lost founder." The academy came of age as an institution despite, even in opposition to, a Jeffersonian and then Jacksonian society that failed to grasp or appreciate a need either for a truly professional army or for an effective, energetic federal government.

Yet it is nonetheless true that Jefferson *was* West Point's founder. The Jefferson image that emerged during the 1790s was in many ways a misleading caricature, the product of partisan polemics during a period of profound crisis in the history of the union when no one could predict the future. For Federalist critics, Jefferson's policy failures as president seemed to confirm the caricature. But Jefferson was no pacifist, and his decision to establish the academy in 1802 was no aberration. He may have been suspicious of military men—given their partisan proclivities, he had every reason to be so—but he had no delusions about enjoying the benefits of peace without preparedness. If he remained somewhat skeptical about the army's self-restraint and professionalism, he was no less determined to achieve a civil-military balance that would protect the Republic from internal as well as external threats.

The essays in this volume offer a more inclusive narrative of West Point's founding and reveal that Jefferson performed a more constructive role than his critics in the army have customarily recognized. They make possible new connections between West Point's founding and the founding of the new American republic.

Military critics, priding themselves on their "realism," charge Jefferson with being a pacifist ideologue, unable to grasp the necessity for energetic government capable of projecting effective power in a dangerous world. Jefferson may in fact be accurately called a "half-way pacifist," inspired by an Enlightenment vision of eventually eliminating the causes of war by dismantling the corrupt institutions of the old regime, including "standing armies."[14] But he never believed that American independence would instantly lead to a republican millennium of peace and prosperity. In 1787, after more than three years of diplomatic frustration in Paris, Jefferson would agree with Hamilton that the new nation had not yet achieved "the happy empire of perfect wisdom and perfect virtue." Fantasies of "perpetual peace" and spontaneous union among the states were predicated on the "deceitful dream" that "the genius of republics . . . is pacific."[15] Jefferson knew that there was a fundamental difference between declaring independence and forcing the powers of the world to recognize it; he also knew that conflicts of interest among the states could easily destroy an increasingly fragile union, thus unleashing counterrevolutionary forces and Europeanizing American politics. He had misgivings about the new Constitution drafted at Philadelphia, but he was convinced that a fundamental reform of the Confederation was absolutely necessary.[16]

Peace, for Jefferson, was the ultimate goal of his republican constitutionalism and not its premise or point of departure. Where he differed from Hamilton, a much more conventional state builder and geopolitician, was in his complex and comprehensive view of the potential sources of conflict that jeopardized peace. The first requirement for a durable republican regime in the New World was constitutional reform in the respective states. The American state-republics might not be naturally peaceful, as Hamilton warned, but at least they could be freed from the despotic rule of predatory ruling classes that, in effect, made "war" on their own peoples. Yet this happy outcome did not follow inevitably from destroying the old imperial regime; it depended instead on drafting proper constitutions according to the precepts of enlightened political science. So, too, Jefferson believed, perpetual peace among the states depended on an effective central government, potent in its own sphere but constitutionally restrained from encroaching on the reserved rights of the states or the liberties of the people. Such a government, he concluded, could promote peace among nations, advancing American interests by working toward a regime of free trade and rising prosperity throughout the commercial world.

Because he believed threats to peace were so pervasive, potentially proceeding from internal as well as external sources, Jefferson was reflexively hostile to claims by the executive or its military minions for unchecked prerogative powers that would enable it to "prepare" for war or make it without regard to civilian authority. War constituted the greatest challenge to the new nation, Jeffersonian Republicans agreed, for the exigencies of mobilizing men and resources in the cause of national independence and self-preservation—the first and highest duty of any government according to the law of nature—tended to obliterate constitutional distinctions among warring powers, thus transforming republics into monarchies with powerful, irresponsible governments—even when they pretended to preserve their republican forms. For the future founder of the military academy at West Point, the Federalists' Quasi-War with France brought these problems to the fore, giving urgent point to well-developed prior concerns about the pernicious implications of loose construction of the federal Constitution and the resulting expansion of the administration's powers for the preservation of the union and peace among the states.

The party conflicts of the 1790s culminated in the Federalists' efforts to suppress the Republican opposition through repressive legislation. The Alien and Sedition Acts of 1798 launched a broad-ranging assault on the administration's domestic enemies even as it prepared for a full-scale war against France. In response, Jefferson and his allies sought to rally their troops against the Federalist juggernaut, calling on American patriots to reenact the Revolutionary struggle against a tyrannical central government. This deepening political crisis made the warnings of Republican ideologues about pervasive threats to peace seem prophetic. The "perpetual union" that had secured amity among the states and their collective security in a dangerous world stood poised on the brink of collapse. In the dark days leading up to the 1800 presidential canvass, an increasingly anxious Jefferson was nearly driven to despair. When, thanks to John Adams's diplomacy, the war crisis dissipated and public opinion recoiled against the administration's mobilization measures, he believed a new day had dawned. Patriotic voters finally came to their senses in the "revolution of 1800," returning to Revolution's first principles and securing their precious union.[17]

The crisis of 1800–1801 was *not* politics as usual. Jefferson's mandate was not as a party leader—he had not "campaigned" for office—but rather as the mere instrument of the people's will. As David Mayer shows, Jefferson's constitutionalism was "contextualist," changing over time "as background political circumstances changed." His inauguration signaled a radical change in circumstances that cast executive authority in an entirely new light. Suspicious of Federalist intentions, he had previously opposed establishing a military academy on strict constructionist grounds. Now that the administration was safely ensconced within its proper sphere of authority, such constitutional scruples could be laid aside.[18] Instead, writes Theodore Crackel, Jefferson initiated a "carefully modulated program of reform" of both civil and military establishments that "would ultimately bring them into line with the broad aspirations and goals of the new Republican regime."[19]

Jefferson's many critics, then and now, have made much of his alleged "inconsistency" and "hypocrisy" on constitutional issues: as long as he was in opposition, he was a strict constructionist; once in power, he was prone to looser, self-serving constructions. Mayer notes, however, that Jefferson's constitutional contextualism always "permitted a broad latitude for the exercise of federal powers within the sphere assigned to the national government under the Constitution, particularly with regard to foreign affairs."[20] Defense of the Republic justified any "necessary and proper" measures, as the first law of nature enjoined, but the same elasticity did not apply to relations between the federal government and the states or individual citizens. Given the Federalists' tendency to interpret the principle of federal supremacy as a license to consolidate all authority in the central government, it was incumbent on the Republican opposition to raise the alarm at any initiative—including the founding of the National Bank, or even the proposal to establish a national military academy—that threatened to expand the ambit of federal authority. But once the government was fully "republicanized"—that is, once it was purged of the "aristocratic," "monocratic" tendencies toward "consolidation" that characterized Federalist administrations—it could be trusted to exercise more expansive powers. "*Federalism* to Jefferson meant far more than the 'states rights' caricature," Mayer concludes, for it led him "to interpret federal powers under the Constitution quite liberally in matters involving foreign affairs." In this respect, he "could be fairly described as a 'nationalist.'"[21]

For fearful Republicans, the internal threat of a consolidationist federal administration seemingly bent on obliterating the states eclipsed external threats from hostile foreign powers in the late 1790s. They could not take the war scare seriously. Could the "sister republic" really want a war with its Revolutionary ally—unless goaded to it by Anglophile Federalists? The strategic horizon changed dramatically as Jefferson assumed office. With the union now secure against internal threat, Jefferson could envision a new epoch of territorial expansion, economic development, and collective security. His claim in his first inaugural address that the United States was "the strongest Government on earth" heralded his new conception of national defense. By any conventional reckoning of military preparedness the claim was absurd on its face. But Jefferson was underscoring the crucial importance of mass mobilization for national security. This was the only regime "where every man, at the call of the law, would fly to the standard of the law, and would meet invasions of the public order as his own personal concern." His formulation conflated the military mobilization of the American Revolution with the political mobilization that saved the Republic and led to his own election, thus conjuring up the iconic figure of the citizen-soldier as the embodiment of patriotic virtue.[22]

Jefferson's rhetorical resolution of civil-military tensions offered a mythic, justificatory narrative of the Revolution (in which, in fact, the relation between "citizen" and "soldier" was profoundly problematic) and of the just-concluded political and constitutional struggle (in which so many benighted voters failed to understand their own true interests). Jefferson was hardly unaware of these discrepancies. His paean to the citizen-soldier and to the transcendent unity of the American people—"we are all Republicans, we are all Federalists"—was instead meant to articulate his administration's goals. "Sometimes it is said that man can not be trusted with the government of himself," Jefferson wrote. "Can he, then, be trusted with the government of others? Or have we found angels in the forms of kings to govern him?" Republicanism was a glorious experiment, an effort to vindicate human nature itself. Its ultimate success depended on the enlightenment of the people, their choice of good leaders, and their willingness to submit to legitimate authority. Everything hinged on the fundamental republican principle that leaders must be drawn from—and responsible to—a vigilant citizenry determined to preserve its liberties. It was precisely for this reason that it was so essential for Jefferson to "republicanize" the military establishment, to create an institutional structure and officer corps that could command the loyalties of citizen-soldiers, and so make the United States the "strongest Government on earth."

A military academy purged of its monarchical and aristocratic tendencies was crucial to Jefferson's goal of republicanizing the officer corps. Notwithstanding his ideological hostility to a professional army, Jefferson had no illusions about dispensing with a military establishment. For a self-governing people to defend itself in time of crisis, a thoroughly republican officer corps must be prepared to lead. The Military Peace Establishment Act of 1802 was not intended to reduce the army, Crackel writes, but it did allow "Jefferson to rid himself of some of his most vociferous detractors in the army" and create "a force that would come to reflect the republican society from which it was drawn." By establishing the military academy, the law "established a source of future Republican officers."[23]

The critical role of a Republican military academy would be to draw future officers from society at large and to inculcate in them a principled commitment to patriotic service. The great danger was that the military establishment would become a quasi-aristocratic caste. The formation of the Society of the Cincinnati, a hereditary association of Revolutionary War officers, pointed ominously in this direction, as did the High Federalism of prominent veterans in the 1790s. For the Republic to survive, Jeffersonian Republicans believed, it was necessary to root out the superstitious awe of the better sort that sustained social hierarchy. Crackel shows that reform of the army was part of a broader campaign to recruit Republicans to all branches of the federal administration and make them more representative of the people. Federalists were most deeply entrenched in a military establishment, a "standing army" whose very existence seemed to jeopardize republican liberty. The new administration's challenge, Elizabeth Samet writes, was to "weaken the pull of organizations such as the Cincinnati by giving future officers something other than the crucible of Revolutionary combat" to unite them as disciplined professionals.[24]

War and peace presented a conundrum to practical Republicans. The Revolution itself demonstrated the central importance of an effective military force in vindicating American independence. Yet that same force could easily take a counterrevolutionary turn—a powerful army with a well-developed esprit de corps and a sense of its own distinctive, corporate interests could seize power at any time. Armies also thrived in a constant state of war that enhanced and rewarded their effectiveness while jeopardizing the liberty, property, and lives of ordinary citizens. How could a republic prepare for war without risking the peace? Aristocratic regimes reproduced themselves, perpetuating privilege and power among ruling families across the generations. Eschewing aristocratic succession, the new republic had to foster new forms of social solidarity, the "brotherhood" of fellow citizens, and a new conception of intergenerational relations. The new nation must find a way to produce "a long line of American Washingtons willing to subordinate themselves to civil power."[25]

The republican obsession with the problem of generational succession was most apparent in ambitious proposals for public education. Educational reformers struggled to overcome formidable resistance from war-weary taxpayers who suspected, with some reason, that publicly financed schools would serve elite interests at their expense. The training of army officers raised particularly acute problems. If American arms had triumphed in the Revolution without benefit of formal military education, why should a military academy be necessary in peacetime? As Don Higginbotham notes, the "tutorial method" of officer training in the midst of the War for Independence "seems to have worked reasonably well," and a "great influx of foreign officers" also gave the army "added military experience and eighteenth-century-style professionalism."[26] But Jefferson and his fellow Republicans were not confident that the Revolutionary experience would be replicated in the next war. On one hand, military skills would atrophy in a period of protracted peace; if, on the other hand, chronic warfare enabled the highly informal, personalistic "tutorial" system to flourish, the growing power of the military establishment would jeopardize the survival of republican government. The Republican solution to this dilemma was the establishment of a formal system of military education. A truly republican academy would recruit widely in the larger society, thus countering the aristocratic tendency of a military caste to reproduce itself, and it would also inculcate republican principles in future officers. The most critical of those principles, the subordination of the military to civilian direction, would be implicit in the very constitution of a federally sponsored academy, established by—and financially dependent on—the people's representatives in Congress.

Education was the republican answer to aristocratic privilege, substituting achievement for the accidents of birth in recruiting a new generation of leaders. Jefferson and other educational reformers were not "agrarian" levelers who would destroy social distinctions. To the contrary, they promoted a conception of what Jefferson called "natural aristocracy," a regime in which merit would be recognized and rewarded. Given Jefferson's meritocratic perspective, the ascendancy of High Federalist warmongers in the late 1790s was particularly disturbing, revealing crypto-aristocratic tendencies that would destroy the republican revolution. One crucial lesson from this crisis was that these tendencies must be countered, not only by the appointment of Republican officials but also by the proper education of the next generation of leaders. Jefferson recognized that there was a paucity of qualified Republicans—particularly in the military—who were qualified for high office. Conscious of the partisan dimensions of this deficit, Jefferson's enthusiasm for educational reform was rekindled in the period leading up to his election.

Historians traditionally have minimized Jefferson's role as West Point's founder because he said so little about the establishment of the academy in his extensive correspondence. The historiographical problem is one of perspective. Because he was determined to republicanize the military—to integrate it thoroughly into the larger society and make it more clearly subordinate to civilian authority—his ambitions for the academy transcended a narrow definition of professional military training. Jennings L. Wagoner Jr. and Christine Coalwell McDonald provide the crucial context for understanding his role in West Point's founding. As they write, "Jefferson was awash in educational ideas, plans, and proposals as the new century ushering in the Republican 'revolution of 1800' dawned."[27] The most progressive approach to military education increasingly emphasized the importance of science and technology, blurring traditional distinctions between professional training in different fields. Early proposals by Pierre Samuel Du Pont de Nemours and Joel Barlow "shared the feature of having special schools, including a military academy, that would operate as components of a national university."[28] In 1806 Barlow recommended moving the academy from West Point to Washington for this purpose; Jefferson and Superintendent Jonathan Williams subsequently favored such a move in order to transform the academy into a "national school of engineering."[29] Jefferson's impulse in these projects was not to dilute military education, but rather to give it additional prestige and public support by linking it with modern scientific and technical training in a comprehensive educational establishment. That Jefferson took this goal seriously is apparent in his openness to military education at his University of Virginia. In 1817, as Higginbotham reveals, he even proposed that the Society of the Cincinnati endow a professorship there![30]

Because the academy stayed at West Point and plans for a national university came to naught, the relevance of Jefferson's educational vision for the institution's history has remained obscure. That obscurity was reinforced by West Point's less-than-glorious early history. Samuel Watson underscores the irony of the belated reception of "Jeffersonian" ideas about democratic access, professionalism, and advanced technical education during Thayer's superintendency (1817–33). The major obstacle to the institution's success in the early years was the tendency of its leaders—including Republican Alden Partridge—to flout the canons of military professionalism. Military men who cherished the aristocratic values Jefferson sought to extirpate—an exaggerated sense of social superiority and personal honor—were prone to resign their commissions at the slightest provocation. An ethos of professionalism, or "regularity," only triumphed at West Point when Thayer's standards of discipline and order fostered "unprecedented uniformity, stability, and predictability."[31] The new professionalism may have constituted the fulfillment of Jefferson's vision, as Watson suggests, but Thayer and his followers did not therefore see themselves as Jeffersonians. Recoiling against the demagogic war hero Andrew Jackson, Jefferson's self-anointed heir, leading military men were drawn into the ranks of the new Whig party. Jefferson's reputation plunged accordingly.

Thayer and his colleagues were able to rebuff Jackson's interference in the academy's administration because they had successfully established a meritocratic institution that could contain and suppress the aristocratic tendencies of the old military establishment. Insulated from the "corruption" of party politics, an increasingly professionalized army identified itself with the nation as a whole and embraced the principle of subordination to civilian authority. In a period of mounting sectional tensions, Watson shows, "the West Point–educated officer corps became the closest thing to a national administrative . . . cadre" in the United States.[32] The academy thus fulfilled Jefferson's original vision of inculcating patriotic values and disseminating advanced technical and scientific knowledge—and did so much more effectively than the University of Virginia, the great project of his declining years. Of course, when he founded the university, an increasingly embittered Jefferson, hypersensitive about encroachments on states' rights, no longer thought in national terms. Fittingly, his new university emerged as a bastion of planter privilege and a hotbed of secessionist sentiment on the eve of the Civil War. As it turned out, however, West Point's "nationalism" proved a frail prop to a disintegrating union. A large number of academy graduates joined the rebellious Confederate forces.

As Merrill Peterson showed many years ago, the "Jefferson image" has been appropriated and reshaped by successive generations of Americans for a dizzying array of often-conflicting purposes.[33] Jefferson should not be seen merely as the passive victim of this process of image construction. Though he strained to sustain an overarching commitment to the republican principles he articulated so eloquently in the heady days of the American Revolutionary crisis, his positions on many fundamental issues changed dramatically over the course of his career. Anxiety about preserving the proper balance between liberty and power—and, particularly, between states' rights and federal authority—would be the crucial pivot for many of these changes. When loyalties to state and union were in perfect accord, as they seemed to be in 1776 and again in 1801 when he ascended to the presidency in the wake of another "revolution," a progressive, optimistic, enlightened Jefferson could look forward to the coming republican millennium. But when reactionary forces jeopardized the federal balance—when, for instance, "restrictionists" sought to ban slavery in Missouri, thus subverting the principle of new state equality and dangerously enlarging the power of the federal government—a despairing Jefferson feared the worst. Perhaps the American Revolution itself had been a tragic mistake, and not the herald of a new epoch in the progress of political civilization.

In his expansive, optimistic mode, Jefferson could envision the development of an energetic, powerful central government. National defense clearly fell within his conception of the federal government's legitimate authority, and there was no constitutional barrier to establishing a military academy that would help secure the nation as a whole from future threats. He also believed that the public had a broad responsibility to educate the rising generation generally, though the role of the federal government was in this case more ambiguous. But if there were scruples about federal sponsorship of a national university—as opposed to a military academy—or to other internal improvements of national significance, it should be easy enough to amend the federal Constitution accordingly. In any event, the caricature of Jefferson as an antistatist libertarian does not hold, either at the federal or state level.

The Jefferson who founded the United States Military Academy believed that power and liberty could be harmonized in an expanding republican empire. His paradoxical project of republicanizing the state depended on making institutions of government that had embodied aristocratic power and privilege responsible and accessible to a self-governing people secure in its rights. For Jeffersonians, the "standing army" was the most dangerously aristocratic institution, the potential tool of the despotic power that Hamiltonian High Federalists had sought to exercise during the Quasi-War crisis. That made the "chaste reformation" of the military establishment such a crucially important component of the broader republican reform program.[34] A republicanized army would be capable of defending the nation against external threats, making the United States "the strongest Government on earth," but would no longer represent the kind of internal threat to the rights of the state-republics and the liberties of the people that had driven Jefferson to the brink of despair in the late 1790s.

The difference between Jefferson and the "realists" who command most respect in military circles is that he had a far more comprehensive vision of potential threats to peace. Where the realist prepared merely to resist the assaults of foreign powers or to project power abroad, the Jeffersonian "idealist" also sought to curb dangerous exercises of power at home. Jefferson thus conceptualized the problem of war and peace in three, interdependent dimensions: to secure a peaceful, progressively improving international order, the federal government had to take the form of a sovereign power capable of exercising conventional military power. At the same time, however, it had to secure the states in the full ambit of their rights as self-governing republics, thus sustaining their "perpetual union" and preempting the possibility of interstate warfare; and, finally, government at every level should be curbed from making war on the sovereign people by encroaching on their rights and violating the fundamental principle of consent. Properly interpreted, the federal Constitution authorized Jefferson to take all appropriate measures to defend the states collectively, but it also functioned as a kind of "peace pact" or supertreaty to secure the states against each other and against the federal government.[35] Bills of rights in the federal and state constitutions defined the rights of individual citizens that were secured through the ordinary operations of republican self-government.

Jefferson's image of the citizen-soldier represented the ultimate convergence of state and society in his republican vision. Evoking a mythic Revolutionary past, Jefferson looked forward to a time when the army would be so thoroughly identified with a self-governing people that civil-military conflict would be unthinkable. But the synthesis of citizen and soldier, like the vision of a more perfect union of sovereign states, was bound to be frustrated. Even in a Jeffersonian republic, citizens and soldiers would have different interests and would see the world differently. The Revolution military men remembered bore little resemblance to Jefferson's; they instead recalled the disjunction of citizen and soldier—and their own thankless struggle to sustain the war in the face of civilian suspicion and neglect. Their future—and the future of the independent United States—depended on the willingness of taxpayers to sustain a peacetime military establishment that could effectively mobilize men and resources in the next war. Perhaps then Jefferson's terms should be reversed: the soldier, not the citizen, should come first and citizens could only "fly to the standard of the law" if the military establishment was prepared to lead them.

But Jefferson did not have to be told that citizens and soldiers constituted distinct interests. As Crackel has shown, Jefferson understood that his great challenge was to republicanize the federal administration, including the army, so that "liberty" would no longer be jeopardized by "power." Only at the highest level of abstraction, in the idea of "popular sovereignty," could this fundamental tension be fully resolved. In the real world, Jefferson knew, government would have to be prepared to act energetically and decisively, sometimes far in advance of public opinion or legislative action. The executive had a clear constitutional mandate to conduct foreign policy, to command the nation's military resources to secure its vital interests. Without an effective military establishment, the president could not perform his most important duties. If the new nation's sovereignty and independence were not secured, the union would collapse, the republican experiment would fail, and liberty would be lost.

Many Federalists, even Jefferson's archrival Hamilton, recognized that Jefferson had no intention of jettisoning the federal administration that Washington and Adams had labored so hard to establish. What remained controversial was the new president's appointment policies. How many Federalist appointees would be purged? Would there be a place for moderate Federalists in the new regime? While Jefferson's appointments inspired some criticism, particularly among hidebound obstructionists who had no intention of cooperating with his administration, he clearly meant to coopt as many former opponents as possible. The appointment of Major Jonathan Williams, a moderate Federalist, as the first superintendent at West Point set the tone for a moderate program of military reform. To the extent that Jefferson relied on the academy to produce a new generation of officers, he was willing to be patient, accepting the necessity of dealing in the meantime with a military establishment that remained overwhelmingly Federalist in sentiment.

What sort of founder does this make Jefferson? The answer is as complicated for the military academy as it is for the nation as a whole. Most obviously, he sponsored and signed the bill that established the academy. He was, in some sense then, the "author" of the founding document, just as he was the author of American independence in his famous Declaration. But if, notwithstanding the efforts of revisionist historians, Jefferson continues to get too much credit for launching the new nation, the army has traditionally minimized his role in the academy's founding, making him a "lost founder." In contrast, the essayists in this volume take a more capacious view, sketching the broad outlines of an intellectual and institutional history that recovers Jefferson's role. If it is so important to know what influences shaped his Declaration—and now to question the extent to which it *is* "Jefferson's" Declaration—is it not also important to know what he had in mind when he authorized the academy's founding?

There is no question that the contributions of West Point's "other founders"—George Washington (deceased by 1802) and Sylvanus Thayer (who arrived some years later, as a young cadet)—have been duly noted and celebrated, and there is no danger that Jefferson will displace them. After all, the corporate identity of a military caste, proud of its own contributions to winning and preserving American independence, demands heroes and founders who come up through the ranks and share its values and worldview. In his famous letter to Henry Lee, setting forth his modest conception of his role in declaring American independence, Jefferson disclaimed any "originality of principle or sentiment," concluding that the Declaration was simply "intended to be an expression of the American mind."[36] But Jefferson could not pretend to express the "military mind." Instead, he challenged the very notion that the military should have a mind of its own, insisting that soldiers were citizens first.

Military men and women would not quarrel with this premise, the foundational principle of civilian supremacy, but they would articulate it in their own language, the language of professional "regularity" and in "concepts of duty, honor, and integrity rooted in disinterested personal accountability" that underscored *differences* between citizens and soldiers.[37] Hostility to Jefferson, and later to Jackson, epitomized the army's almost tribal sense that civilians would never give soldiers the respect and understanding they deserved, that if the military establishment were to function effectively without jeopardizing liberty, it was because the military had so thoroughly internalized professional values. In other words, it was military self-restraint, not the superior wisdom of civilian politicians, that sustained the Republic. From this perspective, Jefferson symbolically functions as an antifounder, the classic embodiment of civilian foolishness.

The authors of the following essays point to a more significant role for Jefferson in the military academy's founding. In emphasizing the deeper affinities between the professional ethos of the officer corps trained at Thayer's academy with the enlightened, meritocratic values espoused by Jefferson and other reformers, Watson illuminates a complex, dialectical process in which an honor-prone quasi-aristocratic military establishment eventually became thoroughly republicanized. This accommodation between army and society may have been set in motion by Jefferson's reform efforts, but it was at least equally the product of the army's alienation from popular politics and partisan meddling. The irony is that, in their Whiggish contempt for the excesses of Jeffersonian and Jacksonian democracy, the officer corps embraced Jeffersonian values. Many of the graduates of West Point in its antebellum heyday may have despised Jefferson. Yet they were truer to the values that he had espoused in 1802, when he founded his military academy, than were the first generations of students at Jefferson's University of Virginia.

Notes

1. The best history of the Declaration's drafting and reception is Pauline Maier, *American Scripture: Making the Declaration of Independence* (New York, 1997).

2. The classic study is Merrill D. Peterson, *The Jefferson Image in the American Mind* (New York, 1960); on Jefferson's image in his own lifetime, see Robert M. S. McDonald, "Jefferson and America: Episodes in Image Formation" (Ph.D. diss., University of North Carolina at Chapel Hill, 1998). For assessments of more recent historiography, see Peter S. Onuf, "The Scholars' Jefferson," *WMQ*, 3rd ser., 50 (1993): 671–99; Jan Ellen Lewis and Peter S. Onuf, "American Synecdoche: Thomas Jefferson as Image, Icon, Character, and Self," *American Historical Review* 103 (1998): 125–36. On the discrepancy between popular and academic attitudes toward Jefferson, see Joseph J. Ellis, *American Sphinx: The Character of Thomas Jefferson* (New York, 1997), 3–23. The most vigorous assault on Jefferson's iconic standing comes from a prominent conservative, Conor Cruise O'Brien, in *The Long Affair: Thomas Jefferson and the French Revolution* (Chicago, 1996).

3. Robert M. S. McDonald, "West Point's Lost Founder: Jefferson Remembered, Forgotten, and Reconsidered," p. 198, this volume. For further thoughts on the contemporary cultural divide, see Jean Yarbrough's afterword, "The Role of Military Virtues in Preserving Our Republican Institutions" at the end of this volume.

4. Elizabeth D. Samet, "Great Men and Embryo-Caesars: John Adams, Thomas Jefferson, and the Figure in Arms," pp. 77–95, this volume. On the founders' concern with their historic reputations, see Joanne B. Freeman, *Affairs of Honor: National Politics in the New Republic* (New Haven, Conn., 2001), epilogue.

5. TJ, Epitaph, (1826), *TJW,* 706.

6. McDonald, "West Point's Lost Founder," p. 203, this volume.

7. TJ to William Stephens Smith, 13 November 1787, *TJP* 12:356; TJ to William Short, 3 January 1793, *TJP* 25:14.

8. TJ, First Inaugural Address, 4 March 1801, *TJW,* 493.

9. Adams to TJ, 14 August 1815, *AJL,* 455.

10. The most thorough account of the period, written from a decidedly neo-Federalist stance, is Stanley Elkins and Eric McKitrick, *The Age of Federalism* (New York, 1993).

11. Marshall Smelser, "The Federalist Period as an Age of Passion," *American Quarterly* 10 (1958): 391–419; John R. Howe Jr., "Republican Thought and the Political Violence of the 1790s," *American Quarterly,* 19 (1967): 147–65.

12. See Charles Royster, *A Revolutionary People at War: The Continental Army and American Character, 1775–1783* (Chapel Hill, N.C., 1979).

13. See the essays collected in James Horn, Jan Ellen Lewis, and Peter S. Onuf, eds., *The Revolution of 1800: Democracy, Race, and the New Republic* (Charlottesville, Va., 2002).

14. Reginald C. Stuart, *The Half-way Pacifist: Thomas Jefferson's View of War* (Toronto, 1978).

15. *Federalist* No. 6 (Hamilton), in *The Federalist,* ed. Jacob E. Cooke (Middletown, Conn., 1961), 35, 31. See the excellent discussion in Gerald Stourzh, *Alexander Hamilton and Republican Government* (Stanford, Calif., 1970), 149–53.

16. The analysis here and in following paragraphs draws heavily on Peter Onuf and Nicholas Onuf, *Federal Union, Modern World: The Law of Nations in an Age of Revolutions, 1776–1814* (Madison, Wis., 1993).

17. Peter S. Onuf, *Jefferson's Empire: The Language of American Nationhood* (Charlottesville, Va., 2000), 80–108.

18. David N. Mayer, "'Necessary and Proper': West Point and Jefferson's Constitutionalism," p. 69, this volume.

19. Theodore J. Crackel, "The Military Academy in the Context of Jeffersonian Reform," p. 100, this volume.

20. Mayer, "'Necessary and Proper,'" p. 55, this volume.

21. Ibid., p. 57, this volume. For further discussion of Jefferson's views on federalism, see David N. Mayer, *The Constitutional Thought of Thomas Jefferson* (Charlottesville, Va., 1994), 185–221, and Onuf, *Jefferson's Empire,* 109–46.

22. All quotations in this and the next paragraph are from TJ, First Inaugural Address, 4 March 1801, *TJW,* 493.

23. Crackel, "The Military Academy in the Context of Jeffersonian Reform," pp. 111–12, this volume. See also the more extensive treatment of this theme in Crackel, *Mr. Jefferson's Army: Political and Social Reform of the Military Establishment, 1801–1809* (New York, 1987).

24. Samet, "Great Men and Embryo-Caesars," p. 85, this volume.

25. Ibid., p. 88, this volume.

26. Higginbotham, "Military Education before West Point," p. 36, this volume.

27. Wagoner and McDonald, "Mr. Jefferson's Military Academy: An Educational Interpretation," p. 131, this volume.

28. Ibid., p. 132, this volume.

29. Ibid., pp. 132–33, 142, this volume.

30. Higginbotham, "Military Education before West Point," p. 42, this volume. See the discussion of this proposal, and its political motivations, in Cameron Addis, *Jefferson's Vision for Education, 1760–1845* (New York, 2003), chapter 2.

31. Watson, "Developing 'Republican Machines': West Point and the Struggle to Render the Officer Corps Safe for America, 1802–33" p. 169, this volume.

32. Ibid., pp. 156–57, this volume.

33. Peterson, *The Jefferson Image.*

34. TJ to Nathaniel Macon, 14 May 1801, in L&B, 10:261.

35. The quotation is taken from David C. Hendrickson's important study, *Peace Pact: The Lost World of the American Founding* (Lawrence, Kans., 2003).

36. TJ to Henry Lee, 8 May 1825, *TJW,* 1501.

37. Watson, "Developing 'Republican Machines,'" p. 167, this volume.

Military Education before West Point

DON HIGGINBOTHAM

Two centuries of discussion and debate about the nature of military education had taken place in the Western world before President Thomas Jefferson established the United States Military Academy at West Point. Jefferson, himself never a soldier, had been interested generally in state-supported education as early as his years in the Virginia legislature during the War for Independence. But his focus had been on education for civilian boys and young men. His elaborate scheme (it failed to secure adoption) had called for a pyramid of institutions. Male students, depending on their performance or financial means, would progress from elementary (girls were included at this first level) and then grammar schools to the capstone institution: the College of William and Mary. To Jefferson, a liberally educated citizenry provided the key to successful republican government.[1] When, after 1800, he finally showed an interest in a national military school, his desire to strengthen republican ideals and practices again came into play. In fact, Jefferson's West Point came into being before the more famous military schools of the nineteenth century, which resulted from the profound changes in warfare during the Napoleonic era.

And yet, given the emphasis of military historians and other students of military education, one might think that officers received little or no academic training before the Prussians created their famous War School. Certainly, whatever institutions that existed get short shrift. Undoubtedly, influential scholars such as Samuel P. Huntington and other American apostles of Emory Upton have played a role in creating this image. Of course, Prussia exercised a profound influence.

In 1807, following its disastrous defeat by Napoleon at Jena and the Treaty of Tilsit, which imposed humiliating terms, Prussia shook up its military establishment. It opened military careers to seventeen-year-olds by competitive examination and revamped military schooling, with its capstone eventually being the War College, associated with Gerhard Johann Scharnhorst, then the best-known military writer in Prussia, and with Carl von Clausewitz, the future father of theoretical and strategic studies. The institution came to prescribe a three-year course in strategy and other advanced subjects. Clausewitz, at one time its director, wrote his famous *On War,* which reached print posthumously in 1832. His quest for fundamental strategic principles took the form of comparing the wars of the French Revolution with those of the old regime.

If Clausewitz failed to offer a satisfactory fare, students of conflict had more down-to-earth alternatives, including the Swiss writer and member of Napoleon's staff Antoine-Henri Jomini, whose *Summary of the Art of War* bristled with maxims about maneuver, attack points, and lines of communication. American officers, including those with West Point educations and West Point educators, found little of relevance in the period before the French upheaval. And surprising as it may seem to us, that included the War for Independence and the life of America's one Great Captain, George Washington.[2]

If Jomini and somewhat later Clausewitz and their interpreters dominated American military writing and teaching, what did eighteenth-century Americans know and think about military education at the time of the imperial wars, the War for Independence, and the subsequent years before the 1802 creation of the United States Military Academy? Americans knew about the rise of the nation-state in the early modern period and the wars that it spawned from the sixteenth century to their own era in the late eighteenth century. They were also aware that there occurred simultaneously what historians now call the "Military Revolution." Part of this change can be explained by technological advances that made for more destructive weaponry, but part of it was owing to the need for a more bureaucratic apparatus to harness the engine of the state to collect heavier taxes and to supply armies and navies made larger by the succession of wars involving the nation-states over nearly three centuries.[3] An examination of military education in Europe and America before the French Revolution shows that on both continents governments and their military men were aware, however imprecisely, of choices in military education between a growing emphasis on institutional learning and a tutorial tradition. In America and possibly elsewhere, these tensions remained alive and well at the end of the century—and even, in the United States, after the founding of the military academy at West Point.

Military schools emerged to provide more systematic training for larger armed forces that now fought and maneuvered in ways brought about by technological innovations. In 1616 John of Nassau, from a distinguished Dutch military family, created an academy for officers, one of the earliest and most influential for its time. His students already had available a body of published soldierly literature in their own language, including at least one illustrated drill manual. Emphasizing distinct, numbered steps for loading muskets and volley fire, the Dutch publications on infantry tactics went through various editions in Danish, German, French, and English. Dutch experts traveled to numerous friendly states to impart the new methods. Gustavus II Adolph of Sweden borrowed and revised these tactical reforms, demonstrating their great potential. A 1726 German military manual showed the continued influence of the Dutch for loading and shooting a musket. In 1653 Prussia established a cadet corps to train officer elites in military science. France, Austria, and Denmark soon followed, as did Russia in 1731.

Thinkers and teachers about war also lavished time on geometric fortifications as the infantry-dominated battlefield increasingly receded in relative importance. In western Europe, at least, what might be termed fortress warfare dominated the landscape. Huge, geometric structures signaled the significance of military architecture and artillery. Officers had to know how to defend or besiege and capture fortresses. Technical awareness became imperative, as artillery and engineering, together or separately, became a distinct branch or component of armies by the eighteenth century. In time, serious soldiers everywhere talked and read about Sebastien Le Prestre de Vauban, Louis XIV's great military engineer, who besides his influence as a teacher and writer, conducted countless sieges and drafted plans for a hundred or more fortresses and other defense works. To Vauban, such citadels served a dual purpose: they guarded against foreign invasion and served as staging points for taking the offensive. His polygonal forts, with their protruding bastions, dotted the landscape of western Europe, especially in the Low Countries and northern Italy, and could occasionally be found in central and eastern Europe as well.[4]

Sieges and siegecraft characterized the climactic campaigns of the Seven Years' War in Britain's thirteen colonies against such French strongholds as Carillion (later Ticonderoga) and Louisbourg. Colonial and British detachments even erected Vaubanseque forts of their own in the wilderness, such as Fort William Henry in New York and Fort Ligonier in Pennsylvania. Siege warfare also formed a major component of the critical stages of the War for Independence, a conflict that began with the siege of Boston in 1775 and ended, for all practical purposes, with the siege of Yorktown in 1781. In between those events were the sieges of Savannah and Charleston, which, unlike the first-mentioned ones, ended disastrously for Americans. But Nathanael Greene and his militia allies used such tactics in reducing several British posts in the South Carolina backcountry. The longest siege of the war, the French and Spanish investment of Gibraltar, brought 40,000 men and fifty ships to bear on the rocky fortress, but after three and a half years the siege ended in failure.[5]

Although military schools became more important in the eighteenth century, it is difficult to generalize about them in terms of their objectives and course of study. And educational institutions, then and now, change for better or worse over time. In Russia, Prussia, and Austria, they served as institutions for inculcating or reinforcing the culture of the nobility. In Russia, the French language, fencing, music, and other cultural arts found their way into the course of study, and the minimum age for entry in 1766 was lowered from thirteen to five because of the fear that older boys might already have acquired bad habits and materialistic values before admission. But until they reached the age of nine, boys were taught by women, because they still needed "maternal sweetness." (The Russian Cadet Corps remained an institution under firm imperial direction until its demise in the Russian Revolution of 1918.)

Similar thinking influenced Prussia's Berlin Cadet Corps, where the age requirement dipped from thirteen to ten. At times, academic standards looked quite rigorous, but many boys complained of being ordered by Frederick II to enroll, and the hazing of newcomers seems to have been a common practice, as would be true later at the United States Military Academy. Some of the more talented young scholars received career options, possibly what we might call the civil service, including the diplomatic branch. Maria Theresa of Austria, like her royal contemporaries elsewhere, saw her newly created military school, the Wiener Neustadt Academy, as a training ground for the next generation of nobles. If the institution lived up to the claims for it, the school may well have been one of the best in that day, with its study of drill, fortifications, artillery, mathematics, and foreign languages.[6]

In Britain, fewer opportunities existed for formal military education than in these continental kingdoms. The only military school of note before the American Revolution was the Royal Military Academy at Woolwich, founded in the 1740s, which focused on officers for the artillery and engineers. If technical military education received the greatest emphasis in Russia, Prussia, and elsewhere, it seems to have been all that Woolwich offered, except for languages. Not until about the time of West Point's founding did Britain have a formal institution, Sandhurst, to train infantry and cavalry officers.[7]

It would have been unthinkable for the British elite to have attended Woolwich and entered an inferior branch of the army. High rank and field command did not go to officers with such a background. At best, writes William B. Willcox, "any such quasi-specialist who rose above the junior grades was as likely as not to find himself governing a city or commanding an expedition."[8] One reads of rare exceptions. Major General William Phillips of the artillery came from modest origins, a sound officer who earned the respect of his social superiors, as did another commoner, Major General James Robertson, who served as military governor of New York City between 1780 and 1783.[9] One reads biographies of Britain's ranking generals in the War for American Independence—Gage, Howe, Clinton, Burgoyne, Cornwallis, and Carleton—without learning much if anything of their having formal military schooling in their home country. If an officer really wanted even a smattering of time in the classroom, he might do as Cornwallis did when the young officer traveled to Turin in the Kingdom of Sardinia, where he entered the military academy, reputedly one of the best in Europe. Doubtless he profited from the experience, even though he stayed only a few months and received special treatment, because his father was a friend of King George II's son, the duke of Cumberland, the general who put down the Scottish Rebellion of '45 in ruthless fashion.[10]

Another junior officer enrolled at Brunswick, and two more studied at Caen, including the son of General Jeffery Amherst, who gained fame in the conquest of Canada. The complexity of our subject is reflected in a comparison between Britain and Prussia. The absence of a stigma upon an officer with a formal military education is seen in Frederick's Prussia, with a third of its generals having been in the Berlin Cadet Corps.[11]

In any case, it is clear that France under the leadership of Choiseul, Saint Germain, and Gribeauval led the way in military innovation and education in the latter half of the eighteenth century.[12] Low-level academies had existed for years, but by the eve of the French Revolution, a variety of advanced specialized schools had appeared. Reformers were sounding off well before 1789, or even 1763, the year of France's humiliating treaty concluding the Seven Years' War. The heated discussions over field artillery and cannon design have been called the "Star Wars" debate of its time. French military reformers, according to Ken Adler, "refashioned the artillery service into a new kind of military machine that, in conjunction with the Revolutionary mass armies, spearheaded the destruction of the old Europe under the command of their disciple, Napoleon Bonaparte." (Americans would later be mindful of these innovations.) More than any other influence, the French inspired armies of the time to increase the use of artillery as opposed to other arms, a greater proportional shift than would be witnessed again until the twentieth century.[13]

A variety of officer training schools also exposed young officers to new ideas about the use of light infantry, to the mixed order of line and column, and to the separation of armies into large administrative components—which during the wars of the French Revolution would become combat divisions. Napoleon, to be sure, was hardly a typical general. But his early soldierly career shows the possibilities available. He attended the Royal Military School at Brienne, where during those five years, he gained some of his most important ideas. Graduating in 1784, he entered the École Militaire in Paris, completing its two-year program in one. Three years later he matriculated at Auxonne, studying at the preeminent artillery school in France.[14]

Even though military education differed in some measure from one country to another, with the French certainly out in front after 1763, some commonalties held true for a majority of them during much of the period in question—ones not yet discussed. Rulers displayed an intense interest in military schools and their officer corps in general. The preference for officers from the nobility reflected the monarch's desire to increase the loyalty of the highest elites to the reigning monarch. The notion stands out with particular clearness in looking at Louis XIV, Frederick II, Maria Theresa, and George II.

In a sense, the crown's behavior retarded the development of creative military leadership. Senior officers often remained in the dark as to national goals and planning, including orders given to other generals in the same campaign, a characteristic of Frederick II's dealings with his uniformed underlings. For an army or naval officer to cross the king, or to be perceived engaging in a political flirtation with the king's opponents, or to bring humiliating defeat to his arm of the service could result in court martial or death. Although the American revolutionaries eschewed monarchy, the early days of independence witnessed concerns about where the loyalty of military men rested. Was their allegiance to Washington or, later, to the Federalists or, later still, to President Jefferson and the Republicans? And was there danger that an American military school would be politicized?

Many officers as late as the American Revolution and afterward either had no opportunity for formal military schooling or they rejected the concept even if such a possibility existed. Professionalism, as the word would be used in the nineteenth century, did not exist even for those who gained valuable know-how from Woolwich, the Wiener Neustadt Academy, or similar schools. At best, officers were highly proficient technicians. A general was born, not made, declared Marshal Saxe, the eighteenth-century French commander. "Application rectifies ideas," he pronounced, "but does not furnish a soul, for that is the work of nature." These views he shared with other military writers, including Henry Loyd and the comte Guibert.[15]

In an era before Clausewitz and Jomini, generals had no strategic or theoretical doctrine to draw on. They did not know how to analyze a problem from different vantage points and seek the best of several approaches. If they saw themselves as professionals, they looked amateurish to a later age. Sir Henry Clinton, alone among Britain's military commanders in the War for Independence, seemed capable of some measure of analytical thinking.[16] But even he, like his colleagues, had no clear understanding of the difference between strategy and tactics. Indeed, strategy seems to have been a word little used. Stratagem appears, but usually in the context of describing a ruse or a surprise. If a general spoke of grand tactics, as opposed to elementary tactics, which applied to the battlefield, he likely meant the movement of armies over large spaces, outside or beyond the field of action.

General John Burgoyne, who lost an army at Saratoga, illustrates the deficiencies of British military leadership. He plunged into the wilderness of upper New York in 1777 without a sense of the obstacles that lay ahead. He lacked a clear-cut objective for the campaign. And he failed to seek any agreement with General Sir William Howe in New York City as to the manner in which their respective forces would cooperate with or complement each other. "Gentleman Johnny" brought with him through the woods and thickets along the Hudson more than a dozen wagons carrying his own personal wardrobe, store of wine, and other personal effects, as well as those of his mistress. And yet Burgoyne predicted an easy triumph over the Americans because, as he put it, the rebels lacked "men of military science."[17]

Burgoyne, Clinton, and the rest of the ranking generals in America had never held major commands, nor had they seen active service for many years. To a degree, Thomas Gage stands out as an exception, for he held the post of commander in chief in North America from 1763 to 1775. But his duties were strictly administrative until he arrived in Boston after the Tea Party and the Intolerable Acts. Certain generals even found ways during their assignments to put down the American rebellion to obtain leaves of absence to return to England for a time. Whatever their seemingly valid excuses, such as to see a dying wife, the truth is that a desire to lobby for a better command or to attend Parliament usually provides the real explanation. The records of those officers who commanded British naval forces in America hardly excelled those of the generals in terms of hands-on commitment during their careers. Richard Howe, Augustus Keppel, and Charles Hardy had not been before the mast for fifteen years or more before the colonial uprising.

In fact, the tutorial or apprenticeship method provided most officers with the tools of their trade, just as it did for young men in fields such as law and medicine. Despite the existence in Europe of some medical schools and institutions for legal training, including the British Inns of Court, direct observation and hands-on training predominated in all fields.[18] Observers noted repeatedly that one learned soldiering from fighting in battles and not from sitting in the classroom. For the young man with military aspirations or for the father who had them for his son, some experts recommended the provision of toy soldiers (metal ones were available by 1600 or so). Instead of childish things like wooden horses, dolls, and toy carts, a boy by the age of ten might be knowledgeable about drawing up companies, posting sentinels, and storming walled cities. Despite Frederick II's heavy investment in the Berlin Cadet Corps and lesser institutions, most Prussian officers considered assignments in the field to be the most valuable experience of all.[19]

George Washington, as the youthful commander of the Virginia Regiment in the Seven Years' War, illustrated how the tutorial system worked at its best. He observed the command techniques of such able British superiors as Colonel Henry Bouquet and General John Forbes; he took notes on useful ideas and information; he read military treatises; and he took fencing lessons. He could not take the so-called grand tour of Europe, an experience available to British and continental officers. To the extent that other nations permitted it, which depended on the relations between a young man's kingdom and the states he proposed to visit, an officer might take in a military school, an army encampment, a fortress, and a famous battlefield such as Bergen (Clinton went over the terrain for four hours), as well as engage in a series of conversations with foreign officers—in the course of much socializing—on their soldierly profession.

Washington, denied the chance to travel in Europe, made the most of his opportunities to develop informative relationships with British officers in America, including Colonel Thomas Gage, with whom he subsequently corresponded. Gage became his first military antagonist in the Revolutionary War, because Washington commanded the New England forces that besieged Gage's troops in Boston.[20] What he learned from Gage and other crown officers in the 1750s he then imparted to the officers who served under him. No doubt Washington also drew on accounts from his brother Lawrence, who held a royal commission for a time and led Virginia troops that participated in the Cartagena expedition against the Spanish in the early 1740s. In his Mount Vernon office, Washington placed only one painting on the wall: Lawrence in his crimson regimentals. Washington stressed to his Virginia officers military reading, firm discipline, uniform dress, and new drill techniques introduced into the British army by the duke of Cumberland. Since Washington and his Virginia Regiment received high praise from several able royal officers, it is safe to conclude that he had learned a good deal. His letters show that he enjoyed military life, even to the point of trying hard but unsuccessfully to obtain a British regular commission and to have his Virginia Regiment placed on the regular establishment.[21]

Reading constituted a form of military education that seems to have had fairly wide appeal to officers in Europe and America, whether they attended war schools or pursued the tutorial method of Washington and Sir Henry Clinton and many other British officers. But it is difficult to measure the effect of such literature on the ability of bookish officers to influence their peers or to conduct campaigns in ways that reflected their learning. Ira D. Gruber provides helpful accounts of the British army, based particularly on new information about Sir Henry. Several decades after William B. Willcox published his magisterial biography of Clinton, *Portrait of a General,* significant sources on the general's reading habits became available to historians: eleven "small leather-bound books containing notes and reflection on nearly thirty years" of military reading. Gruber's study of the inventories of sixteen other officers' libraries reveals reading tastes remarkably similar to those of Clinton. After the mid-eighteenth century, these Britons increasingly devoured French writings on war, which had not been the case in the previous fifty years.[22] Clinton hardly stood alone in recording his thinking about his reading, nor did he lack company in digesting, in addition to the standard exercise manuals, an array of literature that included histories, biographies, and memoirs. Fluent in French, Clinton agreed with his colleague who proclaimed the French language an essential pedagogical tool because the "best modern books upon our profession are written in that language."[23]

A comparison of Clinton's reading with that of Washington is worthwhile, because during the War for Independence, Clinton served as deputy British commander in chief or as the supreme commander from 1776 to 1782, roughly paralleling Washington's slightly longer tenure as commander in chief of the Continental army. Gruber persuasively argues that "Clinton's actions in America do seem to have been remarkably consistent with his ideas about war" recorded in his reading notes.[24] He advocated building support among the civilian population—the loyalists—and he recognized the importance of sea power. He displayed a reluctance to engage in large-scale battle unless he had a numerical advantage and an opportunity to flank the enemy. He admired generals who achieved their ends by maneuver and avoidance of battle.

Clinton, who owned or consumed more than thirty military tomes, had more reading material available than did Washington, and we lack the kind of notes for Washington that Clinton used to preserve his interpretation of his reading. But it is certain that Washington read a good deal, and that in both the Seven Years' War and the Revolution he encouraged his subordinates to do so as well. On the whole, Washington was much better read than we have realized, not only on warfare but on other topics as well. He informed Jonathan Boucher, who tutored his stepson Jackie Custis, that "I conceive a knowledge of books is the basis upon which all other knowledge is to be built." In time, he possessed a library of over 900 volumes.[25]

For Washington what would be an ongoing process for many years of acquiring military literature began as early as age twenty-three, when the recently appointed colonel of the Virginia Regiment ordered from London Humphrey Bland's *A Treatise of Military Discipline*—"Old Humphrey," as generations of officers referred to the work, which went through nine editions. This British staple for drill and regulations had sat on the shelves of Lawrence

Washington's study, where his young brother probably first encountered it. Now he sought his own copy, and only a month later he encouraged his officers of the Virginia Regiment to do the same. Reminding them that there was more to being an officer "than the Title," he said, "let us read." "Bland's and other treatises," he insisted, "will give us the wished for information." For the colonel the message became a refrain. "Leisure hours," he said, should be devoted to the "study of your profession."[26] By the time Washington resigned his commission as the war wound down on the Virginia frontier and as he prepared to marry Martha Custis and bring his bride and her children to Mount Vernon, his "knowledge in the Military Art," as he phrased it, had grown substantially. Since he knew the names of the great captains of history, it is reasonable to assume he had heard a good deal about them, possibly even encountering books covering their careers. He ordered from his business agent in Britain statue busts of Julius Caesar, Oliver Cromwell, Marlborough, Charles XII of Sweden, Prince Eugene of Austria, and Frederick the Great. He initially found the biographies of Charles and Frederick to be unavailable, but he later acquired them.[27]

Washington must have been encouraged by the outburst of military publishing in 1775 as Americans prepared for war. The quality is questionable of some of these guides and manuals, which usually appeared in pamphlet form, but Americans snapped them up, because, for the time being at least, such works were scarce. The printers invariably gave Washington complementary copies, beginning when he was a member of the Continental Congress and some weeks before he received his appointment as commander in chief of the Army of the United Colonies on June 15, 1775. Hugh Henry Ferguson dedicated his edition of a British work, *Military Instructions for Officers Detached in the Field,* to Washington, the Virginian's first honor of that nature. Washington himself began to purchase military tracts. He joined other subscribers to finance the publication of Thomas Hanson's *The Prussian Evolutions.* Committing to buy eight copies, which arrived on May 20, 1775, he also opened his purse for several other military tracts while still in Congress, which he failed to name, merely describing them as "5 books—Military."

A good sense of what Washington had read—or what he considered the best of his reading—can be gotten from his response to sought-after advice from Colonel William Woodford of Virginia. As for Washington's recommendations, he replied on November 10, 1775, with a list of five works, all a part of his library: Bland's *Treatise of Military Discipline;* the comte de Turpin de Crisse, *An Essay on the Art of War,* an English translation; Roger Stevenson, *Military Instructions for Officers Detached in the Field;* Captaine Louis de Jeney, *The Partisan: Or, the Art of Making War in Detachment,* another translation; and William Young, *Manoeuvres, Or Practical Observations on the Art of War.*[28]

The absence of reading notes limits what we can detect about these books' influence on him, but his awareness that French specialists were now au courant cannot be mistaken. His superiors in the 1758 Fort Duquense campaign, General Forbes and Colonel Henry Bouquet, a Swiss soldier of fortune, recommended de Crisse, who urged his readers to study military writings and to be mindful of adequate procurement and logistics, topics often neglected. The French essayist de Jeney underscored the growing European interest in light infantry and skirmishers, who might be deployed behind enemy lines to engage in partisan or guerrilla activity.[29] Marshall Saxe's *Reveries,* another favorite of Forbes and Bouquet, influenced the Forbes campaign against Fort Duquesne, and likely made an impression on their subordinate Washington. These writers maintained that even infantry lines could move effectively through rough, uneven terrain if they had received some light infantry training.

Though committed to a traditional war, with an army built largely along European lines, Washington put a premium on logistical considerations and recognized the value of de Jeney's message, which doubtless underscored lessons he had learned on the frontier, especially in the Braddock disaster. Certainly, he put to good use Daniel Morgan's regiment and other rifle-carrying units from the backcountry, and he temporarily detached Morgan's unit to assist General Horatio Gates in the campaign against Burgoyne. It was the corps, reported Gates, that "the army of General Burgoyne are most afraid of." By 1779 every Continental regiment received some light infantry training. That year a special light force under General Anthony Wayne captured the British post at Stony Point, New York, in a night attack.[30]

If Washington carried his prized books with him throughout the war, even buying "a green baise bookcase" to hold them, so did many other officers bring along the primers of the soldier's profession.[31] Numerous officers had served in the militia in the Seven Years' War, including Benjamin Lincoln, Philip Schuyler, and Benedict Arnold. Several former British officers residing in the colonies received commissions from the Continental Congress, including Generals Charles Lee, Horatio Gates, and Richard Montgomery. Nathanael Greene, Henry Knox, Anthony Wayne, and John Sullivan—too young for service in the 1750s—later served in the militia and took a serious interest in military reading and training. Greene frequented Knox's Boston bookstore in the early 1770s and discussed the latest books then being consumed by British officers. Greene seemed to admire most Marshall Saxe and Frederick II. Knox agreed with Greene that Saxe was the first resort for the principles of war, but, for his growing personal interests, artillery and engineering, he held up the famous Vauban and John Muller, "Professor of Artillery and Fortification" at Woolwich, as the preeminent authorities.[32]

At times Washington's generals turned to military history to answer questions the commander in chief put to them concerning a course of action for the army, a reflection perhaps of his continued emphasis on the importance of "the study of Military authors."[33] For example, after American reversals at Brandywine and Germantown in Pennsylvania in 1777, Washington queried them as to whether the army should strike back, possibly continuing the campaign into the early winter, or whether it should go into quarters until the spring; and if so, should they make their encampment relatively near the enemy in Philadelphia. Their written responses brimmed with references to the maxims and conduct of Pyrrhus, Marius, Maurice, Charles XII, Marlborough, Saxe, the duke of Brunswick, and Montcalm, along with others, including Hannibal.[34] Not surprisingly, Greene, probably better read than any of Washington's senior American officers with the possible exception of Knox, cited authorities from Hannibal to Frederick II in arguing for suspending campaigning and taking up secure positions relatively close to Howe's army.[35]

Captain Johann Ewald, a Prussian officer, believed that Americans took military reading more seriously than their opponents, "who consider it sinful to read a book or to think of learning anything during the war." He discovered that captured American haversacks contained "the most excellent military books translated in their language" such as "the *Instructions* of the great Frederick to his generals[, which] I have found more than one hundred times. Moreover, several among their officers had designed excellent small handbooks and distributed them in the army." German and British officers preferred to fill their portmanteaus with bags of powder, sweet-scented hair dressing, and playing cards.[36]

Ewald went on to make a point about Washington's army that is not now appreciated. At the time of his writing, December 1777, the war had been going on for only two and a half years, and he had witnessed two recent American reversals, at Brandywine and Germantown in southeastern Pennsylvania. Yet he could write that the Americans have "excellent officers."[37] A few weeks later, another German, Captain Johann Heinrichs of the Hessian Jaeger Corps, also saw real potential in the American army. He informed his minister of state that it would take only "Time and good leadership to make . . . [it] formidable."[38] In some ways, Washington and Congress had wanted an army that resembled its British counterpart and other European establishments. Although America had no congressionally mandated military school, a subject to which we shall shortly return, what we have described as the tutorial method seems to have worked reasonably well. Officers' experience with battles and campaigns was already extensive—Boston, Quebec, Long Island, Manhattan, Trenton, Princeton, Brandywine, Germantown, and Saratoga. Americans were reading, as Ewald observed, at just about the point in time when Washington's councils of war were responding with historical allusions to his quest for advice on whether to conclude the campaign of 1777 before the onset of winter.

Washington, like European monarchs, wanted an officer corps composed of elites, or of the better sort at least. He did so at the time when in Prussia and France men outside the nobility were being denied entry into the military and others, who were already officers, were being removed at the conclusion of wars. The very social character of America meant that it would be impossible for Washington to confine his officer corps even to an American kind of aristocracy, a home-grown one based on wealth, education, and lifestyle, although officers such as the Monroes, Marshalls, Laurens, Hamiltons, Schuylers, Livingstons, and Habershams showed that many men above the rank and file could at least measure up to what Washington called gentlemen. For, like his European counterparts, Washington believed that only gentlemen would likely have dedication, commitment, and respect from those they commanded. Colonel Henry Beekman Livingston, frustrated because he could not recruit enough officers who bore the good marks of family and high character, suggested to the commander in chief that he be allowed to enlist "gentlemen adventures" from Canada.[39] Washington sensed the likelihood of political opposition to the idea, especially since he felt inundated by foreign officers sent over from Europe by American diplomats.

Even so, the great influx of foreign officers in the Continental army also gave it added military experience and eighteenth-century-style professionalism. Although some foreign appointments were extremely controversial—because a few Europeans were given preferential rank and station over able American senior officers such as Knox and Greene, and also because some were both arrogant and incompetent—it is fair to say that a substantial percentage were sound and gained the respect of Washington and his lieutenants.[40] This admixture of Europeans is an example of how the American officer corps bore some resemblance to the polyglot nature of European armies. In addition to the numerous Frenchmen, there were Germans, Poles, and, among other nationalities, at least one Russian. Some of these men were typical European soldiers of fortune, having served in several different European armies. Charles Lee, for instance, the former British army major, spent time in various capacities with the Polish, Turkish, and Russian armies before settling in Virginia in the early 1770s.[41]

Aside from the Marquis de Lafayette, whose influential political connections helped cement the Franco-American alliance of 1778, the greatest foreign contributions came from Friedrich Wilhelm von Steuben, the Prussian, and a cluster of French engineers, especially Louis le Begue de Presle Duportail. Steuben's arrival coincided with a growing concern on Washington's part. Although there was now almost a surfeit of military treatises available after two years of war (and varying decidedly in quality), the commander in chief needed a manual to simplify and codify standards and procedures for the Continental army. Indeed, "a regular system of discipline, manoeuvers, evolutions, [and] regulations" was imperative.[42] He turned to Steuben, who had extensive experience as both an infantry and staff officer under Frederick II. Working closely with Washington and other officers, Steuben mixed practices from the British, French, and Prussian armies, adapting them to the backgrounds and needs of Continental soldiers. He slowly formulated his ideas for such a book, experimenting with various procedures as he drilled the Continentals during the Valley Forge winter and into the following campaigning season. He also drew upon his staff experience in Europe in spelling out the duties and responsibilities of regimental officers and men, from the commanding officer to the lowest level of the rank and file.

Once Steuben had completed his manuscript, Washington voiced his general approval, but he requested greater clarity of diction, because the translation of Steuben's prose into English left some matters obscure. And he made additions and alterations before recommending to Congress that Steuben's revised draft be adopted, published, and distributed throughout the army.[43] Steuben had simplified the manual of arms, added more bayonet training, increased the pace of march, and instituted greater battlefield flexibility. It won the praise of both American and foreign officers.

The Washington-Steuben collaboration resulted in the most important piece of American military writing to come out of the war, a conflict that generated a remarkable political literature from men like Thomas Jefferson, John Adams, and James Madison. There were no comparable military treatises, no parallel to the volumes of Clausewitz or Jomini that emerged from the Napoleonic era. Even so, Steuben's *Regulations for the Order and Discipline of the Troops of the United States* met a critical need in handsome fashion. The first edition comprised three thousand copies of what became known as the Blue Book, since most of them were bound in blue paper boards, although Steuben insisted that Washington's personal copy be tooled in gold leaf with leather binding.[44] As for Steuben himself, his value to the army continued to grow. Appointed inspector general, he functioned as the army's chief administrator and became, in effect, Washington's chief of staff.

As for the French volunteers, they contributed most significantly to the American corps of engineers. There were fewer needs in the artillery owing to the talents of the self-educated Knox, who headed the American artillery throughout the war. The chevalier de Mauduit du Plessis, a notable exception, graduated from the prestigious Grenoble artillery school and proved himself to Washington and Knox at Germantown and Fort Mifflin and demonstrated his teaching abilities at Valley Forge.[45] Doubtless Knox and Colonel John Lamb, a fine New York artillery officer, shared the contents of their personal libraries with their fellow officers. Time and again that arm of the service proved its effectiveness—at Trenton, Monmouth, Yorktown, and elsewhere, earning the praise of the French artillerists, unexcelled in Europe, as the two armies conducted the siege of Yorktown. The chevalier de Chastellux, the second-ranking French officer, exclaimed that his troops marveled at the American artillery's "extraordinary progress." Knox's men had approximately as many heavy weapons as the French army commander, the comte de Rochambeau, who reportedly had already participated in fourteen sieges.[46]

By contrast, the French engineers proved indispensable to Washington, for Americans were without talent or experience in that military branch. The French minister of war, Saint-Germain, ensured that the American engineers would not be plagued with incompetents or fortune seekers by, in effect, assigning four highly qualified officers to Washington's army. Louis Le Bègue de Presle Duportail, their ranking officer, so impressed Congress that he received promotion to brigadier general and command of the engineers, which put him on an equal footing with General Knox of the artillery. Duportail then recruited able engineers from France and received superb assistance from

Colonel Thaddeus Kościuszko, a Pole who received his engineering education in France.[47]

Duportail himself had his own library and used his tomes in providing some classroom instruction at West Point late in the war. By the standards of the day, the corps of engineers may well have been the ablest branch of the Continental army. It constructed bridging trains and temporary and permanent fortifications (some of their constructions at West Point and across the river at Constitution Island can be seen today, especially Fort Putnam, which has been completely rebuilt). Combat engineers, called sappers and miners, built the entrenchments and tunnels that allowed Knox's artillery to move into close range at Yorktown. Civil engineers and others with surveying experience constituted the topographical staff. Washington, a former surveyor and mapmaker, relied heavily on this group of officers. A Scot named Robert Erskine, a civil engineer from New Jersey, coordinated six mapmaking teams.[48] According to a leading authority, "the resulting maps equaled those of the French in accuracy and were vastly superior to anything available to British commanders."[49]

Although the last years of the war saw the Continental army suffer from shortages of supplies and pay, to say nothing of desertions and occasional small-scale mutinies, Robert K. Wright is surely correct when he writes that it "fought well under a variety of conditions. The army's organization achieved sophistication; its leadership down to the company level grew experienced, tough, and competent. The 'Europeanization' of the Continental army reflected the contributions of foreign volunteers and also the wisdom of Washington and other American leaders in selecting only those concepts that would work in America."[50]

What the army lacked in professionalism, as defined by that century, was a military school. Although various people proposed such institutions, their endeavors either failed or met with modest, temporary success. Multiple reasons seem to explain the outcome. It was unclear whether Congress—an extralegal body for several years—could create national structures. It did not even establish the Continental army. Instead, it adopted the New England forces besieging Boston at the request—*urging* is a better word—of Massachusetts authorities. The constitutional question hardly faded away with the implementation of the Articles of Confederation in 1781, nor, for that matter, did it disappear completely with the ratification of the Federal Constitution. The innovations in warfare taking place in military systems after midcentury—the employment of light infantry and skirmishers, mobile artillery, and large, self-sufficient divisions—were not dramatic enough to alter thinking about officer education. These were evolutionary developments that failed to bring profound transformations before the wars of the French Revolution and Napoleon.[51]

The attempts to found military schools were haphazard and uncoordinated. James Alcock, announcing the opening of a military school in September, 1775, in Annapolis, Maryland, declared that "there appears at this time a great alacrity among all ranks of people to perfect themselves in the Military Art."[52] It is not unreasonable to assume that other such quick fixes were available to would-be soldiers. A month before the colonies declared their independence, Congressman John Adams, who became a voracious reader of books on war, wrote Knox that "the Public" should establish "Accademies for the Education of young Gentlemen in every Branch of the military Art." Several months later Adams repeated his desire, for "Time, Study and Experience alone must make a sufficient Number of able officers." "This day," he continued, "I had the Honour of making a Motion for the appointment of a Committee to consider of a Plan for the Establishment of a military Academy." Congress responded by appointing Adams to such a committee, but, for whatever the reason, it presumably never presented a report. In fact, it is possible that three separate proposals for military schools were afloat in Congress. Opinions differed on whether to favor general or specialized educational institutions.[53]

Later, when the Continental army encamped at Pluckemin, New Jersey, Knox opened an informal school and rotated his officers through it for brief periods of time. There they read John Muller of Woolwich's *Treatise on Artillery* and the works of other writers.[54] From 1777 to 1779, some educational training took place at Carlisle, Pennsylvania, for an unknown number of artillerymen, but the main purpose of the facility was to repair and make ordnance. The only other attempt at formal instruction resulted from Congress's creation of the Corps of Invalids, a concept adopted from the British army of using men unfit for combat to perform garrison functions. It was to include a "Military School for Young Gentlemen," who would eventually return to active duty as ensigns. Headed by Colonel Lewis Nicola, author or translator of several military tracts and a former British army engineer, the Invalids' educational mission received scant attention. But the unit engaged in important custodial work for the remainder of the war.[55]

It should come as no surprise that efforts to create one or more military academies had met with failure and that informal institutions presided over by Knox, Nicola, and possibly others had not been noteworthy. The fact is that the record of the Continental army, as Robert K. Wright observed, was remarkably good considering the circumstances, for it steadily improved by means of the tutorial method still prevalent in Europe, a method that had served Washington and doubtless other provincial officers rather admirably in the Seven Years' War. The components of their tutorial approach included battlefield experience, military reading, and conversation and observation involving professional officers. Those opportunities had been available to Washington's officers. Even so, Washington, Adams, Knox, and others were undoubtedly correct in seeing infinite value in military schools. The point is that the need was not critical at the time.

But with the war drawing to a close, a better case might now be made for Congress's creating permanent educational facilities. In a future war, there might not be time to get the hands-on training, and there might not be foreign officers available to teach skills that few Americans would know. Whatever the nature of the postwar military system in America, it would surely be small, possibly too small to inculcate the tutorial training of the past. It seemed unthinkable, given the low American opinion of European standing armies, that young men from Virginia, New York, and other states would go to the Old World for a military education or even take the grand tour of the continent, visiting battlefields and conversing with officers in Prussia, Austria, and elsewhere as young Englishmen such as Clinton and Burgoyne had done before the American war. Washington took a dim view of such excursions. American young men would succumb to principles "unfriendly to republican government" and "the rights of man." So did Jefferson, who, in his 1785 letter to John Banister Jr., condemned European education in general and the corrupting influence of old regime society, which would lead American youths to extravagant and immoral lives, including a passion for whores "destructive" of one's "health" and "fidelity to the marriage bed."[56]

When in the spring of 1783 Congress appointed a committee chaired by Hamilton to assess the postwar military needs of the United States, it gave Washington and, through him, his senior officers an opportunity to voice their opinions.[57] The commander in chief received a multitude of proposals, all of which addressed officer education. Most were reasonably sound if sometimes unrealistic. Quartermaster General Timothy Pickering feared an American military academy might generate a kind of nobility—perhaps an indication that he was thinking of current trends in Prussia and France. He then contradicted himself, saying that American officers who wanted formal instruction might enroll in European war schools. Governor George Clinton of New York, who had a modest military background, responded to Washington's solicitation by opposing a specific institution for officer training. But he, as well as one other respondent, broached the establishment of a professorship in military science at one college in each of the thirteen states, an interesting idea in view of such developments years later at land grant institutions and even earlier at some antebellum schools. (Jefferson, long a highly visible archenemy of the hereditary Society of the Cincinnati, urged the society in 1817 to endow such a professorial chair at his new University of Virginia, even—and he must have swallowed hard—promising to name it the Cincinnati professorship.)[58]

Some of the more serious ideas included the creation of three regional academies, near military arsenals so that training facilities and weaponry would be available. Another recommendation advocated a three-year curriculum featuring a thorough grounding in mathematics and the sciences, with some attention as well to geography, literature, and French. Some proposals favored educating men for all branches of the army, not just a standard course leading to engineering and artillery assignments. Summers would be occupied in field training. Breadth in academic education and in preparation for all the military branches particularly appealed to Knox and Steuben. These proposals had merit, although the creation of three army schools would have been exceedingly expensive and would have involved a thin distribution of other resources. And the suggestion, appearing in an occasional proposal, for a naval academy was ahead of its time.[59]

Washington, whose task was to respond to Congress after analyzing these plans, had little to say about military education in a document that focused on maintaining a small, well-trained army and a greatly improved militia under a degree of federal supervision. A total realist, Washington realized the Confederation was contracting at the war's end. Congress's request for advice on the military needs of the nation came almost simultaneously with two events that hardly made the general public look positively on the subject of a sound course for national security: the Newburgh Conspiracy and the founding of the Society of the Cincinnati.[60] Although "an Institution calculated to keep alive and diffuse the knowledge of the Military Art would be highly expedient," Washington doubted Congress's ability to enter "great and expensive Arrangements." What seemed possible for the moment was to offer instruction to young men at artillery and engineering posts. As Washington knew from his recent experience with the Continental army, these were the two branches in which Americans had been deficient and where the greatest need would exist in a time of war. These garrisons, then, would become "a nursery from whence a number of Officers for Artillery and Engineering may be drawn on any great or sudden occasion."[61]

Between Congress's failure to act on Washington's "Sentiments on a Peace Establishment" and the election of Jefferson to the presidency seventeen years later, the subject of an educational institution for the military languished.[62] A dreary succession of schemes for producing well-schooled officers appeared in various places. They lacked the freshness and creativity of the blueprints presented to Washington on the eve of disbanding the army. The army itself hardly acted as a pressure group for new military structures, for its numbers ranged from under one hundred to under a thousand men, as the feeble Confederation limped through the middle and late 1780s. The First Congress under the Constitution created an army, tiny though it was, because of Indian threats in the Northwest. It soon suffered two humiliating defeats at the hands of the tribesmen. In November, 1793, Secretary of the Treasury Hamilton and Secretary of War Knox spoke out in the cabinet for Washington's returning to the cause of a military academy in his forthcoming fifth annual address to Congress, a measure that Secretary of State Jefferson claimed he thought unconstitutional. Hoping to avoid further division among his already-fractious department heads, the president elected to refer the matter to the lawmakers without a precise recommendation. He nonetheless reminded Congress that some "branches of the Military art" could "scarcely ever be attained by practice alone."[63]

If the venerable tutorial approach had achieved results in the Revolution, the explanation lay in large part in the availability of men like Steuben, Duportail, and Kościuszko. Turning to Europe, at least on a large scale, offered no option. The country seethed with anger and hostility between Federalists and Republicans over the French Revolution and its impact on Europe and America. Even during the War for Independence, the European option had generated tensions.

Congress responded somewhat positively to Washington's concerns about officer preparation. In 1794 it established within the army the Corps of Artillerists and Engineers, stipulating the appointment of two cadets for each company and the purchase of books and other instructional materials for their use. The new corps, quartered at the existing army installation at West Point, New York, on the Hudson River, showed the continuing French influence in these areas of specialization and revealed, as in the Revolution, the shortage of qualified Americans for high positions. Three of the five most senior posts went to Lieutenant Colonel Stephen Rochefontaine, the ranking appointee, a former officer in the French and American armies; Major Louis Tousard, another veteran of French and American service; and John Jacob Rivardi, a Swiss-born officer in the Russian army before arriving in America, who had already been employed by Knox to supervise several fortifications under construction on the Atlantic coast. Secretary of War Timothy Pickering, who succeeded Knox in that office, admitted American deficiencies in technological experience. "To become skillful in either branch of their profession," artillery or engineering, would demand "long attention, study and practice." Although there might be complaints about the selection of "foreign officers" for "this object," they alone seemed well qualified, and several were available in America.[64]

West Point in the 1790s hardly appears as a school in the making. The junior officers resented being treated as students required to attend classes by the imperious Rochefontaine. What Theodore Crackel calls "this experiment in military education" lasted "just a few months" because of rebellious engineers and artillerists and a mysterious fire that destroyed the old Revolutionary War provost building on the plain, where classes met. Tensions increased when Rochefontaine and a junior officer fought a duel.[65] Formal education, such as it was, ended. Moreover, part of the corps moved to other stations, some companies to the coast and some to the interior. Whatever Rochefontaine's failings, he had endeavored to create a respectable military library at West Point. A surviving inventory lists twenty-seven titles and a total of forty-three volumes, mostly artillery, mathematics and science, and fortification studies. But unfortunately the library fell victim to the fire.[66] Even the XYZ affair, followed by the Quasi-War with France, scarcely led to the creation of a truly educational facility. Although one intent of the 1794 law creating the Corps of Artillerists and Engineers was to educate cadets (young men not yet holding officers' commissions), as late as 1798 there had been no cadets appointed. Hamilton, nominal head of the enlarged army during the French crisis, called for a "permanent academy for naval and military instruction" and secured from General Duportail, the head of army engineers in the Revolution, a "plan for a military school."[67]

The Federalists, never working together, especially from 1798 through the end of Adams's one-term presidency, favored an academy without being of one mind about how to achieve it. Secretary of War James McHenry now opted for a proposal submitted by Major Louis Tousard for a school at Carlisle, Pennsylvania, or Springfield, Massachusetts. Adams agreed to it, but Congress did not. Never to be outdone, Hamilton returned to the fray, proposing an academy made up of five schools, a ridiculous idea, including everything from cavalry to naval curricula. Moreover, it was terrible timing, because the Federalists were by then feeling a political backlash throughout the country because of, among other things, their efforts to vastly increase the size of the army. Even so, the Adams administration went along with a scaled-down version of Hamilton's grandiose blueprint for military education. But the Federalist internal bickering, the Republican opposition, and the election of 1800 all contributed to the future of a military academy being uncertain at best when Jefferson took office.[68]

The story of the Federalists' last efforts to create a school is, in fact, more complicated than what is outlined here. Adams and his secretary of war even decided they could have a de facto academy, whatever it was called, by vigorously implementing the 1794 law, appointing faculty and cadets for instruction at West Point. But Adams, for one, wearied of appointing Frenchmen to army posts, a practice he seems to have felt had been employed too often since the beginning of the War for Independence. Reacting to a freshet of French names, he exclaimed that "I have an invincible aversion to the appointment of foreigners, if it can be avoided."[69] The new scheme was never fully implemented before Adams left office.[70]

In America, as in Europe, there was always some tension between formal military education and the tutorial approach to learning about warfare. And in the new nation, it would continue into the nineteenth century, fueled in part by the age-old myth that the militia constituted the first line of defense in a free country. Of course, neither of the two approaches really supported the militia myth, but that myth further muddied the waters of rational debate. Some congressmen voiced skepticism of "scientific soldiers." General and later President Andrew Jackson was no friend of Jefferson's military academy. Prior to the American Civil War, only one West Point graduate had risen to the rank of general officer: Joseph E. Johnston in 1860. Yet the military academy survived. To those who still had an eighteenth-century fear of professional officers and standing armies, one could always respond (whatever the truth of the matter) that West Point was primarily an institution for training engineers. But most Americans probably gave little thought to the school. It was not located in a highly visible metropolitan area, although there had been talk in its early days of moving it to New York City. It continued to be out of sight, nestled in the highlands of the Hudson.

Moreover, although new ideas are always unsettling to some people, West Point hardly became associated with innovation. After all, the War for Independence had failed to produce original ideas about how soldiers learned their craft. Even the advanced thinking that one might encounter in French artillery and engineering schools after 1763 seems to have had modest impact on officers on both sides of the Atlantic before the 1790s. An examination of the Continental army and the new federal army of the 1790s, in terms of education and most other matters as well, reinforces the prevailing view that the Revolution looks militarily conservative. To the extent that Americans advocated formal military education, they were mostly of one mind about where it should start, and that was with artillerists and engineers—a strictly European idea.[71]

The influence of French authors, of great significance to military readers in the War for Independence, continued to be felt in the Corps of Artillerists and Engineers at West Point in the 1790s and later. And the impact of America's former ally hardly diminished over the long run at the military academy. Jonathan Williams, the first superintendent, was recognized first and foremost for translating two French military texts. Jefferson himself recommended French titles for the library. In 1803 forty of the one hundred technical books at the school were in French. Superintendent Sylvanus Thayer, a committed Francophile, saw to the wholesale purchasing of French tomes. Alan Aimone writes that "by 1822 books and manuals about engineering, fortification, military art and tactics . . . included only 67 English titles as compared to 174 French manuals and reference books."[72] Frenchmen graced the faculty, and the most famous professor, Dennis Hart Mahan, was a devoted follower of Jomini. The list could go on.[73]

A few concluding comments about the debate over the military academy's origins seem in order. Jefferson's motives in 1801 remain cloudy. He, of course, had opposed such an institution earlier. There now seems less interest in demonstrating a genuine concern for military education on his part. The third president is pictured as desiring to further science or to create an institution with wide-ranging benefits to society. Or, in the opinion of Crackel, Jefferson was out to republicanize the army with Republicans. After all, that was not much different from the Federalist attempt to stock the officer corps of the enlarged army in 1798 with Federalists.[74]

But if military education was not Jefferson's preeminent motive, it should be stressed that it was not number one with Washington either. Surely he saw much value in a well-educated officer corps, but he had avoided the details of a war school, just as he had advocated major constitutional reform in 1787, content to leave the architecture to Madison and others. Washington wanted a military academy first and foremost for the same reason that he long urged the creation of a national university: that is, to create a more centralized government and to foster more national unity. He often remarked that bringing men from the different states into the army during the Revolutionary War had created "a band of brothers," a sense of oneness that would have taken countless years in the normal course of exchanges between Americans from the far-flung regions. Washington repeated those sentiments to Hamilton in 1796 as the two men worked together on what would become known as his Farewell Address, which first appeared in the press on September 19, 1796. Despite Washington's ardent wish to talk about the national benefits of federally sponsored education in the Farewell Address, Hamilton urged him to keep his valedictory to the American people general in nature and to avoid specificity, pointing out that the president's eighth annual message to Congress would provide him with such an opportunity before stepping down as chief executive. Washington gave in, but only in part. Hamilton reluctantly inserted two sentences toward the middle of the Farewell Address recommending "Institutions for the general diffusion of knowledge."[75] Two months later, in Washington's final speech to the lawmakers, he called for a bold program of federal activity, including a national university and a national military academy.[76] Congress has never seen fit to establish a national university, but, as we have noted, it did, albeit in faltering fashion, finally cooperate with a subsequent president, Jefferson, in the establishment of the United States Military Academy. In the army, at least, the new school fostered that sense of oneness that Washington had passionately advocated since his appointment as commander in chief of the Continental forces more than twenty years earlier. West Point has always done that. Let us hope it always will.

Notes

1. Jefferson's ideas on education while in the Virginia legislature are nicely summarized in Noble E. Cunningham Jr., *In Pursuit of Reason: The Life of Thomas Jefferson* (Baton Rouge, La., 1987), 58–60. For Jefferson's proposed legislation, see "A Bill for the More General Diffusion of Knowledge," *TJP* 2:526–28.

2. The best introduction to Clausewitz is Peter Paret, *Clausewitz and the State: The Man, His Theories, and His Times,* 2nd edition. (Princeton, N.J., 1985). For the origins and development of military thought and practice from the Renaissance through the Napoleonic era, Peter Paret, ed., *Makers of Modern Strategy: From Machiavelli to the Nuclear Age* (Princeton, N.J., 1986), chapters 1–7 is indispensable. Russell F. Weigley, *Towards an American Army: Military Thought from Washington to Marshall* (New York, 1962), is still the best study of American writers.

3. Geoffrey Parker, *The Military Revolution: Military Innovation and the Rise of the West, 1500–1800* (Cambridge, UK, 1988); Clifford J. Rogers, ed., *The Military Revolution Debate* (Boulder, Colo., 1995).

4. Henry Guerlac, "Vauban: The Impact of Science on War," in Paret, *Makers of Modern Strategy,* chapter 3.

5. Lee Kennett, *The French Forces in America, 1780–1783* (Westport, Conn., 1977), 143; Piers Mackesy, *The War for America, 1775–1783* (Cambridge, Mass., 1964), especially chapters 14, 18, 21, 28, 29.

6. Joseph L. Wieczynski, ed., *Modern Encyclopedia of Russian and Soviet History,* 6 vols. (Gulf Breeze, Fla., 1976–2000), 6:86–89; Mary West Case, "Catherine the Great, Ivan Ivanovich Betskoi, and Their Schools for a New Society" (M.A. thesis, University of North Carolina at Chapel Hill, 1976), 94–105; Christopher Duffy, *The Army of Frederick the Great* (New York, 1974); Christopher Duffy, *The Army of Marie Theresa* (New York, 1977).

7. John Smyth, *The History of the Royal Military Academy, Woolwich, the Royal Military Academy, Sandhurst . . .* (London, 1961).

8. William B. Willcox, *Portrait of a General: Sir Henry Clinton in the War of Independence* (New York, 1964), 14. In 1803 President Thomas Jefferson's secretary of war, Henry Dearborn, stressed the distinct place of engineering officers in the command system of armies. Engineering officers, he wrote, were staff specialists, and neither in America nor Europe had they been given authority over line officers. See Thomas Elliott Shaughnessy, "Beginnings of National Professional Military Education in America, 1775–1825" (Ed.D. diss., Johns Hopkins University, 1956), 134.

9. Robert P. Davis, *Where a Man Can Go: Major General William Phillips, British Royal Artillery, 1731–1781* (Westport, Conn., 1999); Milton M. Klein and Ronald W. Howard, eds., *The Twilight of British Rule in Revolutionary America: The New York Letter Book of General James Robertson, 1780–1783* (Cooperstown, N.Y., 1983).

10. Franklin and Mary Wickwire, *Cornwallis: The American Adventure* (Boston, 1970), 49–50.

11. Duffy, *Army of Frederick,* 29.

12. The Duc de Choiseul, foreign minister; the Count de Saint German, minister of war; and Gribeauval, the most influential reformer, who in 1776 won the new post of inspector general of artillery and held it until his death in 1789, a man who profoundly influenced Napoleon's thinking about heavy weaponry.

13. Ken Adler, *Engineering the Revolution: Arms and Enlightenment in France, 1763–1815* (Princeton, N.J., 1997) chapters 1–3, 3 (quotation); R. R. Palmer, "Frederick the Great, Guibert, Bulow: From Dynastic to National War," in Paret, *Makers of Modern Strategy,* 105–13.

14. A good introduction to warfare in Napoleon's day, with appropriate emphasis on Bonaparte himself, is Robert A. Doughty and Ira D. Gruber, *Warfare in the Western World: Military Operations from 1600 to 1871* (Lexington, Mass., 1996), chapters 6–7. For greater detail, see David G. Chandler, *The Campaigns of Napoleon* (New York, 1966); Owen Connelly, *Blundering to Glory: Napoleon's Military Campaigns* (Wilmington, Del., 1987).

15. Maurice de Saxe, *My Reveries upon the Art of War,* trans. R. R. Phillips (Harrisburg, Pa., 1955), 297.

16. Willcox, *Portrait of a General,* and his "Sir Henry Clinton: Paralysis of Command," in *George Washington's Opponents: British Generals and Admirals in the American Revolution,* ed. George Athan Billias (New York, 1969), 73–102.

17. Edward B. de Fonblanque, *Life and Correspondence of John Burgoyne, General, Statesman, Dramatist* (London, 1876), 484. Burgoyne's social life while campaigning was disturbing to the wife of the German Brunswicker general. Marvin L. Brown Jr., ed. and trans., *Journal and Correspondence of a Tour of Duty: Baroness von Riedesel and the American Revolution* (Chapel Hill, N.C., 1965), xxxi, 55–56.

18. For the evolution of professionalism in various fields and disciplines, see Howard M. Vollmer and Donald L. Mills, eds., *Professionalization* (Englewood Cliffs, N.J., 1966).

19. J. R. Hale, *War and Society in Renaissance Europe* (New York, 1985), 144–46; Karl Demeter, *The German Officer Corps in Society and State, 1650–1945* (New York, 1965), 68; Don Higginbotham, "Military Leadership in the American Revolution," in *Leadership in the American Revolution,* Library of Congress Symposia on the American Revolution, 3 (Washington, D.C., 1974), 91–95, 98–99.

20. For the Washington-Gage correspondence and other numerous references to Gage during Washington's Virginia military career, see W. W. Abbot, et al., eds., *The Papers of George Washington: Colonial Series,* 10 vols. (Charlottesville, Va., 1983–95), esp. the index to vol. 10 (hereafter cited as *PGW: Col. Ser.*)

21. Don Higginbotham, *George Washington and the American Military Tradition* (Athens, Ga., 1985), esp. chapters 1–2.

22. Ira D. Gruber, "The Education of Sir Henry Clinton," *Bulletin of the John Rylands University Library of Manchester* 72 (1990): 131–51. This essay is the latest of Gruber's pieces in his ongoing study of eighteenth-century British military education. See also his "Classical Influences on British Strategy in the War for American Independence," in *Classical Traditions in Early America,* ed. John W. Eadie (Ann Arbor, Mich., 1976), 175–90; "British Strategy: The Theory and Practice of Eighteenth-Century Warfare," in *Reconsiderations on the Revolutionary War,* ed. Don Higginbotham (Westport, Conn., 1978), 14–31, 166–70; "The Anglo-American Military Tradition and the War of American Independence," in *Against All Enemies: Interpretations of American Military History from Colonial Times to the Present,* ed. Kenneth J. Hagan and William R. Roberts (Westport, Conn., 1986), 21–47. J. A. Houlding, *Fit for Service: The Training of the British Army, 1715–1795* (Oxford, UK, 1981), notes the absence of French works in earlier British reading habits. But he finds a "plethora of manual and platoon exercises . . . that appeared regularly from 1716 through 1746." See chapter 3, 187 (quotation).

23. Fonblanque, *Political and Military Episodes,* 19.

24. Gruber, "Education of Sir Henry Clinton," 142–48, 143 (quotation).

25. Washington to Boucher, 9 July 1771, *PGW: Col. Ser.* 3:50–51. Washington's supposed unappreciated interest in reading and books receives a firm corrective in Paul K. Longmore, *The Invention of George Washington* (Berkeley, Calif., 1988), 213–26.

26. *PGW: Col. Ser.* 2:208–9, 251, 4:344.

27. Ibid., 1:223, 6:355, 358n77, 400. Particularly helpful on Washington's military reading before the Revolution is Oliver L. Spaulding Jr., "The Military Studies of George Washington," *American Historical Review* 29 (1924): 675–80.

28. W. W. Abbot, et al., eds., *The Papers of George Washington: Revolutionary War Series,* 13 vols. to date (Charlottesville, Va., 1987–), 2:346–47 (hereafter cited as *PGW: Rev. War Ser.*)

29. I owe a huge debt to Ellen McCallister Clark, staff member at the Society of the Cincinnati Library in Washington, D.C., for sharing with me her excellent unpublished essay "George Washington's Reading List: Ten Books that Shaped the Continental Army." She not only compiled an important list but analyzed its contents.

30. Don Higginbotham, *Daniel Morgan: Revolutionary Rifleman* (Chapel Hill, N.C., 1961), 70 (quotation); Robert K. Wright, *The Continental Army* (Washington, D.C., 1983), 149.

31. (Worth Bailey), *General Washington's Swords and Campaign Equipment* (Mount Vernon, Va., 1944), 10.

32. North Callahan, *Henry Knox: General Washington's General* (New York, 1958), 18–20, 29–30, 35–36; Theodore Thayer, *Nathanael Greene: Strategist of the American Revolution* (New York, 1960), 22–24, 44–45, 47–48 61; J. Mark Thompson, "Citizens and Soldiers: Henry Knox and the Development of American Military Thought and Practice" (Ph.D. diss., University of North Carolina at Chapel Hill, 2000), 12–13, 62–63, 103–4; Robert J. Taylor et al., eds., *The Papers of John Adams: Series III, General Correspondence . . .,* 10 vols. to date (Cambridge, Mass., 1977–), 4:190; Houlding, *Fit for Service,* 252–53.

33. General Orders, 8 May 1777, *PGW: Rev. War Ser.* 9:368.

34. For examples, see ibid., 12:55, 56–57, 477–81, 532–33, 549, 552.

35. Greene to Washington, 1 and 3 December 1777, in Richard K. Showman, et al., eds., *The Papers of General Nathanael Greene,* 11 vols. to date (Chapel Hill, N.C.: University of North Carolina Press, 1976–), 2:225–29, 231–38.

36. Joseph P. Tustin, ed., *Diary of the American War: A Hessian Journal* (New Haven, Conn., 1979), 108.

37. Ibid. There are similar references and inferences about American military abilities elsewhere in Ewald's diary.

38. Johann Heinrichs, "Extracts from the Letter-Book of Captain Johann Heinrichs of the Hessian Jaeger Corps, 1778–1780" *Pennsylvania Magazine of History and Biography* 22 (1898): 137–40. That same year a French artillery officer serving with Washington, Louis de Recicourt de Ganot, saw Continental officers as possessed of considerable potential. Durand Echeverria and Orville T. Murphy, eds., "The American Revolutionary Army: A French Estimate in 1777," *Military Affairs* 27 (1963): 1–7, 153–62.

39. *PGW: Rev. War. Ser.* 9:32.

40. Stanley J. Idzerda, et al., eds., *Lafayette in the Age of the American Revolution: Selected Letters and Papers, 1776–1790,* 5 vols. to date (Ithaca, N.Y., 1977–), 1:11, 68–67.

41. John R. Alden, *General Charles Lee: Traitor or Patriot?* (Baton Rouge, La., 1951), chapter 2.

42. See, for example, Washington to Alexander McDougall, 23 May 1777, *PGW: Rev. War Ser.* 9:506.

43. Washington to Steuben, 26 February, 11 March 1779, Washington to the president of Congress, 11 March 1779, in John C. Fitzpatrick, ed., *The Writings of George Washington,* 39 vols. (Washington, D.C., 1931–44), 14:151–52, 227–28, 230.

44. Published by Styner and Cist in Philadelphia in 1779, seven other editions of the *Regulations* appeared by 1785. It was also used extensively by the state militias. For a facsimile repro-

duction of the first edition, as well as information on reprintings, see Joseph R. Riling, *Baron Von Steuben and His Regulations* (Philadelphia, 1966).

45. Wright, *Continental Army,* 140.

46. For Lamb, see Isaac Q. Leake, *Memoirs of the Life and Times of John Lamb* (Albany, N.Y., 1858). Chastellux's praise of the Continental artillery is in Howard C. Rice Jr., ed., *Travels in North America in the Years 1780, 1781 and 1782 by the Marquis de Chastellux,* 2 vols. (Chapel Hill, N.C., 1963), 1:282. See Evelyn M. Accomb, ed., *The Revolutionary Journal of Baron Ludwig von Clossen, 1780–1783* (Chapel Hill, N.C., 1958), 156, for the comment on Rochambeau. Knox's role at Yorktown is examined in Thompson, "Citizens and Soldiers," 210–16.

47. Elizabeth S. Kite, *Brigadier-General Louis Begue Duportail* (Baltimore, 1933).

48. Paul K. Walker, ed., *Engineers of Independence: A Documentary History of the Army Engineers in the American Revolution, 1775–1783* (Washington, D.C., 1981), is an invaluable source on the subject. Albert Heusser, *George Washington's Map Maker: A Biography of Robert Erskine,* ed. Hubert G. Schmidt (New Brunswick, N.J., 1966) is an antiquarian volume but useful for Erskine's correspondence.

49. Wright, *Continental Army,* 132.

50. Ibid., 152. See also Paul David Nelson, "Citizen Soldiers or Regulars: The Views of American General Officers on the Military Establishment," *Military Affairs* 43 (1979): 126–32. In *The Age of Battles: The Quest for Decisive Warfare from Breitenfeld to Waterloo* (Bloomington, Ind., 1991), 234, Russell F. Weigley declares that the Continentals "made deep inroads into British tactical superiority" and that some American regiments, particularly Maryland and Delaware units, "attained parity with the British in soldierly skills."

51. Parker, *Military Revolution,* chapter 5; Hew Strachan, *European Armies and the Conduct of War* (London, 1983), chapter 3; Weigley, *Age of Battles,* chapter 11.

52. *Maryland Journal,* 6 September 1775.

53. John Adams to Henry Knox, 2 June and 29 September 1776, in Paul H. Smith, ed., *Letters of Delegates to Congress,* 26 vols. (Washington, D.C., 1976–2000), 4:115, 5:261. For the tangled story of proposals for military education before Congress in late 1776, see Thomas Elliott Shaughnessy, "Beginnings of National Professional Military Education," 32–39.

54. Thompson, "Citizens and Soldiers," 88–91; Shaughnessy, "Beginnings of National Professional Military Education," 54–55.

55. Wright, *Continental Army,* 136–37; Shaughnessy, "Beginnings of National Professional Military Education," 39–48.

56. *Writings of Washington,* 34:59–60n; TJ to John Banister Jr., 15 October 1785, *TJP* 8:636–37.

57. Hamilton to Washington, 9 April 1783, *AHP* 3:322. Washington asked for some time before replying so he could consult others before formulating his response; Washington to Hamilton, 16 April 1783, ibid., 331–32. In fact, two days earlier Washington had requested such opinions; see, for example, Washington to Steuben, 14 April 1783, *Writings of Washington,* 26:315–16, 316n.

58. Shaughnessy, "Beginnings of National Professional Military Education," 71–72; Minor Myers Jr., *Liberty without Anarchy: A History of the Society of the Cincinnati* (Charlottesville, Va., 1983), 208.

59. Shaughnessy, "Beginnings of National Professional Military Education," 63–71, 72–74; Lawrence Delbert Cress, *Citizens in Arms: The Army and the Militia in American Society to the War of 1812* (Chapel Hill, N.C., 1982), 78–84. Most originals of the letters from Washington's subordinates are in the Washington Papers, Lib. Cong. *Correspondence of the Revolution: Being Letters of Eminent Men to George Washington,* 4 vols. (Boston, 1853), 4:27–31.

60. Richard H. Kohn, *Eagle and Sword: The Federalists and the Creation of the Military Establishment in America, 1783–1802* (New York, 1975), chapter 2; Myers, *Liberty without Anarchy,* chapter 1.

61. *Writings of Washington,* 26:374–98, especially 396. Before Congress asked for Washington's views, it had received a detailed plan of military education from Secretary at War Benjamin Lincoln, which probably did not receive serious consideration. The lengthiest plan, thoughtful and comprehensive but hardly possible to adopt at the time, came from Major Jean Baptiste Obrey de Gouvion, a French professional soldier on Lafayette's staff. Shaughnessy, "Beginnings of National Professional Military Education," 59–60, 60n, 63–66.

62. Hamilton's congressional committee accepted Washington's "Sentiments" in somewhat modified form, but Congress failed to adopt any part of the Hamilton report. Shaughnessy, "Beginnings of National Professional Military Education," 77–83; Report on a Military Peace Establishment, (18 June 1783), *AHP* 3:378–97, especially 382, 391, 396 for the committee's cautious approach to military schooling.

63. Memorandum of Matters to be Communicated to Congress, (November 1793), Fifth Annual Address to Congress, 3 December 1793, *Writings of Washington,* 33:160–61, 166–67. The best treatment of efforts to put in place a program of military education in the 1790s is Theodore J. Crackel, *West Point: A Bicentennial History* (Lawrence, Kans., 2002), chapter 2, which has significantly influenced my treatment of the decade. For Jefferson's thinking on a military academy in the 1790s, see TJ, Notes of a Cabinet Meeting on the President's Address, 23 November 1793, *TJP* 27:428; David N. Mayer, *The Constitutional Thought of Thomas Jefferson* (Charlottesville, Va., 1994), 213–14.

64. Report to Military Committee, House of Representatives, 3 February 1796, quoted in Crackel, *West Point,* 33.

65. Crackel, *West Point,* 34–35.

66. Alan C. Aimone, "Genesis of the U.S. Military Academy Library," an unpublished study by a member of the USMA Lib. staff, who is an authority on the early history of the institution.

67. Hamilton to Louis Duportail, 23 July 1798, Duportail to Hamilton, 9 December 1798, *AHP* 22:28–29, 339.

68. Shaughnessy, "Beginnings of National Professional Military Education," 103–10; *AHP* 24:69–75, 308–12; Crackel, *West Point,* 38–40.

69. *WJA* 9:65–66; Crackel, *West Point,* 40–43.

70. No scholar has yet demonstrated that Federalist efforts to create a military school had a positive effect on Jefferson. Indeed, Hamilton's bold vision of several educational institutions would likely have shocked Jefferson. Even Washington, who received a copy of Hamilton's detailed measure, delicately declined to comment on its specifics, although he offered his general support. Hamilton to Washington, 28 November 1799, Washington to Hamilton, 12 December 1799, *AHP* 24:79–80, 99–100. See also Crackel, *West Point,* 43–44.

71. Weigley, *Towards an American Army,* chapters 1–2; William B. Skelton, *An American Profession of Arms: The Army Officer Corps, 1784–1861* (Lawrence, Kans., 1992), chapters 1–3.

72. Aimone, "Genesis of the U. S. Military Academy," 12.

73. Skelton, *Profession of Arms,* 99–100, 102, 115, 123, 240–41, 249, and chapter 10; Weigley, *Towards an American Army,* chapters 4–5.

74. Theodore J. Crackel, *Mr. Jefferson's Army: Political and Social Reform of the Military Establishment, 1801–1809* (New York, 1987), introduction, chapters 1–4, and *West Point,* chapter 2.; Don Higginbotham, *War and Society in Revolutionary America: The Wider Dimensions of Con-*

flict (Columbia, S.C., 1988), chapter 9; Robert Gough, "Officering the American Army, 1798," *WMQ,* 3rd ser., 43 (1986): 460–71. For a review of interpretations of the origins of the United States Military Academy, which have appeared in print before 2001, see James W. Rainey, "Establishing the United States Military Academy: Motives and Objectives of Thomas Jefferson," *Assembly* 59 (2001): 42–44, 57.

75. *AHP* 20:311–12, 316, 318–19, 320; Farewell Address, 19 September 1796, *Writings of Washington,* 35:230.

76. Washington introduced the matter in a short paragraph: "I have heretofore proposed to the consideration of Congress, the expediency of establishing a national University; and also a Military Academy. The desirableness of both the Institutions, has . . . constantly increased with every new view I have taken of the subject." Washington, as well as Presidents Jefferson, Madison, and Monroe, emphasized the need for military education as a way to guarantee the future safety of the nation against aggressive powers. All seemed at pains to advocate formal learning without a suggestion that such an educational institution would lead to an enlarged professional army. Eighth Annual Address to Congress, 7 December 1796, *Writings of Washington,* 35:316–17. As Academy graduates left the military service, their knowledge would be imparted to society at large by means of their serving later in their own state militias. What Washington implied here some subsequent chief executives made explicit. Washington himself had, at the conclusion of the War of Independence, recommended to state governors the appointment of veteran Continental army officers to positions of leadership in the militias. *Writings of Washington,* 26:394; Harrison E. Ethridge, "Patrick Henry and the Reorganization of the Virginia Militia, 1784–1786," *Virginia Magazine of History and Biography* 85 (1977): 436. See also the splendid treatment of the Farewell Address and Washington's Eighth Annual Message to Congress in Joseph J. Ellis, *Founding Brothers: The Revolutionary Generation* (New York, 2001), chapter 4.

"Necessary and Proper"

West Point and Jefferson's Constitutionalism

DAVID N. MAYER

When Henry Adams wrote that, as president, Thomas Jefferson "gave up" the "Virginia dogma" of "States-rights," he voiced a criticism that modern scholars frequently have echoed.[1] Pointing particularly to the Louisiana Purchase and the Embargo, Adams and other scholars—whether otherwise admirers or critics—have charged that Jefferson was, if not outright hypocritical, at least inconsistent in his adherence to the so-called "strict constructionist" constitutional views he had espoused in opposition to Federalist programs in the 1790s.[2] To critics like Adams, the lesson seems clear: Jefferson's strict constructionist "dogma" was an unrealistic reading of the Constitution that gave way to the practical need to broaden the scope of the national government's powers.[3] Conservative and libertarian scholars, conversely, who generally applaud his strict constructionism as a faithful reading of the Constitution (as well as good public policy), point to his actions as president—especially the Louisiana Purchase—as evidence of the corrupting influence of power: even someone as pure as Jefferson, in his limited-government theory, will succumb to power when he himself is wielding it.[4]

The widely accepted view that Jefferson was inconsistent in his constitutionalism is wrong, however. It errs in taking a simplistic and erroneous view of his theory of constitutional interpretation, mistakenly caricatured as a "states' rights" or "strict constructionist" theory. Instead, his theory of constitutional interpretation can be best described as "contextualist." What mattered most to Jefferson was the context of a particular provision within the overall purpose of the Constitution, and not the text of the provision alone. When seen in light of such a contextualist approach to constitutional interpretation, the apparent inconsistencies in his constitutional thought are not really inconsistencies at all. Rather, he was remarkably—though not perfectly—consistent in interpreting fairly strictly the power-granting clauses of the Constitution and in interpreting fairly liberally, or broadly, its power-limiting or rights-guaranteeing clauses.[5]

Moreover, with regard to the power-granting clauses, Jefferson further distinguished those powers shared with the states from those powers exclusively assigned to the national government. The former he interpreted far more strictly than the latter. In other words, Jefferson's contextualist theory permitted a broad latitude for the exercise of federal powers within the sphere assigned to the national government under the Constitution, particularly with regard to foreign affairs. This explains, among other things, Jefferson's acceptance of broad congressional powers over foreign commerce in the enforcement of the Embargo during his second term as president.[6] Thus, with regard to the necessary and proper clause of the Constitution, Jefferson interpreted the terms "necessary" and "proper" differently, depending on the scope of the enumerated power to which a particular exercise of "necessary and proper" powers related.[7] What he regarded as "necessary" and "proper" for the exercise of exclusive federal powers was much broader than what he regarded as "necessary" and "proper" for the exercise of powers shared with the states and thus capable of raising federalism problems under the Tenth Amendment.[8]

Jefferson's support for the establishment of the United States Military Academy at West Point provides an interesting test case for assessing his theory of constitutional interpretation. At first glance, it appears to fit the overall model of inconsistency that many scholars have posited, for Jefferson dramatically shifted his position with regard to the constitutionality of a national military academy. When a Federalist member of President George Washington's cabinet proposed the idea in 1793, Jefferson vigorously opposed it as going beyond the "specified powers" given Congress by the Constitution. Following the so-called "Revolution of 1800," however, with Jefferson as president and Republicans in control of Congress, he called for the establishment of the academy. Thus, as one scholar concluded, "it was truly ironic that this institution was brought into being by the signature of Thomas Jefferson, who hated war, loved peace, and had denied the constitutional power of the federal government to create such an agency."[9]

The irony, however, is more apparent than real when not only his contextualist theory of constitutional interpretation but also the political circumstances of the times are considered fully. Jefferson's eventual support for the establishment of West Point was fully consistent with his mature constitutional theory. His earlier opposition can be explained essentially as an instinctive, but not well-considered, knee-jerk reaction against Hamiltonian Federalism as he perceived it in the 1790s. Like much of his constitutional thought, however, his eventual acceptance of the legitimacy of West Point—and, with it, his mature interpretation of the necessary and proper clause—evolved as a result of his dialectic with the Federalists.

Jefferson's theory of constitutional interpretation—neither "strict" nor "loose" constructionist, in the traditional sense—is best described as contextualist, because his interpretation of any particular provision of the Constitution depended on its context, in two senses: its place in the document as a whole and in the context of the document's overall purpose of limiting the powers of the federal government to encroach on either the legitimate powers of the states or the rights of individuals. Thus, Jefferson's theory of constitutional interpretation emerges from his view of the basic purpose of constitutions, generally—to limit governmental power—as well as his view of the particular purpose of the United States Constitution, which was to limit the powers of a national government within a federal system of divided governmental powers.

A constant throughout Jefferson's long life in politics was his dedication to liberty above all else.[10] He followed the English radical Whig writers on history and government—writers who had a profound influence on the Revolutionary generation—in recognizing the perpetual need to safeguard liberty and, correspondingly, to limit governmental power. As he once wrote, "the natural progress of things is for liberty to yeild and government to gain ground." Like John Locke, Algernon Sidney, and lesser-known English radical Whig political philosophers, Jefferson understood that government, which was created to "secure" individual rights, posed the greatest danger to those rights through the abuse of its legitimate powers. Hence Jefferson, like other good Whigs of his time—and like the classical liberals of the nineteenth century—was profoundly distrustful of concentrated political power and intensely devoted to the ideal of limited government.[11]

The essential purpose of a constitution, as Jefferson saw it, was to limit government—to keep its powers within safe bounds. He reached this basic understanding fairly early—certainly by the time he penned his criticisms of the 1776 Virginia Constitution in his *Notes on the State of Virginia*—but his view of how the federal Constitution achieved this objective evolved more slowly over time, from his first reactions to the Constitution in 1787–88 to his postretirement reflections on republicanism around the year 1816.[12] By the time Jefferson's theory reached its full maturation, he regarded three basic structural features of the Constitution as fundamental means to fulfill its purpose. These were, first and foremost, federalism—the system of dividing powers between the federal government and the states, with the federal government limited to certain powers enumerated in the text of the Constitution; second, separation of powers—the system of separating the legitimate federal powers into three distinct functional branches, complemented by those exceptions to separation of powers we call "checks and balances"; and third, the addition of the Bill of Rights to the Constitution, providing the safeguard of additional checks on the means by which the federal government carried out its enumerated powers. He also recognized a fourth feature, not a structural feature found within the Constitution itself but rather one he regarded as paramount to the Constitution: the people's overall control over the federal government through the Constitution itself and the amending process.[13] Although Jefferson, in many respects, regarded this feature as far more important than the structural ones in keeping federal powers within safe bounds, his understanding of each of the three structural features of the Constitution best explains his contextual theory of constitutional interpretation.[14]

Federalism—the division of powers between the federal government and the states, with federal powers limited to those enumerated in the Constitution—was the starting point of Jefferson's theory. It should be stressed that *federalism* to Jefferson meant far more than the "states rights" caricature, for federalism could cut both ways. With regard to those powers assigned to the federal government by the Constitution, Jefferson could be fairly described as a "nationalist," one who interpreted rather broadly legitimate federal powers—for example, Congress's power to regulate foreign commerce, as his Embargo policy during the second term of his presidency so dramatically illustrates. Similarly, he tended to interpret federal powers under the Constitution quite liberally in matters involving foreign affairs, which he regarded as an exclusive responsibility of the national government since the time of the Articles of Confederation. As a result, to label Jefferson a "literalist" or a "strict constructionist" is not only insufficient but also quite misleading.[15]

Nevertheless, it is possible to identify a general rule of thumb that Jefferson used in interpreting the power-granting clauses of the Constitution. It was the rule he stated at the outset of his 1791 opinion on the constitutionality of Alexander Hamilton's proposed bill to charter the Bank of the United States. He maintained that the Tenth Amendment—which provides that "powers not delegated to the United States by the Constitution, nor prohibited by it to the States, are reserved to the States respectively, or to the people"—should be considered "the foundation of the Constitution." It reiterated the general principle of federal powers expressed in the language of article 1: that the legislative powers of the federal government, vested in the Congress of the United States, were limited to those "herein granted" in the Constitution. "To take a single step beyond the boundaries thus specifically drawn around the powers of Congress," he wrote, "is to take possession of a boundless field of power, no longer susceptible of any definition."[16]

As epitomized by the procedure he followed in his opinion on the bank bill, Jefferson's approach was to consider, one by one, each of the "boundaries" found primarily in article 1, section 8. These enumerations of congressional power should be read, Jefferson later contended, "according to the plain and ordinary meaning of the language, to the common intendment of the time and those who framed it." Thus, as he concluded in his 1791 opinion, "the incorporation of a bank, and other powers assumed by this bill, have not . . . been delegated to the U.S. by the Constitution." He found them neither among the powers specially enumerated nor within the "general phrase" of the necessary and proper clause. Laws of the United States could not exceed those powers enumerated in the Constitution and those corollary powers that were "necessary and proper" to carry into execution the enumerated powers.[17]

Federalism, as Jefferson understood it, also provided the context for his understanding of those corollary powers. He interpreted the words "necessary" and "proper" quite strictly, rejecting the loose construction given by Hamilton (and years later, by Chief Justice John Marshall)[18] as tantamount to merely "convenient" and destructive of the entire enumerated powers scheme of the Constitution. "If such a latitude of construction be allowed to this phrase as to give any non-enumerated power," he feared, "it will go to every one, for there is no one which ingenuity may not torture into a *convenience, in some way or other*, to *some one* of so long a list of enumerated powers." Otherwise, the necessary and proper clause "would swallow up all the delegated powers, and reduce the whole to one phrase," essentially giving Congress a blank check to exercise whatever powers it regarded as conducive to the national welfare. Such a sweeping reading of the clause would violate a cardinal rule of constitutional interpretation as he understood it, the "established rule of construction," that where a phrase will bear either of two meanings, it should be given "that which will allow some meaning to the other parts of the instrument, and not that which would render all the others useless." In other words, Jefferson interpreted corollary powers under the necessary and proper clause in the same way that he interpreted the enumerated powers: in light of the overall context of the Constitution as confirmed by the Tenth Amendment. It was a system establishing a national government of certain limited powers, reserving all else to the states or to the people.[19]

It is clear what Jefferson regarded as an erroneous interpretation of the necessary and proper clause, but what was his view of how the clause *should* be interpreted? In general, given his basically strict approach to the power-granting clauses of the Constitution, Jefferson's interpretation of the clause closely approximated the approach legal scholar Randy Barnett has identified as "Madisonian." To truly fall within the scope of the clause, a given exercise of power must meet two tests: it must be "necessary," in the sense that it is a means directly related and incidental to a specified enumerated power, and it must be "proper" in the sense that it is consistent with the limited character of the national government under the Constitution.[20] In his opinion on the bank bill, Jefferson concluded that chartering a national bank was neither "necessary" to the enumerated powers he discussed—the powers to tax, borrow money, and regulate commerce—nor "proper" for the federal government to exercise.[21]

Given, moreover, Jefferson's overall contextualist approach to interpretation, the precise meaning of the terms "necessary" and "proper" varied with the nature of the enumerated power to which they were tied, as well as the nature of the claimed incidental power. With regard to the bank bill, he was especially concerned that the proposed national bank would exercise powers in conflict with many state laws, such as "those against Mortmain, the laws of alienage, the rules of descent, the acts of distribution, the laws of escheat and forfeiture, the laws of monopoly." Given the preemptive effect of federal law—a consequence of the article 6 supremacy clause of the Constitution—the proposed bank would bypass these state common law restrictions. As he wrote in his 1791 opinion, "nothing but a necessity invincible by any other means"—certainly not mere convenience, he argued—"can justify such a prostration of laws which constitute the pillars of our whole system of jurisprudence." Hence, where the measure proposed interfered with state law, as he argued was the case with the bank bill, Jefferson applied the most stringent test for necessity: means not only directly incident to enumerated powers, but "those means without which the grant of the power would be nugatory."[22]

When, however, the measure proposed related to an exclusive federal power—for example, Congress's power to regulate foreign commerce or commerce with the Indian tribes—he followed a less stringent test for necessity. To Jefferson, federalism meant keeping both the federal and state governments within their respective spheres. It cut both ways, as his statements in his first inaugural address confirmed. Here, on the one hand, he affirmed his "support of the state governments in all their rights, as the most competent administrations for our domestic concerns, & the surest bulwarks against anti-republican tendencies." On the other hand, he argued for "the preservation of the General government, in it's whole constitutional vigour, as the sheet anchor of our peace at home, & safety abroad." Although he viewed matters of "domestic" government—"all legislation and administration, in affairs which concern their citizens only"—the exclusive concern of the states, he also viewed foreign or federal matters—"whatever concerns foreigns, or the citizens of other states"—as concerns of the national government, provided its powers were limited to the few functions enumerated in the Constitution.[23]

Federalism, although a key element of Jefferson's constitutionalism, was not the only structural feature that defined and thereby limited federal governmental powers. Equally important to Jefferson's contextualist theory of interpretation were the principle of separation of powers and the explicit rights-guaranteeing, or power-limiting, provisions of the Constitution.

Because separation of powers was fundamental to his conception of republicanism, Jefferson took the doctrine quite seriously—indeed, arguably, more seriously than any other president in United States history has.[24] In interpreting constitutional provisions regarding the allocation of federal powers among the three branches, therefore, he was indeed a strict constructionist. Thus, for example, he had qualms about President Washington's plan to issue a neutrality proclamation, because he feared it might undercut the power to declare war, vested in Congress alone by article 1, section 8 of the Constitution. Similarly, as president, Jefferson deliberately sought authorization from Congress for the United States naval operations in the Mediterranean commonly called the Barbary War. And, both when he was advising Washington as secretary of state and when holding the presidency himself, he viewed the presidential veto power quite narrowly. Believing that on mere policy differences, presidents should defer to Congress, he considered constitutional objections to be the only legitimate ground for use of the veto power.[25]

Jefferson's narrow view of the veto power illustrates quite aptly how his commitment to separation of powers influenced his constitutional interpretation. The veto, of course, is an example of one of the so-called "checks and balances" of the Constitution. It is an instance of a shared power and thus is an exception to the separation doctrine. Article 1 vests the national government's legislative powers generally in Congress, but the provision specifying the procedure for law making—the so-called presentment clause of article 1, section 7—gives the president power to either veto or sign bills into law. Because it was an exception to the general rule of separation of powers, Jefferson construed it narrowly and hence believed that presidents could exercise the veto power only on constitutional grounds. Similarly, when considering an exception to separation of powers that cut the other way—such as the Senate's power to confirm presidential appointments—he also construed the exception "strictly," taking the position that the Senate lacked the power to negate the grade of a diplomatic appointment as well as the person appointed.[26]

Finally, Jefferson generally interpreted liberally the Bill of Rights and other provisions in the Constitution that guaranteed rights or limited the exercise of governmental power. Perhaps the best examples of how broadly Jefferson construed rights-guaranteeing or power-limiting clauses may be found in his arguments against the constitutionality of the Alien and Sedition Acts in his Kentucky Resolutions of 1798. There, for example, he took a broad view of the Fifth Amendment's due process clause as well as Sixth Amendment rights to a jury trial—held in public, with benefit of counsel and the opportunity to cross-examine witnesses—in arguing that the Alien Act's provisions empowering the president to order deportations were unconstitutional. He similarly took a broad view of the First Amendment freedoms of speech and press in maintaining the unconstitutionality of the Sedition Act. Moreover, in holding that Congress did not have the power to pass the Alien Act, he made the novel argument that it violated the article 1, section 9 provision that "the migration or importation of such persons as any of the states now existing shall think proper to admit, shall not be prohibited by the Congress prior to the year 1808." Here, he disregarded the generally understood intent of the clause—protection of the foreign slave trade—and instead followed the language of the text quite literally.[27]

Jefferson's broad view of rights-guaranteeing and power-limiting clauses was consistent with his generally strict view of the power-granting clauses of the Constitution, for by drawing this vital distinction, he remained faithful to the overall purpose of the document in limiting the reach of the national government and confining it to its legitimate scope. Jefferson summarized his approach to constitutional interpretation in the Kentucky Resolutions, where he wrote that "free government is founded in jealousy, and not in confidence; it is jealousy and not confidence which prescribes limited constitutions, to bind down those whom we are obliged to trust with power." Viewing the Constitution as having "fixed the limits to which . . . our confidence may go," he maintained, "In questions of power, then, let no more be heard of confidence in man, but bind him down from mischief by the chains of the Constitution."[28]

Those "chains," as Jefferson understood them, comprised all the various structural devices found in the Constitution for limiting power and safeguarding rights. To extend the metaphor, the chains were not all of equal size or strength but varied according to the need for restraint. His theory of constitutional interpretation, being contextualist, varied in application, depending on both the nature of the clause and the particular exercise of power under consideration.

When Henry Knox, the secretary of war, proposed in a cabinet meeting in late fall 1793 that Washington recommend to Congress the establishment of a military academy, Jefferson opposed the proposal. He objected that "none of the specified powers given by the [C]onst[itutio]n to Congress would authorize this."[29] The other cabinet member present, Attorney General Edmund Randolph, "said nothing" about the proposal, according to Jefferson's notes on the meeting. But apparently Jefferson so strongly protested against it that Washington, not wishing "to bring on anything which might generate heat and ill humor," ordered the subject to be dropped.[30] Washington made only a very guarded allusion in his message to Congress of December 3, 1793.[31] Nevertheless, Congress took the first step toward establishment of a military academy several months later, on May 7, 1794, when it authorized the recruitment of a Corps of Artillerists and Engineers to be garrisoned at West Point.[32]

Jefferson was right about none of the specified powers given Congress by the Constitution authorizing it to establish a military academy, but what about the article 1, section 8 power "to raise and support armies"? Comparing the brief explanation for his opposition to Knox's proposal as he gives it in his notes with the thorough analysis he had given Hamilton's bank bill three years earlier, it is evident that Jefferson was giving the constitutional question rather scant attention. Clearly, his cursory, almost cryptic explanation ignores the issue of the necessary and proper clause.

Considering the political circumstances in which this cabinet meeting took place, Jefferson's lack of attention to the matter of a military academy might be understood. The Washington administration—and Jefferson, particularly, as secretary of state—at the time was heavily engaged in dealing with the diplomatic crisis resulting from the bellicose activities of the volatile French ambassador to the United States, Edmond Charles Genet. Indeed, the basic purpose of the cabinet meeting was to prepare Washington's address for the forthcoming meeting of Congress, in which the United States government's response to Genet's conduct was a key topic.[33] Under these circumstances, Jefferson was not only uninterested in giving serious consideration to the notion of a national military academy but was also generally hostile to any further actions, particularly those initiated or proposed by the executive branch, which might give further impetus to Federalist attempts to bring the United States into war against France. Thus in the cabinet meeting, Jefferson opposed on policy grounds both the proposal for a military academy and Knox's other proposal, that Washington recommend to Congress the fortification of principal harbors.

Beyond the immediate political circumstances of the neutrality crisis in 1793, there were the overall political circumstances of the 1790s, virtually an entire decade in which Jefferson viewed with intense distrust any proposal originating from Hamilton or members of Hamilton's faction within the government.[34] Jefferson, reacting against Hamilton's broad views of federal power generally and executive power specifically, tended to adhere especially strictly to the principles of federalism and separation of powers as he understood them.[35] This was especially true with regard to military matters, about which Jefferson harbored near-paranoid fears. He believed, for example, that Federalists planned to use the Society of the Cincinnati to establish a hereditary aristocracy in America.[36]

His opposition to Hamiltonian Federalist programs in the 1790s prompted him to take the strictest—or narrowest—interpretation of other article 1, section 8 powers. In 1796, for example, when James Madison proposed in Congress that the federal government undertake a survey for a national post road from Maine to Georgia, Jefferson asked his good friend and political confidant whether he had "considered all the consequences of your proposition respecting post roads? I view it as a source of boundless patronage to the executive, jobbing to members of Congress and their friends, and a bottomless abyss of public money."[37] Jefferson observed that the enumerated power "to *establish* post roads" might be interpreted as either the power "to *make* the roads" or the power to "only *select* from those already made those on which there should be a post," and then he suggested that the latter was the "safest" interpretation. He feared that the power to build roads, which "permits a majority of Congress to go to cutting down mountains and bridging of rivers," would open the door to wholesale spending. "You will begin by only appropriating the surplus of the post-office revenues," he warned, "but the other revenues will soon be called in to their aid, and it will be a scene of eternal scramble among the members who can get the most money wasted in their state, and they will always get most who are meanest."[38]

Interestingly, Madison's proposal in 1796 reminded Jefferson of Knox's proposal for fortifying harbors, raised at the same cabinet meeting, three years earlier, at which Knox proposed a military academy. He noted that "the fortification of harbours was liable to great objection" but that "national circumstances furnished some color." With regard to post roads, however, "there is none"—that is, no colorable pretext for the exercise of national government powers—for "the roads of America are the best in the world except those of France and England."[39]

Washington in his last message to Congress invited it to create a military academy.[40] Yet Congress did not act—even after Washington's successor, John Adams, in 1800 transmitted to Congress an elaborate plan for a military academy prepared by Secretary of War James McHenry.[41] At the height of anti-French war fever in the summer of 1798, Congress had authorized Adams to appoint four teachers of the "Arts and Sciences" for the instruction of the cadets and young officers in the Corps of Artillerists and Engineers stationed at West Point.[42] Although the Department of War had gathered there a number of prospective students and made an attempt to organize a school, nothing came of it, largely because of Adams's inability to find suitable teachers.[43]

By the end of Adams's presidency, with war hysteria abating, other considerations dampened Congress's enthusiasm for further action, including fears of a professional military.[44]

Stephen Ambrose has noted in his history of West Point that "as President, Jefferson abandoned the constitutional objections he had once raised against a national academy and urged his Secretary of War, Henry Dearborn, to continue and even speed up the work McHenry and Adams had begun."[45] By September 1801, with a student body of twelve cadets, ranging in age from ten to thirty-four, and a teacher finally in residence, the first class was held.[46] By this time, Jefferson had dispatched to West Point Jonathan Williams, a scientist with no military experience, who served as the army's inspector of fortifications. When Williams arrived in December 1801, the academy itself still had no formal legal status. At Jefferson's request, however, on March 16, 1802, Congress authorized him to organize a corps of engineers, to consist of not more than twenty officers and cadets, which "shall be stationed at West Point . . . and shall constitute a military academy." The law authorized the secretary of war to purchase books, implements, and apparatus for the institution's "use and benefit" and provided that the commander of the corps, the chief engineer, would also "have the superintendence" of the academy.[47] Williams, as the ranking engineer at West Point, became the academy's first superintendent.[48]

Jefferson's support for the 1802 act can be explained, in part, as a consequence of his strict adherence to the principle of separation of powers and, accordingly, the qualms he probably felt about establishing a military academy by presidential discretion alone. Given his views about separation of powers, he understood that the establishment of the academy needed to be authorized explicitly by legislation.

More important, however, was Jefferson's support for the institution itself. Clearly, as president, Jefferson had no constitutional scruples about Congress's power to establish the academy at West Point. By this time he had come to see the establishment of such a school as falling comfortably within the "necessary and proper" powers incident to the authority "to raise and support armies."[49] His partisan disagreements with Knox and Hamilton might have pushed him to reject their proposals in the 1790s, but by the time of his presidency, he had come to agree with most of his contemporaries, Federalist and Republican alike, who viewed establishment of a military academy by the federal government to be both "necessary" and "proper." It was necessary because

Americans in the early national period widely believed that neither the state governments nor the private sector would create an institution like the academy.[50] It was proper because it fit within the authority allocated to the national government under the Constitution. Specifically, article 1, section 8 authorized Congress not only "to raise and support armies" but also "to provide for organizing, arming, and disciplining, the militia."[51]

Two other factors should be emphasized in explaining Jefferson's stance after 1801. First was the critical change in political circumstances: the Republicans' electoral triumphs in the "revolution of 1800," which gave them control of both houses of Congress as well as the presidency and thus effected what Jefferson regarded "as real a revolution in the principles of our government as that of 1776 was in its form." With the American people having restored their government to its "true principles," as he saw them—and having elected to power men who adhered to those principles—he no longer feared a Federalist conspiracy to use the military to undermine republicanism by erecting an aristocratical and monarchical establishment.[52] Indeed, as Theodore Crackel persuasively argues, the permanent establishment of a national military academy after 1801 provided a wonderful opportunity for Jefferson to "republicanize" the army under the command of Republicans.[53]

Second, to some extent, both the limited size and scope of the academy as first established during his presidency made Jefferson comfortable with the institution. As Dumas Malone observed, "if little concerned about the professional training of army officers in time of peace, he fully recognized the usefulness of engineers in peace or war and valued the infant Academy chiefly for its potential scientific contributions." Malone exaggerated only slightly when he characterized the academy during Jefferson's presidency as "a military school in little more than name."[54] Superintendent Williams certainly seemed to emphasize scientific rather than military endeavors. It should be noted, however, that Jefferson endorsed Williams's recommendation that the academy be placed under the definite authority of the president and that it be moved to Washington. When Williams drafted a report proposing enlargement of the academy and its transformation into a national scientific institution that would train militia officers, Jefferson recommended the report to Congress, suggesting the plan would help to make America's defenses more uniform.[55]

Jefferson's support for the establishment, and even for the expansion, of the academy at West Point was consistent with his approval, as president, of other federal programs directly tied to enumerated powers. For example, he pointed to Congress's article 1, section 8 power "to provide and maintain a navy" as the constitutional basis for his proposal in 1802 to construct in the Washington Navy Yard a dock in which vessels could be "laid up dry and under cover from the sun"—an economy measure that Federalist congressmen derided as a "visionary scheme." He similarly considered an act for the building of piers in the Delaware River as an adjunct to the power to provide and maintain a navy, because, he maintained, that power was tantamount to the power "to provide receptacles for it, and places to cover and preserve it."[56]

In both these cases, Jefferson tied the projects directly to enumerated powers. Each plan so clearly employed enumerated powers (although, strictly speaking, they were warranted only under the necessary and proper clause) that Jefferson thought of them as essentially tantamount to the direct exercise of enumerated powers. In contrast, consider his position on two proposals not tied to any of the enumerated powers, the chartering of a company to mine copper and the establishment of a national university.

Shortly before his presidency, Jefferson criticized a House bill incorporating a company for the Roosevelt copper mines in New Jersey. He pointed out that it was "under the *sweeping clause* of the constitution, & supported by the following pedigree of necessities. Congress are authorized to defend the country: ships are necessary for that defence: copper is necessary for ships: mines are necessary to produce copper: companies are necessary to work mines: and 'this is the house that Jack built.'" This was the same kind of reasoning with respect to the necessary and proper clause that he had condemned in his opinion on the bank bill in 1791. Creation of a corporation, whether a bank to assist the government in its financial operations or a mining company to assist in national defense, was too remote a means to the enumerated ends.[57]

Although Jefferson as president did favor the idea of establishing a national university, he understood that a constitutional amendment was required in order to give Congress the authority. When he formally proposed the idea along with Secretary of the Treasury Albert Gallatin's plan for a comprehensive system of national roads, canals, and other "internal improvements," Jefferson noted the necessity of an amendment, "because the objects now recommended are not among those enumerated in the Constitution, and to which it permits the public monies to be applied." Indeed, Jefferson floated the idea to Congress early—at a time when the treasury was beginning to accumulate a surplus, even though the national debt had not yet been retired—in order to give sufficient time for Congress to propose, and the states to ratify, a constitutional amendment.[58]

Besides the Embargo, which can be justified as a broad exercise of what Jefferson regarded as the clear federal power to regulate foreign commerce, three other examples of apparently broad, or "loose constructionist," use of federal powers during Jefferson's presidency ought to be cited: the Louisiana Purchase, the Lewis and Clark expedition, and the National Road. Of these three, only the last demonstrates a real inconsistency in his constitutionalism. Rather than showing hypocrisy, Jefferson's reluctant acquiescence in the Louisiana Purchase—and abandonment of his plan to press for a constitutional amendment explicitly sanctioning it—demonstrate the seriousness of his constitutional scruples. He was loath to imply federal powers to acquire new territory and incorporate it into the United States even though these clearly were not powers that could be exercised by the states. Thus, unlike the bank bill, the Louisiana Purchase did not jeopardize the principle of federalism; it did not threaten any powers reserved to the states by the Tenth Amendment.[59] What is remarkable about Jefferson's position regarding Louisiana, in fact, is that he was so willing to jeopardize the purchase in order to use a constitutional amendment "to set an example against broad construction, by appealing for new power to the people," as he explained in an important letter to Wilson Cary Nicholas, one of the Republican leaders in Congress.[60]

When in a special, secret message to Congress on January 18, 1803, he requested an appropriation of $2,500 for what later became the Lewis and Clark expedition, he considered it "for the purpose of extending the external commerce of the U.S." As Ambrose has explained in his account of the expedition, Jefferson's message emphasized the opportunity to establish contacts with native tribes along the Missouri River and thus possibly to steal the fur trade from the British. He concluded that "the interests of commerce place the principal object within the constitutional powers and care of Congress, and that it should incidentally advance the geographical knowledge of our own continent can not but be an additional gratification."[61] Thus, as with the academy and his dry dock proposal, he linked the project to an enumerated power, although its constitutionality really was based on a relatively broad reading of Congress's commerce power—and hence, a more "sweeping" interpretation of the necessary and proper clause. As with the Embargo, however, because this was a power exclusively given Congress under the Constitution, he had no constitutional problem with it. Like the Louisiana Purchase itself, it raised no Tenth Amendment problem of federal preemption of a legitimate state matter.

Finally, Jefferson supported construction of the National Road, extending from Cumberland, Maryland, to Ohio. His treasury secretary, Albert Gallatin, conceived of the project, to be financed from a fund established when Ohio became a state in 1802. Unlike broader plans for internal improvements, such as the comprehensive plan he suggested to Congress in 1806, he did not regard it as requiring a constitutional amendment.[62] Perhaps he viewed the National Road as falling under the same category as another project he instituted as president in 1804, the construction of a new post road to New Orleans, which he saw clearly as an exercise of the article 1, section 8 power to establish post roads, as well as perhaps article 4, section 3, which authorized Congress "to dispose of and make all needful rules and regulations respecting the territory" of the United States. In light of the concerns he raised in his 1796 letter to Madison about broad use of the power to establish post roads, however, Jefferson should have been troubled about the precedents these projects might set. Indeed, his own experience in coping with the demands of local communities, which pressed for deviations from the most direct feasible route, exposed Jefferson firsthand to the very thing about which in 1796 he warned Madison—"the political hazards of federal responsibility for fixing routes of trade," as Merrill Peterson aptly phrased it.[63]

Jefferson was remarkably, although not perfectly, consistent in adhering to a contextualist theory of constitutional interpretation. Awareness of how his interpretation of particular provisions of the Constitution was affected by his fundamental commitment to core constitutional principles—such as federalism, the separation of powers, and rights guarantees—helps explain many of the apparent inconsistencies. Although it is not fair to charge Jefferson with hypocrisy, as critics from his own time to the present day have done, it is evident that his position with regard to certain proposed federal programs—such as a national military academy and federal funding of "post roads"—changed over time, as background political circumstances changed. When the intensely partisan politics of the 1790s had abated, in the wake of the "revolution of 1800," Jefferson abandoned his earlier, knee-jerk opposition to a military academy and supported establishment of the United States Military

Academy at West Point. The man who once questioned the constitutionality of the institution became its founder.

Notes

1. Henry Adams, *History of the United States of America during the Administrations of Thomas Jefferson* (New York, 1986), 614, 1239.

2. Adams, discussing the Embargo, puts it succinctly: "He [Jefferson] had undertaken to create a government which should interfere in no way with private action, and he had created one which interfered directly in the concerns of every private citizen in the land. He had come into power as the champion of States-rights, and had driven States to the verge of armed resistance." Ibid., 1239.

3. To be sure, Adams denounces the Embargo as disastrously bad policy and the "ruin" of Jefferson's presidency (ibid., 1245) but is almost gleeful in describing the Louisiana purchase as a precedent "too striking to be overlooked" which "gave a fatal wound to 'strict construction'. . . ." Ibid., 363, 389. When he added that "the Jeffersonian theories never again received general support," however, he not only exaggerates but overlooks most of nineteenth-century American constitutionalism. Jefferson's strict reading of federal powers was followed by most of his successors as president—not only his immediate Republican successors, James Madison and James Monroe, but also, most famously, perhaps, by Democratic presidents Andrew Jackson and Grover Cleveland, in their exercise of the presidential veto power. Here Adams makes the same mistake that many modern scholars do, in reading twentieth-century broad, or "Hamiltonian," readings of the Constitution back into the nineteenth century.

4. For example, Albert Jay Nock seems implicitly to accept the charge of inconsistency when he rationalizes both the Louisiana Purchase and the Embargo as "responsible" exercises of power: "It is mere idleness to think of the author of the Embargo Act as a doctrinaire enemy of strength in government. . . . His instinctive objection was not to strength, but to irresponsibility; not to centralization in itself, but as an engine of exploitation. . . . In purchasing Louisiana and in the matter of the Embargo, he had acted as an elected agent, answerable for the exercise of discretion in extraordinary circumstances." Albert Jay Nock, *Mr. Jefferson* (Washington, D.C., 1941, 1926), 271.

5. Thus, for example, Jefferson's strict interpretation of article 1, section 8 powers in his 1791 opinion on the bank bill can be squared with his liberal interpretation of various power-limiting provisions in his 1798 Kentucky Resolutions. See David N. Mayer, *The Constitutional Thought of Thomas Jefferson* (Charlottesville, Va., 1994), 194.

6. Ibid., 215, 217–18.

7. "The Congress shall have power . . . [t]o make all laws which shall be necessary and proper for carrying into execution the foregoing powers, and all other powers vested by this constitution in the government of the United States, or in any department or officer thereof." U.S. Constitution, article 1, section 8, clause 18.

8. See Mayer, *Constitutional Thought of Thomas Jefferson*, 215–16 (contrasting the bank bill with the Louisiana Purchase).

9. Leonard D. White, *The Jeffersonians: A Study in Administrative History, 1801–1829* (New York, 1951), 259–60.

10. See David N. Mayer, "'The Holy Cause of Freedom': The Libertarian Legacy of Thomas Jefferson," in *The Noblest Minds: Fame, Honor, and the American Founding,* ed. Peter McNamara (Lanham, Md., 1999), 97–119.

11. TJ to Edward Carrington, 27 May 1788, *TJP* 13:208–9. On English radical Whig ideas and their influence, see David N. Mayer, "The English Radical Whig Origins of American Constitutionalism," *Washington University Law Quarterly* 70 (1992): 131–208.

12. See Mayer, *Constitutional Thought of Thomas Jefferson,* 59–63, 89–144.

13. On Jefferson's unique views regarding the importance of constitutional amendments and popular control over constitutions, see ibid., 295–319. It was in his theory of constitutional change and its associated assumptions (including the importance of popular participation in and vigilance over government) that Jefferson made his most distinctive contributions to American constitutionalism. Ibid., 297.

14. This is not to say that Jefferson's unique views regarding constitutional change are unimportant or irrelevant to his theory of interpretation. Rather, for the purposes of this paper, it is not necessary to explore the ramifications of this aspect of his constitutional thought. It suffices to observe that Jefferson's ready acceptance of the notion of frequent, explicit constitutional change helped reinforce his strict interpretation of the power-granting clauses of the Constitution. As he observed in his 1803 letter to Wilson Cary Nicholas urging a constitutional amendment sanctioning the Louisiana Purchase, "When an instrument admits two constructions, the one safe, the other dangerous, the one precise, the other indefinite, I prefer that which is safe & precise. I had rather ask an enlargement of power from the nation where it is found necessary, than to assume it by a construction which would make our powers boundless. . . . Nothing is more likely than that their enumeration of powers is defective. This is the ordinary course of all human works. Let us go on then perfecting it, by adding by way of amendment to the Constitution, those powers which time & trial show are still wanting." See TJ to Wilson Cary Nicholas, 7 September 1803, *TJW,* 1139–41.

15. See Mayer, *Constitutional Thought of Thomas Jefferson,* 217–18, 194.

16. TJ, Opinion on the Constitutionality of the Bill for Establishing a National Bank, 15 February 1791, *TJP* 19:275–80.

17. In his opinion on the bank bill, Jefferson also discussed the so-called general welfare clause of article 1, section 8, clause 1 as a "general phrase," but it is clear that he did not so regard it. Rather, he saw the words "provide for the . . . general welfare of the United States"—technically, a phrase and not a clause—as words limiting the scope of Congress's taxing power, the subject of the clause. Years later, after his retirement from the presidency, when he commented approvingly on his successor's veto of an internal improvements bill, he pointed to the proper interpretation of the "general welfare" phrase as an essential difference between the Republican and Federalist parties. "Our tenet ever was . . . that Congress had not unlimited powers to provide for the general welfare, but were restrained to those specially enumerated." He again emphasized the phrase was not an independent grant of power; rather, it was a limitation on power to lay and collect taxes. See Mayer, *Constitutional Thought of Thomas Jefferson,* 191–92, 219–20.

18. See *McCulloch v. Maryland,* 17 U.S. (4 Wheaton) 316 (1819).

19. TJ, Opinion on the Constitutionality of the Bill for Establishing a National Bank, 15 February 1791, *TJP* 19:275–80 (emphasis in the original). It is interesting to note that the justice on the current United States Supreme Court who comes closest to Jefferson's contextualist theory of interpretation, particularly with regard to the way it takes seriously the Tenth Amendment, is Justice Clarence Thomas. See David N. Mayer, "Justice Clarence Thomas and the Supreme Court's Rediscovery of the Tenth Amendment," *Capital University Law Review* 25 (1996): 339–423.

20. Randy E. Barnett, "Necessary and Proper," *UCLA Law Review* 44 (1997): 745–93. Although Barnett calls this approach "Madisonian," for he focuses primarily on Madison's theory of interpretation, he acknowledges that Jefferson's view was essentially similar. Ibid., 755. In explaining the "proper" part of the clause, Barnett cites the work of two other legal scholars who have devised a test that seems quite Jeffersonian, or contextualist, in its features:

> In view of the limited character of the national government under the Constitution, Congress's choice of means to execute federal powers would be constrained in at least three ways: first, an executory law would have to conform to the "proper" allocation of authority within the federal government; second, such a law would have to be within the "proper" scope of the federal government's limited jurisdiction with respect to the retained prerogatives of the states; and third, the law would have to be within the "proper" scope of the federal government's limited jurisdiction with respect to the people's retained rights. In other words, . . . executory laws must be consistent with principles of separation of powers, principles of federalism, and individual rights.

Ibid., 773 (quoting Gary Lawson and Patricia B. Granger, "The 'Proper' Scope of Federal Power: A Jurisdictional Interpretation of the Sweeping Clause," *Duke Law Journal* 43 [1993]: 267, 297).

21. See Mayer, *Constitutional Thought of Thomas Jefferson*, 191–93.

22. Ibid., 193–94.

23. Ibid., 185–86.

24. See, generally, Ibid., 130–35 (discussing separation of powers and Jefferson's "tripartite" theory generally), 222–56 (discussing presidential powers), and 236–94 (discussing the judiciary and the power of judicial review). On presidential powers, see also David N. Mayer, "Thomas Jefferson and the Separation of Powers," in *The Presidency Then and Now*, ed. Phillip G. Henderson (Lanham, Md., 2000), 13–29, 250–54.

25. See Mayer, *Constitutional Thought of Thomas Jefferson*, 232, 242–44, 228–29; Mayer, "Jefferson and Separation of Powers," 18–20.

26. Mayer, *Constitutional Thought of Thomas Jefferson*, 230–31.

27. Ibid., 203–4.

28. Draft of the Kentucky Resolutions, October 1798, *TJW*, 454–55.

29. TJ, Notes of Cabinet Meeting on the President's Address to Congress, 23 November 1793, *TJP* 27:428. In the same meeting, Jefferson also opposed "the expediency" of a proposal to Congress to fortify principal harbors. His notes indicate that Knox also favored this proposal but that Randolph joined Jefferson in opposing it; Hamilton was absent from the meeting. Ibid.

30. Jefferson continued to oppose both the proposal for a military academy and the recommendation by Hamilton and Knox for fortifying major harbors. See TJ, Materials for the President's Address to Congress, (ca. 22 November 1793), ibid., 423–24 (editorial note).

31. White, *Jeffersonians*, 251. Washington suggested to Congress that "a material feature" in the improvement of the nation's defenses might be "to afford an opportunity for the study of those branches of the military art which can scarcely ever be attained by practice alone." George Washington, Fifth Annual Message, 3 December 1793, in Saul Padover, ed., *The Washington Papers* (New York, 1955), 283.

32. Sidney Forman, *West Point: A History of the United States Military Academy* (New York, 1950), 14. The 1794 act also created the rank of cadet. "Cadets were in effect junior officers: they had the right to command, to sit as members of courts-martial, and to employ servants or waiters." The law further provided for the purchase of books and apparatus for military instruction. Cadets and junior officers were expected to attend classes in a two-story stone building called "The Old Provost." Forman adds, "Some officers became indignant at descending to the grade

of pupils—and by design or accident the Provost, books and instruments were destroyed by fire in 1796." Ibid., 15.

33. See TJ, Materials for the President's Address to Congress, (ca. 22 November 1793), and editorial note, in *TJP* 27:421–24.

34. On Jefferson's perception of Hamilton and the Federalist party—and how his dialectical relationship with Hamiltonian Federalism helped shape his constitutional thought in the 1790s—see Mayer, *Constitutional Thought of Thomas Jefferson*, 107–18.

35. For example, it was in 1793, in the context of the continuing controversy over Washington's neutrality proclamation, that Jefferson urged his friend Madison to take up the pen and write the "Helvidius" essays, to counter the "heresies" of Hamilton's "Pacificus" essays and their broad view of presidential power in the war-making arena. See ibid., 232.

36. See Elizabeth Samet's essay in this volume, "Great Men and Embryo-Caesars: John Adams, Thomas Jefferson, and the Figure in Arms." The fear of a military-aristocratic alliance that Professor Samet describes in her essay is exemplified by Jefferson's views toward the Society of the Cincinnati. He wrote to Madison frankly of his concern that the same Federalist "Monocrats" who were publicly denouncing the Republican party's "democratical societies, whose avowed object is the nourishment of the republican principles of our constitution," were also "themselves the fathers, founders or high officers" of the Society of Cincinnati, which he described this way: "a *self-created* one, carving out for itself hereditary distinctions, lowering over our constitution eternally, meeting together in all parts of the Union periodically, with closed doors, accumulating a capital in their separate treasury, corresponding secretly and regularly," and with their sight "perfectly dazzled by the glittering of crowns and coronets." TJ to Madison, 28 December 1794, *TJP* 28:228–30 (emphasis in original). In light of these concerns, it is not at all surprising that Jefferson would oppose plans for a military academy when proposed by the same men, particularly Knox and Hamilton.

37. TJ to Madison, 6 March 1796, *TJP* 29:7–8. I am indebted to my friend and colleague Brad Smith for calling my attention to this passage, with which he prefaces an excellent article showing how the modern expansive interpretation of the so-called spending clause fosters political rent seeking (i.e., the seeking of special favors from government). Bradley A. Smith, "Hamilton at Wits End: The Lost Discipline of the Spending Clause vs. the False Discipline of Campaign Finance Reform," *Chapman Law Review* 4 (2001): 117–45.

38. TJ to Madison, 6 March 1796, *TJP* 29:7–8 (emphasis in original). In his letter in response, Madison tried to reassure his friend that his proposal had no "dangerous consequences." He emphasized it was "limited to the choice of roads where that is presented, and to the opening them, in other cases, so far only as may be necessary for the transportation of the mail." This was, he posited, "fairly within the object of the Constn." He also sought to allay Jefferson's fears about federal spending, suggesting that once the route was fixed for the post road, "the local authorities will probably undertake the improvement &c. of the roads; and individuals will go to work in providing the proper accommodations on them for general use." Madison to TJ, 4 April 1796, ibid., 55. Madison's bill was defeated in the Senate; see TJ to Madison, 6 March 1796, ibid., 8n.

39. TJ to Madison, 6 March 1796, ibid., 8.

40. "[A] thorough examination of the subject will evince that the art of war is at once comprehensive and complicated, that it demands much previous study, and that the possession of it in its most improved and perfect state is always of great moment to the security of a nation," Washington noted. Washington, Eighth Annual Address, 7 December 1796, *Washington Papers*, 301.

41. McHenry's plan combined elements of proposals he received from two sources, Alexan-

der Hamilton and Louis de Tousard, a veteran of the Revolutionary War under General Lafayette and a major in the First Regiment of Artillerists and Engineers. Hamilton's plan called for the establishment of four schools: a "fundamental school" at West Point, to give basic instruction in all branches of the army and navy; a school for engineers and artillerists; a school for cavalry and infantry; and a school for the navy. All cadets would spend two years at the fundamental school and then two more at the specialized institutions. Tousard's plan called specifically for the "formation of a School of Artillerists and Engineers" and recommended, in the words of Stephen Ambrose, "a complete course in the basic sciences, practical field instruction, the best possible faculty, and rigid discipline." McHenry's 14 January 1800 report to President Adams proposed that the government establish Hamilton's four suggested schools, each organized in accordance with Tousard's plan. See White, *Jeffersonians,* 252; Stephen E. Ambrose, *Duty, Honor, Country: A History of West Point* (Baltimore, 1966), 13–14.

42. Forman, *West Point,* 15 (citing Act of Congress of 16 July 1798).

43. Ibid., 16–17. In January 1801 President Adams appointed as a teacher of mathematics George Baron, an Englishman who had been an instructor at the British military academy at Woolrich. Baron attempted to introduce English methods at West Point, but his civilian status in a military community gave him little authority, Forman notes; held in "contempt" at West Point, Baron remained only thirteen months. Ibid., 17.

44. Stephen Ambrose suggests that the "chief reason" for Congress's inaction was "an unspoken but nevertheless real fear of a trained body of officers"—a fear tied not only to Americans' traditional Whiggish antipathy to standing armies but also to recent history, "their knowledge that the French Revolution had been betrayed by just such officers." Ambrose, *Duty, Honor, Country,* 15. On the Jeffersonian Republicans' distrust of a standing army and its relevance to Jefferson's reduction of the regular army during his administration, see White, *Jeffersonians,* 213.

45. Ambrose, *Duty, Honor, Country,* 19.

46. Ibid. Ambrose notes another milestone: when the teacher, Baron, illustrated his lecture by making marks with chalk upon a standing slate, the blackboard was introduced to America. Ibid.

47. Forman, *West Point,* 18–19; White, *Jeffersonians,* 251 (citing 2 Stat. 132, secs. 26–28 [16 March 1802]).

48. Forman, *West Point,* 23. Williams was the son of a prosperous merchant and a grandnephew of Benjamin Franklin; he came to Jefferson's attention through his service as secretary and vice president of the American Philosophical Society. See Ambrose, *Duty, Honor, Country,* 22. At West Point, Williams devoted less time to the academy than he did to the scientific society he founded, the United States Military Philosophical Society. See ibid., 30–32. Williams resigned in June 1803, following a dispute over his right to command troops. Forman, *West Point,* 25–26.

49. "The Congress shall have power . . . [t]o raise and support armies. . . ." U.S. Constitution, article 1, section 8, clause 12. Establishment of the academy might also follow as a "necessary and proper" exercise of Congress's power, under article 1, section 8, clause 17, to exercise authority over "all places purchased . . . for the erection of forts, magazines, arsenals, dock-yards, and other needful buildings." See Mayer, *Constitutional Thought of Thomas Jefferson,* 214. In this essay, however, I focus on the power to raise and support armies, because use of the latter clause in support of the constitutionality of novel uses of federal property constitutes a kind of circular argument—as the Supreme Court demonstrated in its New Deal–era decision upholding the constitutionality of the Tennessee Valley Authority. See *Ashwander v. Tennessee Valley Authority,* 297 U.S. 288 (1936) (upholding the TVA as a proper exercise of Congress's analogous power under article 4, section 3, "to dispose of and make all needful rules and regulations respecting the territory or other property belonging to the United States").

50. Many years later—after even the most diehard radical Jeffersonian Republicans had come to accept the necessity of West Point, following the War of 1812—John C. Calhoun expressed the prevailing sentiment when, as secretary of war, he reported to the House of Representatives in 1820 that "It ought never to be forgotten that the military science, in the present condition of the world, cannot be neglected with impunity. It has become so complicated and extensive as to require for its acquisition extensive means, and much time to be exclusively devoted to it. It can only flourish under the patronage of the Government, and without such patronage it must be almost wholly neglected." White, *Jeffersonians,* 257 (quoting from *American State Papers: Military Affairs,* II, 76 [February 23, 1820]).

51. Article 1, section 8, clause 16. This clause further provides, however, that "the appointment of the officers, and the authority of training the militia according to the discipline provided by Congress" were powers reserved to the states.

52. TJ to Spencer Roane, 6 September 1819, *TJW,* 1425.

53. See Theodore J. Crackel's essay in this volume, "The Military Academy in the Context of Jeffersonian Reform." Jefferson's efforts to "republicanize" (or Republicanize, as some might say) the military establishment were paralleled by his actions regarding the judiciary. Although he could do little to transform the political composition of the life-tenured federal judiciary, which continued to be dominated by Federalist judges—particularly after Congress with Jefferson's blessing repealed the Judiciary Act of 1801 and thus shrunk the size of the federal judiciary—Jefferson could help counterbalance Federalist judges by using his appointment power to replace Federalists in the critical positions of United States attorneys and marshals. This significant exception to his overall moderate patronage power he rationalized as necessary to effectuate the "revolution of 1800," and the will of the electorate. See Mayer, *Constitutional Thought of Thomas Jefferson,* 122, 265–67.

54. Malone, 5:510.

55. Ambrose, *Duty, Honor, Country,* 30–32, 34–35. Jefferson observed that "as these youths grow up and take their stations in society, they will naturally become militia officers and in a few years, in the ordinary course of events, we should see a uniformity in our militia, resulting from a spirit of emulation, which the reputation of having received a military education would naturally excite." Ambrose notes that Jefferson's argument probably did not help win support for the academy in Congress, where many Republicans were suspicious of Williams because he was a Federalist, while southerners wanted a school of their own in the South. Observing that politicians generally were hostile because they wanted the exclusive right to grant commissions, Ambrose concludes that Congress opposed the plan because it meant "fewer militia commissions the political parties could use as patronage—a practice that would plague West Point until well into the twentieth century." Thus, Congress ignored most of the Williams's proposals, although in 1808 it authorized an increase in the number of cadets to 256 in light of America's growing troubles with France and England. Ibid., 35.

56. Mayer, *Constitutional Thought of Thomas Jefferson,* 214.

57. TJ to Robert R. Livingston, 30 April 1800, in Ford, 7:446.

58. TJ, Sixth Annual Message, 2 December 1806, ibid., 8:494. After his retirement from the presidency, Jefferson continued to support a constitutional amendment to authorize internal improvements. See Mayer, *Constitutional Thought of Thomas Jefferson,* 219–20.

59. Ibid., 215–18, 244–51.

60. TJ to Wilson Cary Nicholas, 7 September 1803, *TJW,* 1141.

61. Stephen E. Ambrose, *Undaunted Courage: Meriwether Lewis, Thomas Jefferson, and the Opening of the American West* (New York, 1996), 78. More troubling, as a potential precedent

for broad construction, was the beginning of the United States Coastal Survey, under the auspices of Jefferson's administration and pursuant to an 1806 appropriation for the survey of the coast between Cape Hatteras and Cape Fear. See Merrill Peterson, *Thomas Jefferson and the New Nation* (New York, 1970), 857–58.

62. Mayer, *Constitutional Thought of Thomas Jefferson*, 219.

63. See Peterson, *Thomas Jefferson and the New Nation*, 857.

Great Men and Embryo-Caesars

John Adams, Thomas Jefferson, and the Figure in Arms

ELIZABETH D. SAMET

"Every hero," Ralph Waldo Emerson observed in *Representative Men* (1851), "becomes a bore at last." Yet while he reigns, the hero elicits unseemly adulation. "Hear the shouts in the street!" Emerson affirms, "The people cannot see him enough. They delight in a man. Here is a head and a trunk! What a front! what eyes! Atlantean shoulders, and a whole carriage heroic, with equal inward force to guide the great machine!" Emerson goes on to suggest that the very phrase *great man* contributes to society's degeneration because it connotes a predestined virtue exclusive to the few, unattainable by the many. "Is there caste?" he demands, "Is there fate? What becomes of the promise to virtue?" It is not the heroic type per se that so vexes Emerson but rather the apparent loss of self that accompanies an ordinary citizen's surrender to hero worship. Too readily dazzled by vulgar, triumphant display, humanity tends to miss those quieter sorts of heroism that enlarge rather than oppress. The hero Emerson describes makes his adherents ever smaller. Seducing them from themselves, he leaves his adorers paralyzed, not empowered, by his example. In short, the hero becomes our alibi. "What indemnification is one great man for populations of pigmies!" exclaims Emerson. "His attractions warp us from our place. We have become underlings and intellectual suicides."[1] In whatever measure we allow the great man to do our living for us—to whatever degree, in Emerson's metaphor, we "sun" ourselves in his "light" but imagine it our own—by so much does our individual dignity diminish and our self-reliance, that Emersonian quintessence, erode.[2]

Nothing, for Emerson, more clearly revealed humanity's descent from a state of dignity to one of dependence than did the world's seemingly inexhaustible craving for heroes. He perceived that societies exist always in a state of anticipation, a condition in which the only thing that successfully weans them from one great man is the rise of another. And thus the worshippers take an antidote as dangerous as the disease. Over a decade before, in his 1837 Phi Beta Kappa address at Harvard, Emerson had articulated a psychosomatic model of hero worship in which the acolytes subordinate even their bodies to the hero's cause: Individuals willingly "perish," he asserts in "The American Scholar," "to add one drop of blood to make that great heart beat, those giant sinews combat and conquer."[3]

Emerson's reflections on the "Uses of Great Men" have an eighteenth-century paternity. His precursors might have titled such an inquiry "The Uses and Abuses of Great Men." The seductiveness of heroes, especially that of great military conquerors, was a favorite preoccupation of political thinkers on both sides of the Atlantic throughout the 1700s. In *Cato's Letters,* John Trenchard and Thomas Gordon charted the historical devolution of the hero from a "brave disinterested" figure into something altogether different. They believed that the term *hero* had become a byword for *conqueror* in the modern world. Mock heroes had replaced the real. "Whereas the primitive heroes were the bulwarks of society, and the preservers of men," Trenchard and Gordon contended, "those who pretended to succeed them, were the disturbers of society, and the destroyers of men." After all, "Alexander deified himself, and Caesar was deified by others, for being universal murderers. . . . Mischief is inseparable from the profession of a present hero, whose business and ambition is to multiply conquests." Among the figures most often cited in contemporaneous admonitory essays on the modern military hero were Marlborough, Louis XIV, and Cromwell. Trenchard and Gordon attributed the tendency toward mischief on the part of such men to the wildness of their "nature" and the impudence of their "ambition." "There is no trusting of liberty," they insisted, "in the hands of men, who are obeyed by great armies."[4]

Half a century later, during the American Revolution, the same theme would appear in the correspondence of Lieutenant Colonel Alexander Hamilton, who suggested to James Duane in 1780 that it was a weak federal government that made possible the rise of conquering generals. Hamilton's prediction for America was far from sanguine. "Already some of the lines of the army would obey their states in opposition to Congress," he wrote, "notwithstanding the pains we have taken to preserve the unity of the army—if any thing would hinder this it would be the personal influence of the General, a melancholy and mortifying consideration."[5] Hamilton here suggested the perils of depending on the charisma of a general—even when that general was someone as irreproachable as George Washington himself—to rescue a republic from civil strife.

By the turn of the century, Napoleon had provided Americans with a fresh example of the military demagogue's ability to gain absolute power through personalism. In "The Nature and Basis of Bonaparte's Power," Fisher Ames noted the ease with which revolutionary peoples become "blind instruments in the hands of ambitious men." Under such circumstances, Ames continued in this 1801 essay, "the power of an army, of necessity, falls into the hands of one man, the general-in-chief, who is the sole despot and master of the state."[6] Military men, Thomas Jefferson affirmed, were particularly sympathetic to the royal aspirations of their commanders: "Some officers" of the Continental army, he reported, "trained to monarchy by military habits, . . . proposed to Genl. Washington . . . to assume himself the crown, on the assurance of their support."[7]

Such suspicions notwithstanding, it was Jefferson's administration that established, and John Adams's that had planned for, an institution designed precisely to train young men in military habits. In 1802, the same year in which Napoleon founded the *École Spéciale Militaire* at Fontainebleau, Congress authorized the founding of the United States Military Academy. This essay examines the academy as the creation of two deeply ambivalent founders who were persuaded, on the one hand, of the political dangers posed by military men and, on the other hand, of the growing necessity to provide well-disciplined troops for the national defense. It also situates West Point's founding within late eighteenth-century conceptions of military ambition and republican virtue.

It is useful to recall how low the age's opinion of professional soldiering was. Edward Gibbon's dismissal of the modern European mercenary as "the meanest, and . . . the most profligate, of mankind" was typical. As the preservation of "the public freedom" had given way to schemes of conquest, Gibbon observed in *The Decline and Fall of the Roman Empire,* war had degenerated into "a trade."[8] Mary Wollstonecraft likewise posited that soldiers had become wholly unfit for republican citizenship. Standing armies were fundamentally "incompatible with freedom," she wrote, "because subordination and rigour are the very sinews of military discipline."[9] Believing that the agricultural and commercial advances of the modern world had made a "nation of soldiers" in the ancient Greek sense obsolete, Hamilton affirmed that standing armies were "the inseparable companion of frequent hostility" in republics.[10]

Nevertheless, Hamilton's federalism, combined with his soldier's understanding of the practical considerations of drill and discipline, forced him to conclude that without some national "force constituted differently from the [state] militia to preserve the peace of the community," the citizenry would be unable to resist local tyrants. If threatened by those who would usurp power, "citizens must rush tumultuously to arms, without concert, without system, without resource; except in their courage and despair."[11] In *Federalist* No. 25, Hamilton reminded his readers of the militia's uneven performance during the Revolution. Valiant and "valuable" as they had been, he insisted, militiamen could not have won the war "by their efforts alone. . . . War," Hamilton continued, "is a science to be acquired and perfected by diligence, by perseverance, by time, and by practice."[12] Hamilton here captured a central difficulty facing the architects of the United States, namely, how to balance the needs of national defense with the demands of liberty.[13]

Lacking confidence in an unsupervised militia, Hamilton argued in 1799 that "The Institution of a Military Academy [would] be an auxiliary of great importance."[14] Adams and Jefferson came to the same conclusion, of course, but their enthusiasm was tempered by anxieties about the politics of military men. Furthermore, a belief in war's allure and in the appeal of military tyrants stimulated their periodic warnings about the potential dissolution of the Republic. Adams often observed that war would eventually distract Americans from the republican project. "All animals," he wrote to Benjamin Rush during the War of 1812, "take more pleasure in fighting than in eating."[15] Democracy was ephemeral, Adams told John Taylor, and strife was its inevitable termination. Individuals might occasionally be able to overcome their destructive passions, but "nations and large bodies of men, never."[16] Chief among these passions was that "for distinction." In Adams's political psychology, man's desire for distinction was both society's necessary engine and its ultimate destroyer. This passion drove not only the tyrants and villains but also the "patriots and heroes, and most of the great benefactors to mankind." In *Discourses on Davila,* Adams reminded his readers that "even in these esteemed, beloved, and adored characters, the passion, although refined by the purest moral sentiments, and intended to be governed by the best principles, is a passion still." It was, "like all other human desires," both "unlimited and insatiable."[17]

Elsewhere in *Davila* Adams gave to this double-edged passion the name *emulation,* and he argued that "next to self-preservation," it constitutes "the great spring of human actions." Only a "well-ordered government," he asserted, could "prevent that emulation from degenerating into dangerous ambition, irregular rivalries, destructive factions, wasting seditions, and bloody, civil wars."[18] In Adams's political vision, dangerous ambition always seems to resolve itself into military conquest. Not surprisingly, he discovered in military hierarchy an ideal figure for civil society's culture of emulation. "The soldier compares himself with his fellows, and contends for promotion to corporal. The corporals vie with each other to be sergeants. The sergeants will mount breaches to be ensigns. And thus every man in an army is constantly aspiring to be something higher, as every citizen in the commonwealth is constantly struggling for a better rank, that he may draw the observation of more eyes."[19] "Napoleon and all his generals," Adams informed Taylor, "were but creatures of democracy."[20]

Convinced that military ambition could never be anything other than an ambition to conquer, Adams nevertheless had a realist's attitude toward the periodic necessity of force in the preservation of liberty. And throughout his career he took a keen interest in the training and education of military men. Adams was the first to admit that he was no warrior himself. When, on the eve of revolution in 1775, his friend Mercy Otis Warren noted how much he had lately been consumed by the present crisis, Adams replied in humorously self-deflating style that, patriot though he was, he considered himself "too old to make a Figure in Arms the Profession to which We must for the future perhaps be obliged for our Safety and our Liberty as much as formerly we were to that of the Law. If the Standards should be erected, and A Camp formed," he added, "ten to one but he flies to it, but whether it will be for shelter, or as a volunteer, Time alone must discover."[21] Time discovered that Adams would become a patriot of the pen, not of the sword, but he recognized the centrality of soldiers to the establishment and future maintenance of the Republic. Acutely aware of the obligation civilians incurred to military force, Adams worked as a member of the Continental Congress Board of War throughout the Revolution to preserve civilian supervision of military affairs.

Adams took great pride in having been, as he claimed, the first founder to recognize the need for a national military academy. Referring to Adams as the academy's "first mover," Charles Francis Adams calls special attention to his grandfather's vision and passion for the initiative in his edition of Adams's *Works.*[22] In his capacity as a member of the Board of War, Adams corresponded frequently with officers. "This day," he notified then-Colonel Henry Knox in an October 1, 1776, postscript to a letter written a few days before, "I had the honour of making a motion for the Appointment of a Committee to consider of a Plan for the Establishment of a military Accademy in the Army."[23] Here soliciting Knox's opinions about the enterprise, Adams continued throughout the conflict to serve enthusiastically on the board.

In contrast to Adams's self-deprecation, Jefferson demonstrated a disproportionate sensitivity about his own lack of military service. He went to great lengths, for example, to refute the charges of cowardice that Henry ("Lighthorse Harry") Lee leveled at him in *Memoirs of the War in the Southern Department* (1812). Lee attacked him for his conduct during Simcoe's Raid on Richmond in December 1780, when Jefferson, then wartime governor of Virginia, had supposedly fled before the enemy. Dumas Malone suggests that while it is difficult to ascertain the truth, there seems little evidence that a terrified Jefferson ran away in a panic. "If no Don Quixote," Malone concludes, "neither was he Falstaff."[24] But the episode still rankled in 1826, when Lee's son, who was preparing a revised edition of *Memoirs,* visited Jefferson at his deathbed to set the record straight. Jefferson had smoothed the way with a written apologia to Lee a few months before:

> I may with confidence challenge any one to put his finger on the point of time when I was in a state of remissness from any duty of my station. But I was not with the army! true; for first, where was I? second, I was engaged in the more important function of taking measures to collect an army; and, without military education myself, instead of jeopardizing the public safety by pretending to take its command, of which I knew nothing, I had committed it to persons of the art, men who knew how to make the best use of it.[25]

It is interesting to note the way Jefferson's expedient emphasis on military expertise and soldiers as "persons of the art" dovetails with contemporary rationales for founding a military academy. It is also easy to account for Jefferson's discomfort. As Douglass Adair and others have shown, martial virtue—that of the citizen as opposed to the professional—was never very far from the eighteenth-century notions of fame and republican citizenship absorbed by the founders. To men like Hamilton (whose hero happened to be General Wolfe), citizenship's arms-bearing component played a potentially outsized role.[26]

Perhaps nothing better illustrates the philosophical differences between Hamilton and Jefferson than their respective definitions of greatness. Adducing Hamilton's choice of heroes as proof of his true "political principles," Jefferson recalled to Rush that Hamilton had not recognized his busts of Bacon, Newton, and Locke. When Jefferson told him that "they were my trinity of the three greatest men the world had ever produced," Hamilton, pausing "for some time," evidently replied that "the greatest man that ever lived, was Julius Caesar."

Jefferson used this vignette as evidence for Hamilton's belief "in the necessity of either force or corruption to govern men."[27] Republican suspicions of a widespread susceptibility to greatness in the Federalists—especially to the greatness of Washington—found voice in the campaign slogan *Principles, not men!* There is much evidence for Republican claims. Illuminating similarities between the birthday celebrations for Washington and those for King George II half a century before, Simon Newman has shown how the Federalists constructed a "cult" around Washington. Newman suggests that the winning of independence "did not signal the end of monarchical traditions of veneration for a single individual who effectively symbolized national unity and purpose."[28]

But Jefferson was disturbed less by Washington himself than by those officers who lionized him. This anxiety fueled his opposition to Hamilton's militarism and to any argument for a standing army, which was in his eyes, as Joanne Freeman notes, one of the "tools of monarchy."[29] Washington's apparent indifference to the worship paid him made Jefferson uneasy. Believing that there "never was a moment in which [Washington] would not have died" for the Republic, Jefferson nevertheless worried that Washington's own staunch principles prevented him from perceiving the dangerous ambitions of subordinates such as Hamilton, Knox, and Steuben.[30] One clumsy scheme had been initiated near the end of the Revolution by Colonel Lewis Nicola, who attempted to convince Washington of "the weakness of republicks" and then invited the general to become a king.[31] Washington's rectitude—and his unequivocal rebuff of Nicola—did not console Jefferson, who continued to ferret out other, more subtle monarchists.

More worrisome were the conspiracies of Knox and Steuben, whom Jefferson accused of trying to gain Washington's acquiescence in a military coup before the army disbanded. Jefferson also bridled at what he perceived to be an attempt on the part of officers to form a network of secret societies. The same Newburgh, New York, encampment that witnessed an aborted officer mutiny in 1783 later saw the drafting of a charter for the Society of the Cincinnati, a hereditary organization called into being by Knox and others for the purpose of commemorating the dangers and privations they had shared in the battle for liberty. Much of the original charter, which referred to the organization as a "society of friends," outlined procedures for the disbursement of funds to indigent officers, widows, and orphans.[32] Yet Jefferson believed that "the charitable part of the institution," coupled with the society's hereditary nature, would create a class of men who would come to view themselves as superior to the "industrious farmer." The society would authorize the "lazy lounger, valuing himself on his family, too proud to work, & drawing out a miserable existence by eating on that surplus of other men's labour which is the sacred fund of the helpless poor." The charitable allowance was at once too little and too much: "A pitiful annuity will only prevent them from exerting that industry & those talents which would soon lead them to better fortune."[33]

The officers' stated vow to follow the example of Cincinnatus "by returning to their citizenship" did nothing to mitigate Jefferson's vexation at their desire to preserve a division between civil and military cultures.[34] In a 1786 response to a French correspondent, Jefferson explained why the society had not excited more animated protests from American citizens. Americans had "no more idea" of "distinction by birth or badge" than they did "of the mode of existence in the moon or planets." Only Europeans, accustomed to the historical "evils" of "arbitrary distinction," he reasoned, could summon the appropriate "horror" at a hereditary order that was nothing other than "a detestable parricide."[35]

Jefferson complained to several correspondents that the Cincinnati were busy fomenting plots. The society, he told James Madison in 1794, was "carving out for itself hereditary distinctions, lowering over our constitution eternally, meeting together in all parts of the Union periodically, with closed doors, accumulating a capital in their separate treasury, corresponding secretly and regularly." Jefferson asserted that the officers had been "perfectly dazzled by the glittering of crowns and coronets."[36] In their secret meetings, they would continue to "collate their grievances, some real, some imaginary, all highly painted" and "communicate to each other the sparks of discontent" that could enflame the entire republic. The order's very existence would "continue a distinction between the civil & military which it would be for the good of the whole to obliterate as soon as possible."[37] Here Jefferson was only reiterating what he had told Washington himself on April 16, 1784, when he insisted "that a distinction is kept up between the civil & military, which it is for the happiness of both to obliterate." Washington himself may have been blameless, Jefferson added, but he would not live forever:

> When the members assemble they will be proposing to do something, & what that something may be will depend on actual circumstances; that being an organized body under habits of subordination, the first obstructions to enterprize will be already surmounted; that the moderation & virtue of a single character has probably prevented this revolution from being closed as most others have been, by a subversion of that liberty it was intended to establish; that he is not immortal, & his successor, or some of his successors, may be led by false calculation into a less certain road to glory.[38]

As time went on, Jefferson's fears about the splintering of civil and military communities were only exacerbated by the Federalist military program, especially by the specter of Hamilton's New Army, and, a few years later, by the Burr Conspiracy.[39]

And thus Jefferson saw in the military academy a political opportunity. Could not this institution weaken the pull of organizations such as the Cincinnati by giving future officers something other than the crucible of Revolutionary combat to unite them by investing them with a degree of professionalism and discipline? As Theodore Crackel has noted, the academy formed part of a larger Jeffersonian reconstitution of the army as a reflection of republican society at large, an organization loyal to republican principles.[40] Jefferson's reforms succeeded in wresting the army from Federalist control and in increasing the number of Republican appointees. With the establishment of a national academy, officers, disgruntled or otherwise, could no longer quite so easily form their own communities at the Republic's margins.

The academy's founding in 1802 also realized Washington's own earlier vision. It was he who had first publicized the need to transmit "the knowledge . . . acquired thro' the various Stages of a long and arduous service." It would have been regrettable, he observed, should that particular legacy be allowed to "become extinct." "Until a more perfect system of Education" could be adopted, an academy could provide continuity by "instructing a certain number of young Gentlemen in the Theory of the Art of War, particularly in all those branches of service which belong to the Artillery and Engineering Departments." Homegrown soldiers would also reduce American dependence on foreign allies, particularly the French.[41]

It is important to remember that Jefferson's distrust of military culture did not obscure for him either the importance of fielding trained soldiers or the fundamental unpredictability of the militia. The territorial acquisitions that marked his administration made the need for a disciplined force even more pressing. And while he argued that a "well-organized and armed militia" remained the "best security" for a free people, Jefferson also recognized the limitations of its present structure, especially for prolonged or "distant service."[42] In his sixth annual message to Congress, in 1806, he called attention to both the strengths and weaknesses of a decentralized militia. Praising the alacrity with which citizens of the Western territory had "tendered their services in defence of their country" against Spanish troops in Louisiana, he nevertheless noted, alluding to the Burr Conspiracy, that in other parts of the country "a great number of private individuals were combining together, arming and organizing themselves contrary to law, to carry on military expeditions against the territories of Spain."[43]

Jefferson understood that the academy, in contributing to their professional training in engineering and artillery, could become a place where citizens acquired the practical knowledge that would prepare them to defend the nation's rapidly expanding borders. West Point also provided one venue for the advancement of scientific study. The academy's focus on technology complemented Jefferson's emphasis on the direct relationship between liberty and science: "the precious blessing of liberty," he wrote to Joseph Willard, "is the great parent of *science* and of virtue."[44] Jefferson was also sympathetic to what today goes by the name of "values education" at the military academy. The March 1825 minutes of the University of Virginia Board of Visitors notes the importance of paying "especial attention to the principles of government which shall be inculcated therein, and to provide that none shall be inculcated which are incompatible with those on which the Constitutions of this State, and of the United States were genuinely based."[45] Properly instructed in the principles of government, military academy graduates might be less likely to join conspiracies.

Jefferson did not, however, conceive of the academy as another University of Virginia committed to the study of abstract ideas or to the wider exploration of liberal arts. Far less intimately connected to the Revolutionary army than Adams had been, he had a somewhat vaguer notion of military curricula. There seems little evidence, Crackel suggests, for seeing the academy as an integral part of a larger Jeffersonian enlightenment project.[46] Practical and political considerations were likewise important to Adams's plan for an academy. In his capacity as a member of the Board of War, Adams had noted a general disrespect for civil authority among officers, particularly among southern officers. He recalled in his *Autobiography* the insubordinate communiqués written by various staff officers and aides—documents "not well calculated to preserve the Subordination of the military Power, to the civil Authority, which the Spirit of Liberty will always require and enforce." The project of instilling republican principles in military men was as dear to him as it was to Jefferson, but almost from the first Adams had a more expansive notion of the kind of intellectual inquiry that might occur at a military academy.

While serving on the Board of War, Adams had been extremely critical of the army's almost complete lack of professional knowledge and skills. "It was my peculiar Province," he wrote in a letter subsequently included in his *Autobiography,* "to superintend every thing relating to the Army. I will add without Vanity, I had read as much on the military Art, and much more of the History of War, than any American Officer of that Army, General Lee excepted." During the war, Adams corresponded with Knox about the need to make translations of European military texts available to American officers, and his *Autobiography* is replete with observations about the shortcomings of the Continental army. Citing Montesquieu on Hannibal and Polybius on discipline, Adams would apprise various officers of their failings. At one juncture he was so "vexed" that he claimed to be "almost . . . resolve[d] to make interest to become a Collonel" himself. Criticized for presuming to instruct the army, Adams commented, "I can only reply, by asserting that it was high time, that the army had some Instructor or other."

One of Adams's insights was that courage without knowledge was insufficient to the formation of a successful officer. "Of the courage of these gentlemen and the Officers in general I had no doubt," he insisted. "But I was too well informed that most of the officers were deficient in reading: and I wished to turn the Minds of such as were capable of it, to that great Source of Information."[47] An academy would thus answer a particular need, and Adams could look forward to the founding of what he would later call "a Nursery for the education of young men in military Science discipline and tactics."[48]

This rhetoric of nurturing is not accidental. West Point's identity as an *academy* certainly harmonized with Adams's insistence on the centrality of education to the perpetuation of a republic, but as his correspondence with various officers attests, Adams also seemed to feel a special paternal interest in their education. In one letter we find him instructing his "young friend" Colonel Tudor in history. Introducing Tudor to the story of the Theban hero Epaminondas, Adams provided a lengthy discourse on the liberation of Thebes from Sparta.[49] Yet, as he wrote several years later to British reformer John Jebb, one had to be careful about confusing liberty with the liberator. "If Thebes owes its liberty to Epaminondas," suggested Adams, "she will lose both when he dies." Adams insisted that "reformation must begin with the body of the people, which can be done only, to effect, in their educations. The whole people must take upon themselves the education of the whole people." "Instead of adoring a Washington," Adams wrote, "mankind should applaud the nation which educated him." The United States Military Academy was one specialized incarnation of that general "system of education" essential to creating a long line of American Washingtons willing to subordinate themselves to civil power.[50]

Under such a system, Adams believed that Americans could realize their republican potential—a potential spoiled by the worship of famous heroes. The "spirit of liberty," he had written earlier, "without knowledge, would be little better than a brutal rage." By supporting schools, citizens would realize the legacy of their colonial forefathers, who had, as Adams noted in his 1765 *Dissertation on the Canon and Feudal Law,* bequeathed "so universal an affection and veneration for those seminaries, and for liberal education, that the meanest of the people contribute cheerfully to the support and maintenance of them every year." At no time was knowledge more important than in times of political turbulence. In the midst of the Stamp Act Crisis, Adams insisted that "every sluice of knowledge be opened and set a-flowing" in the face of British attempts "to strip us in a great measure of the means" through tyrannical duties and restrictions.[51]

By 1821 Adams seemed convinced that the United States Military Academy had indeed become a public seminary of learning. When members of the corps marched to Massachusetts that summer, he addressed them at Quincy. In his oration the former president suggested not only what role the academy might play in the Republic but also what preparation its cadets ought to receive. Adams described the cadets' course as the "pursuit of honor" conducted "under the auspices of the national government." Underscoring once again a universal tendency to prefer military to any other kind of heroism, Adams set his untried audience the task of meditating on the true nature of glory. To be a dashing figure in arms, he averred, was simply not enough. Battlefield heroics had no intrinsic value; heroism derived its worth exclusively from its connection to certain virtues—among them, wisdom, benevolence, equity, humanity, and justice. Adams reminded the cadets that "Conquest and Victory, abstracted from their only justifiable object and End which is Justice and Peace, are the Glory of Fraud Violence and Usurpation." Wars could serve the ends of peace; they could not, when isolated from justice, serve the ends of virtue.

The oration also reveals Adams's perhaps peculiar vision of early nineteenth-century cadet life. The academy's curriculum was largely technical, but Adams conjured a picture of these young men reading "night and day" the biographies of history's "immortal Captains." Somewhat softened by this time in his attitude toward the worship of Washington, he exhorted them as they read to learn to distinguish the bankrupt glory of Caesar and Alexander from the true "Glory of Washington, and his faithful colleagues!" "Models of Excellence," he urged, could be found at home as easily as they could in the annals of European or Ancient tyrannies. Perhaps Adams spotted a skeptic in his midst, for he proceeded, in an allusion to Milton's *Paradise Lost,* to liken the achievements of Alexander and Caesar to the "livid flames . . . which far round illumined Hell."

Adams recognized that it would never be easy for these future officers, upon one day finding themselves in the midst of battle "in the most exalted transports of . . . military ardour," to remember the "dignity" of their "character as . . . American citizens." Indeed, he feared that this was a fight few won, and his trenchant ruminations about conquerors and kings suggest the degree of importance the academy had assumed for him as a nursery of republican ideals. To preserve the Republic, a military academy would have to encourage the study of virtue itself rather than the celebration of its periodic human emanations. At the close of his speech to the corps, Adams instructed the cadets to regard their position as "a sacred trust" that made them responsible to their country and qualified them for any "course of Life." Despite the early academy's lack of humanist pretensions, Adams praised these young men "for attaining eminence in Letters and Science as well as Arms."[52]

Those cadets who had achieved sufficient "eminence in Letters" to tackle Plutarch or Polybius would have been able to make sense of the full significance of the several invocations of Epaminondas that appear in Adams's writings. For Plutarch as well as for his devoted eighteenth-century readers, Epaminondas stood as the archetypal disinterested servant of the people, a safer bet even than Cincinnatus, because he was a liberator rather than an agent of territorial expansion. (The Roman wars against the Aequi can only with difficulty be construed as crusades for liberty.) Epaminondas had also been the great hero of Montaigne, who recognized in him the same virtues Adams would discover: "resolution and valour—not the kind which is sharpened by ambition but the kind which wisdom and reason can implant in the well-ordered soul." Epaminondas never betrayed his "integrity" in a quest for glory; against the Theban's "standard," Montaigne observes, "the sense of right and wrong in Alexander seems subordinate, hesitant, spasmodic, weak and subject to chance."[53] In Thebes and Epaminondas Adams found a parallel to the young American republic of 1785 and its founding general, George Washington. "Perhaps," as he wrote to Colonel Tudor, "there is not in all Antiquity, if there is in universal History, an Example, more apposite to our Situation, than that of Thebes, or a Character more deserving of imitation, than that of Epaminondas."[54] Here was a man who managed somehow to keep his "passion for distinction" in check.

In 371 BCE a combined force of Boeotian farmers and Theban warriors crushed the celebrated Spartan phalanx at the battle of Leuctra, thereby freeing Greece from tyranny and ending the pernicious system of helotage. The Thebans' unconventional attack from the left wing succeeded in crushing Sparta. According to Plutarch, Epaminondas engineered "a rout and a slaughter of the Spartans such as had never before been seen."[55] Plutarch's *Life of Epaminondas* has been lost, but the numerous sketches elsewhere in his writings combine to create the portrait of a man both ascetic and aloof, a general whose authority was moral as well as military.

Moralia, for example, contains the following vignette. Returning finally to Thebes in 369 from his campaign, which had freed more than 200,000 Spartan slaves and united the oppressed city-states of Greece, Epaminondas was put on trial by his political enemies for keeping the army in the field beyond the expiration of his term as Boeotarch. Calm and certain of the rightness of his cause, Epaminondas, in lieu of offering a defense, announced to the judges that his actions alone would suffice. Should they condemn him to death, he asked only that they "inscribe their sentence upon his tombstone, so that," as Plutarch told it, "the Greeks might know that Epameinondas had compelled the Thebans against their will to lay waste Laconia with fire and sword, which for five hundred years had been unravaged; and that he had repopulated Messene after a space of two hundred and thirty years, and had organized the Arcadians and united them in a league, and had restored self-government to the Greeks. As a matter of fact," Plutarch concluded, "all of these things had been accomplished in that campaign." Leaving their ballots behind them, the judges, laughing, walked out of the courtroom.[56] The image of Epaminondas as a great liberator gains further luster in Plutarch's *Life of Pelopidas,* where the historian celebrated him as precisely the kind of citizen-soldier whom the modern world had seemingly—as Hamilton, Gibbon, and Wollstonecraft were quick to note—made obsolete.

Plutarch's influence on Adams can be seen throughout his correspondence as well as in *Thoughts on Government,* where he invoked Epaminondas and Pelopidas as "two sages and heroes" who had "first, to inspire a little understanding and unanimity into their fellow-citizens; then to discipline them for war, and conquer their enemies; and, at last, to frame a good constitution of government."[57] The order of the agenda is its most important feature. Adams implied no direct causal relationship between fighting wars and winning through to virtue. Instead, virtue informs wars. Adams's admonitions provide an important counterpoint to the more seductive and pervasive rhetoric of renovating virtue through bloodshed—calling for the blood of patriots as well as that of tyrants periodically to refresh the body politic—inherited by Jefferson and others from Rousseau.

Adams's refusal to confuse the celebration of battlefield courage with that of the battlefield itself illuminates some of the dangers of the alternative model—a model still extant in, for instance, the recent recommendation of a symposium on American citizenship and military service that "in a society in which male adolescents find it increasingly difficult to discern what it means to be a man or how to become one, we should *promote military service as a rite of passage to manhood.*"[58] The idea of selling an army as a surrogate father underestimates the difficulty of distinguishing between the courage to fight enemies who hope to take liberty from us and the impulse to assert or reinvent ourselves by shedding blood. Such dangerous dissociation of belligerence from deliberation is precisely the disjunction that Adams resisted.

Recently, the myth of Epaminondas as the founder of a "democratic federation" has been reenergized by Victor Davis Hanson, who insists upon the connection that Adams was careful to avoid. In *The Soul of Battle,* Hanson dramatically affirms that the Theban campaign did nothing less than "salvage through battle the very soul of the Greek *polis* itself."[59] Hanson's portrait of the Theban general as the man who invested Greece with "a new sense of political community" and led the first great "army of liberation" also links Epaminondas with two West Point graduates, William Tecumseh Sherman and George S. Patton. Hanson sees both men as inheritors of the "great liberator" tradition.[60] On the face of it, he seems to have discovered in these three men that great succession of Epaminondases for which Adams had hoped. Yet it is difficult to sustain such an image of either man, perhaps especially of Sherman, who while superintendent of the Louisiana Seminary of Learning and Military Academy, in 1861 informed his brother, Senator John Sherman, that military leaders would have to run the world after the war. To his wife he wrote that he had seen enough political chaos to make him "a monarchist."[61] Had Jefferson's fears about soldiers infatuated with crowns perhaps come home to roost?

His bluster, many southern friends, and blatant racism notwithstanding, and despite the fact that he found himself deep in the South at the beginning of the war, Sherman never evinced any doubt about which side of the conflict to choose. Indeed, he manifested a keen understanding of the principles uniting him to military service. These principles easily trumped for him—if not for others—local considerations of geography, self-interest, and personal loyalty. Disappointed by those officers who chose the Confederacy, Sherman was also impatient with West Point graduates in the Union army who could not seem to suspend their petty squabbling to fight a war.

Dennis Hart Mahan, a professor of civil and military engineering at the military academy, had written to his former pupil in 1863, asking him whether he should circulate among his old students a message urging them to rededicate themselves to the Union cause. "I surely will respond to your Confidential Circular," Sherman wrote back, "and will do all I can in War and Peace to reconcile the elements of our Country—so discordant, that they have not only torn asunder the ties that bound the families together by natural affinities, but of our own old Army Circle, that once seemed the very Siamese Twins of Society." West Point itself, he added, could "perform a part" as well. "She has and may continue to teach subordination and combinations," he wrote to Mahan, "and in the sequel can demonstrate how the most gallant, high spirited man can be the proud Soldier, yet humble and obedient citizens."[62]

Sherman was deeply attached to the institution that had educated him, and he took great pride in what he called "the best Military College in the civilized world."[63] The academy took equal pride in the general. At Sherman's death, Superintendent John M. Wilson requested permission for the corps to go to St. Louis to march in the funeral procession. "They loved General Sherman as a father," Wilson told officials in Washington, "and he loved them as his children."[64] Suggestive of an ongoing American pursuit of military fathers, the request is perhaps not one that would have pleased Adams or Jefferson.

The same year that Mahan wrote his letter to Sherman, and a little more than a decade after his ruminations on hero worship in *Representative Men*, Ralph Waldo Emerson was invited by Secretary of War Edwin Stanton to serve on the military academy's board of visitors. Attracted by the institution's ethos of "self-help and ascetic life," Emerson found its administration still troubled by an accusation made in the press to the effect that West Point was "a hotbed of aristocracy." "Rather let them accept it," Emerson advised, "and make West Point a true aristocracy, or 'the power of the Best,'—best scholars, best soldiers, best engineers, best commanders, best men,—and they will be indispensable to their Government and their Country." He predicted that the academy would become "the Shop of Power, the source of instruction, the organization of Victory." Emerson seemed quite carried away by his visit—indeed transported out of his own ambivalence about heroes. According to his son, he took great delight in the parades and drill. Reportedly, he also "talked with cadets and was pleased by their manly bearing and honourable tone and tradition."[65]

Honorable tones and traditions continue to imbue West Point today. This volume and the 2002 bicentennial celebration of which it formed a part were catalyzed by a preoccupation with traditions—more precisely with issues of ownership, legitimacy, and paternity. Deriving comfort and strength from a history rich with heroes, West Point naturally craves presiding geniuses. But is it really Jefferson's military academy? Thayer's? MacArthur's? Washington's? Or, as some of the new monuments that have recently appeared in the academy's Central Area suggest, former superintendent Robert E. Lee's? Moreover, does the military academy need a father at all? Surely it can be no orphan as long as it belongs to the People. As long as it continues to be the nation's military academy, it will never need to depend *solely* on antique heroes to sustain it.

All commemorations run the risk of forgetting Adams's injunction that societies can never be much improved until the people learn to acknowledge themselves "the fountain of power."[66] There remains always a danger that in celebrating our heroes we may lose something of ourselves. We may also lose sight of what Emerson so clearly understood, namely that the "essence of heroism" is "self-trust." Emerson recognized that the past could prove a burden by imposing a predetermined pattern on the future. It does no good to look for the same hero twice, for heroes never reappear in the same guise:

> When nature removes a great man, people explore the horizon for a successor; but none comes, and none will. His class is extinguished with him. In some other and quite different field, the next man will appear; not Jefferson, not Franklin, but now a great salesman; then a road-contractor, then a student of fishes; then a buffalo-hunting explorer, or a semi-savage western general. Thus we make a stand against our rougher masters; but against the best there is a finer remedy. The power which they communicate is not theirs. When we are exalted by ideas, we do not owe this to Plato, but to the idea, to which, also, Plato was debtor.[67]

One of the military academy's necessary responsibilities would seem to be to teach cadets to recognize the *idea* that exalts them and to anticipate the next opportunity to enact it. The reexamination of history prompted by events such as bicentennials—but in fact ongoing every day in the classroom—becomes most valuable when cadets can abstract an ideal from the individual who may for a time embody it. The cadet who can learn to read her past and her heroes in this way will be able to see the course of rectitude even when she finds herself in moral territory into which her heroes never ventured.

Indeed, the institution's overarching academic program goal resonates with this sentiment by emphasizing that intellectually developed graduates must be able to "anticipate and respond effectively to the uncertainties of a changing technological, social, political, and economic world."[68] Emerson would have called this attribute a "military attitude of the soul." "Our culture," he insisted, "must not omit the arming of the man. Let him hear in season that he is born into the state of war, and that the commonwealth and his own well-being require that he should not go dancing in the weeds of peace, but warned, self-collected and neither defying nor dreading the thunder, let him take both reputation and life in his hand, and with perfect urbanity dare the gibbet and the mob by the absolute truth of his speech and the rectitude of his behavior." Emerson here described another type of heroism and another type of war. The war of the battlefield is only, he concluded, heroism's "rudest form."[69] If the academy can teach cadets both to fight the "rudest form" of war when necessity demands and this other kind of war always, then it validates itself and needs no father but becomes its own. Lieutenants thus armed will be able to exist in an enlightened relationship to both the heroes of their past and the particular crises of their future. The frequent errors of history's erstwhile actors, moreover, will not betray them into errors of their own. They will always be able in the end to trust themselves.

Notes

1. Ralph Waldo Emerson, *Representative Men,* ed. Pamela Schirmeister (New York, 1995), 11–21.

2. Ralph Waldo Emerson, "The American Scholar," in *The Essential Writings of Ralph Waldo Emerson,* ed. Brooks Atkinson (New York, 2000), 55.

3. Ibid.

4. John Trenchard and Thomas Gordon, No. 93, 8 September 1722, and No. 25, 15 April 1721, in *Cato's Letters,* 2 vols., ed. Ronald Hamowy (Indianapolis, Ind., 1995), 2:661–64, 1:187.

5. Alexander Hamilton to James Duane, 3 September 1780, in *Alexander Hamilton: Writings,* ed. Joanne B. Freeman (New York, 2001), 72.

6. Fisher Ames, *Equality VII, The Palladium,* 22 December 1801, in *The Works of Fisher Ames,* 2 vols., ed. W. B. Allen (Indianapolis, Ind., 1983), 1:258–59.

7. TJ, "Anas," 4 February 1818, *TJW,* 663–64.

8. Edward Gibbon, *The Decline and Fall of the Roman Empire,* 6 vols., ed. Hugh Trevor-Roper (New York, 1993–94), 1:12–13.

9. Mary Wollstonecraft, *A Vindication of the Rights of Women,* in *Political Writings of Mary Wollstonecraft,* ed. Janet Todd (Toronto, 1993), 86.

10. Hamilton, *Federalist* No. 8, *Alexander Hamilton: Writings,* 192–93.

11. Hamilton, *Federalist* No. 28, ibid., 280–81.

12. Hamilton, *Federalist* No. 25, ibid., 267.

13. On the revolutionary dynamic of liberty and power, see Bernard Bailyn, *The Ideological Origins of the American Revolution,* enlarged ed. (Cambridge, Mass., 1992), chapter 3.

14. Hamilton, Memorandum on Measures for Strengthening the Government, 1799, *Alexander Hamilton: Writings,* 918.

15. Adams to Rush, 26 May 1812, in *The Spur of Fame: Dialogues of John Adams and Benjamin Rush, 1805–1813,* ed. John A. Schutz and Douglass Adair (San Marino, Calif., 1966), 222.

16. Adams, *Letters to John Taylor, of Caroline, Virginia,* XVIII, *WJA* 6:485.

17. Adams, *Discourses on Davila,* VI, ibid., 248–49. Joseph J. Ellis suggests that *Davila* contains Adams's "most candid opinions on the emotional source of all political behavior." See *Passionate Sage: The Character and Legacy of John Adams* (New York, 1993), 165. Noting that Adams perceived "dangerous and beneficial tendencies" to coexist in "the passion for distinction," C. Bradley Thompson argues that "the science of government was reducible" for Adams to "understanding" that passion. Indeed, Thompson adds, Adams believed that "political architecture ought to be

grounded on devising institutional arrangements for the purposes of regulating and channeling" its contrary energies. See *John Adams and the Spirit of Liberty* (Lawrence, Kans., 1998), 156.

18. Adams, *Discourses on Davila,* XIII, *WJA* 6:279. On the progression from the desire for distinction to emulation to ambition, see Ellis, *Passionate Sage,* 166.

19. Adams, *Discourses on Davila,* III, *WJA* 6:240.

20. Adams, *Letters to Taylor,* XVIII, ibid., 485.

21. Adams to Mercy Otis Warren, 3 January 1775, in *The Papers of John Adams,* vol. 2, ed. Robert J. Taylor et al. (Cambridge, Mass., 1977–), 2:210.

22. *Life of John Adams, WJA* 1:257.

23. Adams to Henry Knox, 29 September 1776, in *The Diary and Autobiography of John Adams,* 4 vols., ed. L. H. Butterfield (Cambridge, Mass., 1961), 3:437. On Adams's understanding of martial virtue and his contribution to the development of a national military establishment, see David W. Hazen, "John Adams and the Foundations of American Military Policy" (M.A. thesis, University of North Carolina at Chapel Hill, 1978).

24. Malone, 1:357.

25. TJ to Henry Lee, 15 May 1826, in Ford, 10:387–89.

26. Douglass Adair, "Fame and the Founding Fathers," in *Fame and the Founding Fathers,* ed. Trevor Colbourn (New York, 1974), 3–26.

27. TJ to Benjamin Rush, 16 January 1811, *TJW,* 1236. Yet even Hamilton, whom so many contemporaries accused of tyrannical aspirations, could think of no better way to vilify his archenemy Aaron Burr than to label him a Caesar: "As a public man he is one of the worst sort. . . . [I]f we have an embryo-Caesar in the United States," he wrote, "'tis Burr." See Alexander Hamilton to unknown recipient, 26 September 1792, *AHP* 12:480.

28. Simon P. Newman, "Principles or Men? George Washington and the Political Culture of National Leadership, 1776–1801," *JER* 12 (Winter 1992): 495, 479–80. See also chapter 2 of Ellis, *Passionate Sage.*

29. Joanne B. Freeman, *Affairs of Honor: National Politics in the New Republic* (New Haven, Conn., 2002), 207.

30. TJ, "Anas," 4 February 1818, *TJW,* 662.

31. See John Rhodehamel, ed., Notes, *George Washington: Writings* (New York, 1997), 1106. On the enduring appeal of the monarchy in America, see Barry Schwartz, *George Washington: The Making of an American Symbol* (New York, 1987), 135.

32. "The Institution of the Society of the Cincinnati," Appendix to Minor Myers, *Liberty without Anarchy: A History of the Society of the Cincinnati* (Charlottesville, Va., 1983), 258–65.

33. TJ, Answers and Observations for Démeunier's Article on the United States in the *Encyclopédie Methodique* (1786), *TJW,* 587–88.

34. "The Institution of the Society of the Cincinnati," 258–65.

35. TJ, Answers and Observations, *TJW,* 587.

36. TJ to James Madison, 28 December 1794, *TJP* 28:228.

37. TJ, Answers and Observations, *TJW,* 587.

38. TJ to George Washington, 16 April 1784, ibid., 791.

39. On fears aroused by the Federalist military program, see Theodore J. Crackel, *Mr. Jefferson's Army: Political and Social Reform of the Military Establishment, 1801–1809* (New York, 1987), chapter 1; James Roger Sharp, *American Politics in the Early Republic: The New Nation in Crisis* (New Haven, Conn., 1993), 181–82, 240; Richard H. Kohn, *Eagle and Sword: The Federalists and the Creation of the Military Establishment in America, 1783–1802* (New York, 1975), 302–3; and Joseph J. Ellis, *Founding Brothers: The Revolutionary Generation* (New York, 2001), 193–94.

40. Crackel, *Mr. Jefferson's Army,* 53.

41. Washington, Sentiments on a Peace Establishment, in *The Writings of George Washington from the Original Manuscript Sources 1745–1799,* 39 vols., ed. John C. Fitzpatrick (Washington, D.C., 1931–44), 26:396–97. On the idea of a military academy as "a very republican institution," see Hazen, "John Adams," 168.

42. TJ, Eighth Annual Message, 8 November 1808, *TJW,* 547; TJ to Barnabas Bidwell, 5 July 1806, ibid., 1165.

43. TJ, Sixth Annual Message, 2 December 1806, ibid., 525. On the Burr Conspiracy, see Crackel, *Mr. Jefferson's Army,* chapter 6.

44. TJ to Joseph Willard, 24 March 1789, *TJW,* 949.

45. TJ, From the Minutes of the Board of Visitors, University of Virginia, 4 March 1825, ibid., 479.

46. Crackel, *Mr. Jefferson's Army,* 61.

47. Adams to General Parsons, 2 October 1776 and 19 August 1776, in *Diary and Autobiography,* 3:445–48. For the entire range of correspondence, see 3:431–49.

48. Adams to TJ, 20 August 1821, *AJL,* 573.

49. Adams to Colonel Tudor, 26 September 1776, *Diary and Autobiography,* 3:439. Henry Adams describes West Point in terms that echo his grandfather's: "Great as the influence of this new establishment was upon the army, its bearing on the general education of the people was still greater, for the government thus assumed the charge of introducing the first systematic study of science in the United States." See Adams, *History of the United States of America during the Administrations of Thomas Jefferson,* ed. Earl N. Harbert (New York, 1986), 205. Adams also greatly emphasized the importance of West Point to the winning of the War of 1812. "Perhaps without exaggeration the West Point Academy might be said to have decided, next to the navy, the result of the war." See Adams, *History of the United States of America during the Administrations of James Madison,* ed. Earl N. Harbert (New York, 1986), 1342.

50. Adams to John Jebb, 10 September 1785, *WJA* 9:539–40. For a discussion of this letter in the context of democratic office holding, see Gordon S. Wood, *The Radicalism of the American Revolution* (New York, 1993), 289–90. On the founders' theories of political education, see Gillian Brown, *The Consent of the Governed: The Lockean Legacy in Early American Culture* (Cambridge, Mass., 2001).

51. *A Dissertation on the Canon and Feudal Law,* in *The Revolutionary Writings of John Adams,* ed. C. Bradley Thompson (Indianapolis, Ind., 2000), 32, 27–28, 34.

52. "Written by the venerable John Adams, and delivered before the cadets of the U.S.M.A. & citizens of Boston, in August 1821," Adams file, USMA Archives, West Point, N.Y. Also printed in *WJA* 10:419–20. Adams here echoes Trenchard and Gordon, who write of military virtue as exclusively the product of civil liberty. See No. 65, 10 February 1721, *Cato's Letters,* 1:450–61.

53. Michel de Montaigne, "On the most excellent of men," *The Complete Essays,* trans. M. A. Screech (London, 1991), 855–56.

54. Adams to Tudor, 26 September 1776, *Diary and Autobiography,* 3:439.

55. Plutarch, *Life of Pelopidas,* in *The Age of Alexander,* ed. and trans. Ian Scott Kilvert (London, 1973), 90.

56. Plutarch, vol. 3 of *Moralia,* 14 vols., trans. Frank Cole Babbitt (Cambridge, Mass., 1927), 192c–194c.

57. Adams, *Thoughts on Government,* 1776, *WJA* 4:514.

58. Elliott Abrams and Andrew J. Bacevich, "A Symposium on Citizenship and Military Service," *Parameters* 31 (Summer 2001): 22.

59. Victor Davis Hanson, *The Soul of Battle: From Ancient Times to the Present Day, How Three Great Liberators Vanquished Tyranny* (New York, 1999), 43.

60. Ibid., 49.

61. Sherman to John Sherman, 18 January 1861, and Sherman to Ellen Ewing Sherman, 27 January 1861, in *Sherman's Civil War: Selected Correspondence of William T. Sherman, 1860–1865*, ed. Brooks D. Simpson and Jean V. Berlin (Chapel Hill, N.C., 1999), 43, 47.

62. Sherman to Dennis Hart Mahan, 16 September 1863, ibid., 541–43.

63. John F. Marszalek, *Sherman: A Soldier's Passion for Order* (New York, 1993), 441.

64. Michael Fellman, *Citizen Sherman: A Life of William Tecumseh Sherman* (New York, 1995), 403.

65. Edward Waldo Emerson and Waldo Emerson Forbes, eds., *Journals of Ralph Waldo Emerson, with Annotations*, 10 vols. (Boston, 1909–14), 9:511–14. On Emerson's enthusiasm for law and order and for the figure of the soldier as a postwar development, see George M. Fredrickson, *The Inner Civil War: Northern Intellectuals and the Crisis of the Union* (New York, 1965), 177–78. Christopher Newfield has recently argued for a strain of authoritarianism running through Emerson's entire career. See *The Emerson Effect: Individualism and Submission in America* (Chicago, 1996).

66. Adams to John Jebb, 10 September 1785, *WJA* 9:540.

67. Emerson, *Representative Men*, 14.

68. Office of the Dean, United States Military Academy, *Educating Future Army Officers for a Changing World: Operational Concept for the Academic Program at the United States Military Academy* (West Point, N.Y., 2002), 16.

69. Emerson, "Heroism," *Essential Writings*, 228–29.

The Military Academy in the Context of Jeffersonian Reform

THEODORE J. CRACKEL

In 1981 I published an article on the founding of the United States Military Academy at West Point that ignited a debate that continues until today. In that piece, and in a series of books that followed, I argued that Jefferson's motivation for its creation was the desire to establish a facility that could commission as officers America's Republican sons—young men who were less likely than their Federalist counterparts to have otherwise enjoyed the requisite education.[1] Joseph Swift, who had been appointed a cadet by John Adams, noted that at Jefferson's new academy, "appointments to military office were made from families of prominent Democrats and of less Educated Persons."[2] Swift's observation is supported by the fragmentary application records, in which the political affiliation—the Republican parentage, at least—of applicants was routinely noted in letters of recommendation.[3] The academy would provide them with the rudimentary knowledge of mathematics and drawing that they would need to survey and lay out fortifications, draw maps, properly employ artillery, and perform the other duties required of officers of that day.

In a second article that appeared in 1982, I set the creation of the military academy into the context of a general reform of the military establishment accomplished by the Military Peace Establishment Act.[4] A few years later, I enlarged my examination of that subject in my book, *Mr. Jefferson's Army.* The army that Jefferson inherited upon assuming the presidency "had a Federalist character that was largely a product of the critical and intensely partisan years of 1798 to 1800." This almost wholly Federalist army seemed threatening to the new Republican regime. Many of the officers had "openly expressed contempt for the political philosophy of the new administration." Jefferson, upon assuming office, "undertook a carefully considered program of political and social reform that included patronage, incentives, coercion, and removals."[5] His aim, I argued, was nothing short of Republicanizing the army and thus ensuring its loyalty to his administration.

Here I take that argument a step further, placing Jefferson's creation of the military academy and his overhaul of the military establishment within a broader context of reform. It was not just those in the army who were displeased with his election. Many who occupied the second level of government—those officials appointed by George Washington or John Adams to posts just below cabinet level—had openly expressed contempt for the political philosophy of the new administration and for Jefferson himself. In truth, all of the instruments of governance that Jefferson inherited as president in March 1801 had so absolute a Federalist character that loyalty to him and his policies was in doubt. The Federalist civil service, as Carl Prince maintains, "offered shelter to a paid political cadre devoted to keeping the 'ins' in."[6]

How was the new president to govern if those to whom the execution of his policies was entrusted were not loyal to him? Jefferson's answer was a carefully considered program of reformation that included the replacement of many Federalists, the accommodation of others, an insistence that new appointments go only to the Republican faithful, and, in some cases, the simple expedient of eliminating offices through legislative action. Jefferson reacted in much the same way to both the civil and military establishments that he inherited—he employed a carefully modulated program of reform that would ultimately bring them into line with the broad aspirations and goals of the new Republican regime.[7]

The extensive second echelon of the civil establishment appointed or controlled by the president consisted of treasury agents (in particular the customs and internal revenue officers), the federal attorneys, and the federal marshals.[8] The numerous postmasters were appointed by the postmaster general, but he, in turn, received guidance on this matter from the president. Also appointed by the president, although not answerable to him, were the members of the federal judiciary.

The customs service, by 1801, was operating in all of the sixteen states, the District of Maine, and the new District of Columbia. The top positions in this service were controlled by presidential appointment. These included the collectors of customs, the assistant collectors called "naval officers," and the surveyors of customs. Only the largest ports had a full complement of these senior officials. Ports of medium size usually did without a naval officer, and smaller ports were administered by only a collector—the very smallest by only a surveyor. When Jefferson took office in 1801, there were 124 of these senior customs officers at seventy-one ports of entry.[9]

The internal revenue service was created in 1791 to collect taxes established for certain domestic activities—on stills and distilled spirits, on refined sugars, on paper, on sales at auction, and on carriages. In 1798, when a land tax was imposed to fund the enlargement of the army and an expanded conflict with France—now known as the Quasi-War—land tax commissioners were appointed to assess and collect this tax. By 1801 the internal revenue service (including the land tax commissioners) consisted of roughly 450 men, of whom almost 60 were senior supervisors or inspectors of the revenue who were appointed by the president.

One final group, closely allied by function with the Treasury Department, were the United States commissioners of loans—one in each of the original thirteen states. Although an independent agency, they acted as local agents of the Treasury Department. Their role, in the beginning, was to settle the pre-1789 debts owed by the federal government to the individual citizens. This they generally did by exchanging the old debt for new interest-bearing federal bonds. They then made the quarterly interest and principal payments on the new government securities and paid the pensions due invalid veterans.

Even more numerous than the agents of the Treasury Department were the postmasters. Almost every city, town, village, and hamlet had its own post office and its own postmaster—roughly one thousand by 1801. Appointed by the postmaster general, these officials were, in most communities, the sole resident representatives of the federal government.

Federal attorneys were appointed in each judicial district—usually coincident with state and territorial boundaries. They determined which violations of federal law were to be investigated and decided upon the scope of those investigations. Their purview included violations of the customs laws, the neutrality law, and, later, the Alien and Sedition Acts. Finally, they presented the cases to a grand jury and prosecuted them before the federal bench. United

States marshals were also appointed for each federal judicial district. They seized and detained persons charged with violations of federal law and empanelled the grand juries and petit juries that brought charges and heard cases.

When Jefferson took office in 1801, the federal court system included the Supreme Court, six recently added circuit courts, and eighteen district courts—one in each of the sixteen states and in the District of Maine and the District of Columbia. The judiciary included seven Supreme Court justices, sixteen new judges in the circuit courts, and eighteen district court judges. And, as noted above, there was a federal attorney and a federal marshal in each of the eighteen judicial districts.

The Constitution had provided for a Supreme Court, but it had left the design and creation of the lower federal judicial establishment to the Congress. As part of the Judiciary Act of 1789, Congress established two federal court systems inferior to the Supreme Court—the district courts and the circuit courts of appeal. Each original state was made a judicial district, as was Massachusetts's District of Maine. As the years went by, new districts and new courts were added with the admission of new states—Vermont, Kentucky, and Tennessee—and the establishment of the District of Columbia.

These numerous second-level federal officials exerted great influence in their communities—political and otherwise. Their positions gave them prestige, earned them deference, and provided handsome incomes from salaries and fees. They were not about to hand this over to the Republicans without a fight. They were not barred from politics by either law or custom. Shortly after Jefferson took office, Elbridge Gerry warned him that he faced "a desperate faction" and advised him to place "in every important office" men "in whom you can place implicit confidence." Jefferson should endeavor, he wrote, "as expeditiously as circumstances will permit to clean the Augean Stable."[10]

"Among the primary dispensers of [Federalist] ideology," according to Prince, "were the collectors and, in the larger ports, the naval officers and surveyors of customs. These men were the cardinal party leaders."[11] Typical of them was the customs collector at the small southern Massachusetts port of Dighton, one Hodijah Baylies—a 1777 Harvard graduate and a former major in the Continental army. The combination of his local standing and his office made him Dighton's most prominent Federalist, and his customhouse became the center of local party activity. He was typical of the second rank of federal official and typical of the local Federalist managers in Massachusetts.

Similarly, Nathaniel Fosdick, the collector of customs at Portland in the District of Maine, was his town's acknowledged Federalist leader; he exploited his position to the utmost in public meetings. It was reported that after Jefferson's victory in the election of 1800, Fosdick attempted to incite the American troops in the city to mutiny.[12]

In Pennsylvania, despite Republican victories in 1796, the Federalists remained a powerful and effective political organization. Federal appointments had gone almost wholly to the faithful in that party. George Latimer, the collector of customs at Philadelphia, received a handsome income from his post, and he was, in turn, an active and important political manager. He was one of the prime movers of the party machine in that state. "In Philadelphia as elsewhere," Prince notes, "the officers paid as much attention to political concerns as they did to government business."[13]

Even in Jefferson's Virginia there were Federalist strongholds among the tidewater cities, and in these places the customhouses were as much centers of political activity as they were in northern ports. Charles Simms, who was made collector of customs at Alexandria in 1799, was an ardent Federalist and caustic critic of Jefferson.

The internal revenue service was equally as political as the customs branch. The extensive travel required to visit distilleries and other sites throughout their state enhanced the revenue agents' political utility. It was not unusual, as an election approached, to find the entire service employed in the Federalist cause. Republican Joseph Bloomfield of New Jersey complained bitterly in 1801 that Aaron Dunham, the supervisor of the revenue for New Jersey, had used his subordinates in the revenue office to promote the election of Federalists.[14]

In Virginia, the Federalist revenue supervisor, Edward Carrington, headed a group of ten inspectors of revenue that covered the entire state. Carrington was a major figure in the Federalist party in Virginia and beyond. He had been a close associate of Washington and an adviser to Alexander Hamilton. He was also the brother-in-law of Chief Justice John Marshall. Nine of the ten inspectors under him were also Federalists. They constituted "a partisan force of higher civil servants," observes Prince, "who did much to cement the minority Federalist interest in this large and pivotal state."[15]

Many government loan agents were also politicos of the first order. Jabez Bowen of Providence, Rhode Island, was not atypical. A shrewd politician and crafty businessman, his influence reached almost every corner of his tiny state and beyond. Like many of the others, he had no reservations about employing his office to the advantage of the Federalists. Because the initial appointments to these loan offices came before political parties had coalesced, their numbers contained more Republicans than any other group of federal appointees. Even then, only four of the original thirteen could ultimately be labeled Republicans, and only two of these—Benjamin Harwood of Maryland and John Neufville of South Carolina—remained in office in 1801.[16]

Similarly, in selecting postmasters the Federalists had essentially excluded their political opponents.[17] Jefferson was convinced that these partisan postmasters examined the communications between Republican leaders and then passed on what they learned to the Federalist leadership. His letters were filled with such accusations: "I owe you a political letter," Jefferson wrote in 1798, "Yet the infidelities of the post office and the circumstances of the times are against my writing fully & freely." He knew not, he said, "which mortifies me most, that I should fear to write what I think, or my country bear such a state of things."[18]

Two other critical posts in the partisan executive establishment of 1801 were the federal attorneys and the federal marshals. When Jefferson took office, members of this group were almost uniformly of the Federalist persuasion and active in the political affairs of their states and of the nation. In New Jersey, the federal attorney, Lewis Stockton, was said to have done more damage to Jefferson's prospects in the election of 1800 in that state than any other single individual. In Pennsylvania, Federalist strategy in the presidential election was directed by the federal attorney, William Rawle. And in New Hampshire, one of the most aggressive of those who campaigned against Jefferson was the federal attorney, Jeremiah Smith.[19]

Even so, despite the high level of activity of the federal attorneys, it was the marshals against whom Jefferson reacted most vehemently. The marshals, who enforced the laws, were particularly visible and in a unique position to influence the outcome of cases. It was their ability and willingness to pack or rig juries that enraged Republicans. Their actions had been particularly egregious in the several sedition cases brought by the Federalist administration against Republican newspaper editors.

The Judiciary Act of 1789 created three circuit courts—the eastern, middle, and southern circuits. Two sittings of every circuit court were to be held annually—each to be presided over by two Supreme Court justices and the district judge of the seat at which the circuit court met. No judges were appointed specifically to the three circuit courts. This arrangement had changed in early 1801, however, when the lame-duck Federalist Congress passed a new judiciary act. That law released the Supreme Court justices from the obligation to ride the circuit and created six circuit courts—most with three judges each.[20] John Adams signed the bill, and with the stroke of his pen, almost doubled the number (from eighteen to thirty-four) of judges sitting in the lower federal courts. Then, in the last days of his presidency, Adams filled these new federal benches with the party faithful. This measure was necessary, said Gouverneur Morris, because the Federalists were "about to experience a heavy gale of adverse wind." "Can they be blamed," Morris asked, "for casting many anchors to hold their ship through the storm?"[21]

Those in the Republican camp in 1801 saw the matter in a different light and argued that, so long as the federal bench was so completely in the hands of the opposition, the revolution they had just effected could not be completed. "It is surely a most singular circumstance," wrote William Branch Giles, "that the public sentiment should have forced itself into the Legislative and Executive Department, and that the Judiciary should not only not acknowledge its influence, but should pride itself in resisting its will, under the misapplied idea of 'independence.'"[22] Many others agreed. "It would seem," said a writer from Virginia, "that the friends of order [the Federalists] being beaten out of the executive and legislative posts, are about to mount their cannon . . . and play upon all the Republicans from the Gibraltar of the Judiciary Department."[23]

A federal judgeship seems to have been no bar to political activity, and sitting judges did not limit themselves to mere private manipulation of party matters, but rather engaged in and even headed political campaigns. They spoke, seemingly without restraint, about the ideological issues that pervaded the times. District Judge John Lowell of Massachusetts, for example, was actively and openly involved in the politics of his state, and in July 1800 had been the featured speaker at a Federalist celebration of the Fourth of July. In a highly partisan oration, he denounced the Republicans and opened the campaign there against Jefferson.[24]

Republican concern, however, was not merely a matter of party jealously, but was also a reaction to politically motivated rulings in the courts that the Federalists controlled. "It is clear," writes Prince, who has looked in detail at the Federalist appointees, "that what happened in the district and circuit courts in the 1790s cannot simply be written off as the bias of a few partisan judges involved in a handful of isolated cases. Political prejudice in the courts appears to have been pervasive and deeply rooted in ongoing political involvement on and off the bench."[25] Richard Ellis sounds a similar note in his landmark study of Jefferson and the courts. "The partisan manner in which the Act of 1801 had been passed, and the continued arrogance of some Federalist judges," writes Ellis, "had made the federal judiciary the foremost issue facing the administration."[26]

The mechanisms of governance that Jefferson inherited in 1801—the hundreds of men who occupied the second level of offices in the federal government and who would be charged with executing the policies of the president—consisted almost wholly of those who not only were hostile to the views and programs of the new president, but who also could be expected to oppose him actively and to thwart his policies. Virtually all of these men were Federalists; many of them had electioneered, chaired party meetings, engaged in propaganda programs, coordinated political activities, and in every way sought to use their positions and influence to promote Federalist interests.[27] They had raised "almost violent opposition" to Jefferson, wrote South Carolina's Andrew Pickens, who added that "the same spirit still remains in the enemies of the present administration, and will again attempt to restore their power."[28] Thomas McKean of Pennsylvania had written Jefferson in the same vein: "It appears that the antirepublicans, even those in office, are as hostile as ever, tho' not so insolent. To overcome them they must be shaven, for in their offices like Sampson's locks of hair their great strength lieth."[29]

Facing pervasive opposition to his policies among the second level of federal officials, Jefferson would have been justified in wondering how he was to govern. These men, and in particular Adams's "midnight" appointees, were, as Jefferson explained, "from among my most ardent political enemies, from whom no faithful cooperation could ever be expected, and laid me under the embarrassment of acting thro' men whose views were to defeat mine."[30]

If Jefferson and the Republicans were to govern effectively, they would first have to gain control over the instruments of governance that, even after their election victory, still lay firmly in Federalist hands. Jefferson's plan to accomplish this took shape in the early months of the new administration. Most of the elements of the plan were available for all who would see them. He laid them out in his inaugural address. Many Federalists (and too many historians), however, seem to have stopped reading when they had finished the line

"We are all Republicans, we are all Federalists." Had they read further, or with a more critical eye, they might have discerned what Jefferson was about. "It is proper you should understand what I deem the essential principles of our Government, and consequently those which ought to shape its Administration," he said. These principles contained implicit warnings.

One demanded the "absolute acquiescence in the decisions of the majority." With victory came the right to govern, and to set the course of the ship of state. It also carried the right—even the obligation—to take control of all the instruments of governance. For the Federalists in opposition that meant either their acquiescence to Republican designs or their removal. Another principle was "the supremacy of the civil over the military authority." Those military officers who had been so vociferous in their opposition to Republican ideas and to Jefferson, and their friends in the Congress, should have taken notice. Many of them would also be displaced.

Yet another principle was "freedom of person under the protection of the habeas corpus, and trial by juries impartially selected." Given the repeated Republican outcry about juries packed with Federalists—in particular those enrolled to try Republican editors for sedition—how could Federalists have been surprised when Jefferson made wholesale dismissals of federal marshals? How could Federalists not have understood that all this would temper the moderation he had suggested when he said "We are all Republicans, we are all Federalists"?[31]

Jefferson's plan to take over the reigns of government—to install men aligned with the philosophy of the new administration—had two components. The first involved those things that he could do or inaugurate immediately. The second encompassed those things Congress would have to do on his behalf.

Not long after the inauguration Jefferson outlined even more directly the first component of his plan to take a more Republican crew onto the ship of state. Some Federalists would be removed for political reasons—in particular, the federal marshals who packed juries and the federal attorneys who had aided and abetted them. "Marshals and Attornies to be removed where federal, except in particular cases," noted Jefferson just ten weeks after his inauguration.[32] In addition, Adams's last appointments, Jefferson assured Republicans, would be considered as nullities; new men would be appointed in their stead. More generally, Federalists in key positions who proved incompatible with the new regime would be replaced—under one pretext or another.

Some could be forced out under the threat of being driven out—resigning to avoid the stigma of dismissal. Others "make it a VIRTUE to oppose the Constituted Authorities," reported the Boston *Independent Chronicle,* "and some of them boast of the *honor* of being dismissed from office under the present administration."[33] Other removals would be made for misconduct. In fact, when possible, misconduct would be used as the rationale for dismissal. For collectors, at least, it was a "general rule," noted Jefferson just days after taking office, that none would be removed "till called on for acc[oun]t that as many may be removed as defaulters as are such."[34]

Where practical, of course, Federalists would be wooed to the cause, and there was always the hope that a few removals might prompt moderate Federalists to consider some form of accommodation. The federal attorney in Massachusetts, Samuel Bradford, was an example. "He is a moderate and prudent and will be republican," wrote Jefferson.[35] Others, like Bradbury Cilley of New Hampshire, were spared for a time. "Tho' a federal o[ugh]t not be removed because of his connections."[36] Of course, Republicans would fill all new vacancies.

There was, however, only so much he could do on his own. An outline of the second component of his plan—legislation required of the Congress—was contained in Jefferson's State of the Union message to Congress in December 1801. He asked the legislature not only to repeal the internal taxes but also to abolish the entire internal revenue service. He asked for a reformulation of the army—and saw to it that the bill to answer that need contained a means of removing a number of his more vociferous opponents and provided a mechanism for introducing Republican sons into the officer ranks. Finally, he called attention to the judiciary system and the Judiciary Act of 1801 passed just before the adjournment of the last Congress, and ensured that the bill that would effect the repeal of that act also provided for the dismissal of the judges who had been appointed to courts it had created.[37] All of this was debated and deliberated and then delivered to Jefferson by the Republican-controlled Congress in March and April 1802.

Shaping a government responsive to Jefferson's direction became the core issue for the new administration; it absorbed a great deal of the time and attention of the president and of all those around him throughout their first year in office and beyond. Of all the incumbent Federalist officeholders under his gaze, Jefferson reacted most decisively against the incumbent federal marshals. These, in his view, were the most visible abusers of Republicans. "The practice of the marshals in empanelling Federalists for jury service," writes historian Manning Dauer, "converted the law into an engine of the Federalist political machine."[38] Jefferson replaced ten of the eighteen marshals (56 percent) in 1801, and two more in 1802. By the end of 1806, all but one had been replaced.[39]

Attorneys, of course, were also targets for removal. Fredrick Freilinghuysen, the United States attorney for New Jersey, as well as Charles Marsh of Vermont and Jeremiah Smith of New Hampshire, were staunch Federalists who considered all Republicans foes not only of Adams, but also as likely partisans of the French Jacobins and their campaign against the French aristocracy. These three were among the four attorneys removed in 1801; six more were replaced by Republicans in 1802, making ten of eighteen in all, or 55 percent. By the end of his second term, Jefferson had replaced fourteen of the eighteen federal attorneys (78 percent).

Despite the fact that federal judges could not be removed by the president, some vacancies did occur among the district judges, and those allowed Jefferson to place a few Republicans on the district benches. Three Republicans were appointed to fill vacancies in 1801. His last appointments to these seats came in 1806, after which a total of nine of the eighteen district judgeships had been filled by Jeffersonian appointees.

It was not, however, necessary to replace all of the judges or attorneys or marshals to achieve relief. Jefferson seems to have understood that the replacement of even one of the three key members of the federal judicial apparatus of each state—either the district judge or the federal attorney or the marshal—would mitigate the effect of the Federalist sympathies of the others to an important degree. An "impartial"—that is, Republican—judge might dismiss a purely partisan prosecution; an impartial attorney might refuse to indict on specious grounds; or an impartial marshal would refuse to pack a jury. By the end of 1801, Jefferson had named at least one Republican as either a judge, attorney, or marshal in fifteen (83 percent) of the eighteen judicial districts. Two more districts (making seventeen of eighteen, or 94 percent) were added to that list in 1802. Moreover, in North Carolina, where no Jeffersonian appointments were made immediately, the incumbents were clearly acceptable to the new administration. In 1802 John Spence West, the marshal in that state, was reappointed by Jefferson to another four-year term. In less than two years, the administration had insinuated some measure of influence into the federal judicial process in every state, and the level of influence grew each year.

In other areas, Jefferson moved somewhat more deliberately. "I know that in stopping thus short in the career of removal, I shall give great offence to many of my friends," he wrote to Benjamin Rush.[40] But he seemed to understand that accommodation was more likely to succeed among the treasury officers than among the attorneys or marshals and, in reality, acquiescence to the new administration was sufficient among customs officials. More was required of those with mandates to enforce the administration's policies—the roles attorneys and marshals would play. In any case, all new vacancies would go to Republicans.

The contrast between Jefferson's policy toward the customs officers and his removal of attorneys and marshals could hardly have been greater. Where he had replaced 56 percent of the marshals and attorneys in the first nine months of his administration, he replaced only 9 percent of the customs officers. The number of Jefferson's appointees among the senior officials of the customs service grew to 23 percent by the end of 1802, to just under half during his first term, and to a bit over three quarters by the end of the second. Still, that number and rate of removal was very modest in comparison to his actions relative to the federal attorneys and federal marshals. Yet it is clear that Jefferson moved with more energy in replacing customs officials at the more visible and important posts. In the nation's eleven largest ports, he replaced three collectors (27 percent) in the first year, and four more (for a total of 64 percent) in 1802.[41] By the end of 1806, he had replaced ten of these eleven collectors. It was not until Jefferson was about to leave office that the twelfth—Benjamin Lincoln of Boston—was replaced.

The commissioners of loans, one for each of the thirteen original states, were treated much the same as the collectors at the nation's key ports, for they were of equal stature and prominence. Three of the thirteen (23 percent) were removed in the first year. Among these was Matthew Clarkson of New York, whom Republicans considered, as Prince writes, "one of their ranking tormentors."[42] By the end of his first term, Jefferson had replaced a total of seven—just over half. He would replace ten of the thirteen, or 76 percent, by the time he left office in 1809.

Jefferson's concern about the abuses in the postal system was hardly resolved by the election of 1800, and he continued to hear complaints that correspondence between Republicans remained altogether unsafe.[43] But it was not until Gideon Granger took office as postmaster general in November 1801 that any significant process was made in that area.[44] "Knowing as I did," wrote Granger early the next year, "that most of the officers under me had been in the habits of associating and corresponding as well on politics as on business with those lately in authority . . . it occurred to me that some removals would become necessary." Their purpose, he said, was "to preserve and maintain confidence in the department."[45] Granger, who had the authority to appoint and discharge postmasters and who fully understood the president's aims, immediately set about Republicanizing the postal system.

The second component of Jefferson's plan was put into place late in 1801. On November 27 the president wrote to his daughter, Martha Jefferson Randolph, that "we are now within 10 days of Congress, when our campaign will begin and will probably continue to April."[46] The elements of this campaign were outlined in his message to Congress on December 8. Among his requests, Jefferson called on that body to abolish the internal taxes, to reduce (and reform) the army, and to repeal the Judiciary Act of 1801. Each of these were elements of his plan to gain control over the various instruments of government. He followed up by arranging for selected members of the Congress to introduce bills that the administration had drafted—bills that would accomplish this end.[47]

Jefferson reported in his message to Congress that "the inspectors of internal revenue who were found to obstruct the accountability of the institution, have been discontinued," but his administration's bill that would repeal internal taxes went further.[48] As soon as the taxes due as of the date of repeal (June 30, 1802) were collected, the internal revenue officers would be dismissed. Just in case any of the collectors dragged their feet, the president was authorized by the act to close any office, to consolidate collection activities, or simply to suspend collection, at his sole discretion. By affixing his signature to this bill, Jefferson effectively eliminated the officers of the internal revenue service—one of the most pervasive agencies of the Federalist faction.

The Military Peace Establishment Act was signed and made law on March 16, 1802. This bill allowed Jefferson to rid himself of some of his most vociferous detractors in the army. Their jobs too were simply eliminated.[49] Jefferson restructured the army in a way that allowed his administration to dismiss a substantial number of officers—many of them strong Federalists and among his most outspoken critics. The 1802 law actually offered several benefits. By eliminating the army staff and its senior officers, it ended Federalist domination of the army's internal hierarchy; by restructuring the army in a way that reduced the number of regiments—and, thereby, the number of regimental commanders (and staffs)—it permitted the removal of a number of the more senior officers who were persistent and vocal political opponents of the president; and, finally, by creating the United States Military Academy, it established a source of future Republican officers. This act was the foundation upon which the administration would impose a "chaste reformation" on the army, creating a force that would come to reflect the republican society from which it was drawn—an army whose loyalty to republican principles and the new Republican regime would now be assured.[50]

The administration saw to it that the new officers were drawn from Republican ranks. And, in 1808, when circumstances suggested that the army should be expanded to meet an anticipated French threat, Jefferson's appointees achieved a majority in every rank (from ensign to brigadier general) except major. The army now truly belonged to Jefferson.

The final element of the campaign in Congress was the repeal of the Judiciary Act. Although rather more straightforward than either of the others, it accomplished the same end—reducing Federalist influence. In 1801, only days before Adams was to leave office, the lame-duck Federalist congress nearly doubled the size of the federal judiciary by creating a separate federal circuit court system with its own judges. The repeal of the act in 1802 eliminated these sixteen circuit court judgeships and removed from office the sixteen key federal jurists Adams had rushed to appoint—men whom the Federalists hoped to use to maintain their influence or, as Jefferson saw it, to impede the work of his new administration. On April 29, 1802, when Jefferson signed the repeal of the Judiciary Act of 1801, all of the elements of the plan that would enable him to take control of the various mechanisms of governance had been put in place.

Historians have always had difficulty coming to grips with Thomas Jefferson, for his pronouncements and his actions were so often at odds, or so it has seemed.[51] This issue is no exception. He spoke of moderation in his inaugural speech: "We are all Republicans, we are all Federalists." Yet, almost immediately, he began uprooting Federalist office holders for no apparent reason other than to replace them with Republicans, and he sponsored legislation that would enable the removal of even more Federalists from their government positions.

Henry Adams used the word "moderation" to describe Jefferson's policy, adding that he "could afford to make few removals for party reasons."[52] Many of those who have followed agreed that moderation was a reasonable characterization of Jefferson's policy of patronage. Dumas Malone described the policy as little more than an effort to gain a "balance between parties."[53] Noble Cunningham, in 1963, characterized the administration's effort as simply a "middle-of-the-road, day-to-day removal policy."[54]

In 1970, however, Carl Prince examined the appointment records in detail and came to a remarkably different conclusion. "Jefferson's patronage policy during the first term was as decisive as it was thoroughly partisan," he wrote. "Removals in one form or another for purely political reasons constituted the backbone of his effort to break the Federalists' power, particularly that party's stranglehold on the sensitive and politically potent second-level United States offices in the states." Jefferson's election, he maintained, "was a revolution in the sense that it led to the systematic elimination of a long-standing, heretofore well-anchored aristocracy from the second line of the federal government."[55]

Forrest McDonald, in his 1976 study of Jefferson, concluded, seemingly independent of Prince's work, that to reform the government Jefferson would have to change its personnel or—as McDonald put it, mimicking one of Jefferson's favorite metaphors of that period—"to assemble a loyal crew for steering the sloop of state on a republican tack."[56] Two years later, Robert M. Johnstone Jr., in his *Jefferson and the Presidency: Leadership in the Young Republic,* noted that the president's "appointive power" would allow him to "recast the political complexion of the executive, bringing it into line with the dominant philosophy of his party."[57] Neither McDonald nor Johnstone, however, recognized how far or how fast Jefferson had moved. Johnstone portrayed Jefferson's course as a halfhearted policy that he had reluctantly and belatedly assumed.

In fact, Jefferson fully recognized that to reform the instruments of governance inherited from the Federalists he would have to replace many, if not most, of the Federalists who then occupied the offices of the government. The loyalty and responsiveness of the federal civil and military establishments to the new Republican regime were problematic at best, and that situation was compounded when Adams systematically made appointments to existing vacancies during his last days in office. The second rank of federal offices were filled almost wholly with Federalists, many of whom were openly contemptuous of the political philosophy of the new administration and of Jefferson himself. "It was my destiny to come to the government when it had for several years been committed to a particular political sect," Jefferson wrote a friend. "I found the country entirely in the enemy's hands."[58]

In response, immediately upon assuming office, Jefferson set into motion a carefully considered program of reformation. The first step was the removal of many high Federalists and an insistence that new appointments go only to the Republican faithful. For the civil establishment, this could be effected largely through his power to appoint and dismiss. The second step was the simple elimination of influential Federalist offices through legislative action. To deal with the judges of the federal courts and the disaffected officers of the army, men who could be removed only by established legislative processes, he had to work through the Congress.

Not all the Federalists were oblivious to his efforts. "All of the measures recommended by the President form a consistent plan of mischief," wrote Oliver Wolcott to Roger Griswold as the legislative program was being considered.[59] To Theodore Sedgwick, the repeal of the judiciary system, the removal of Federalist appointees, and the abolition of internal taxes were all part of a effort for "breaking down all the internal Machinery of the government."[60] Both were correct, but neither had plumbed the depth of Jefferson's designs, or divined their full implications.

"So long has the vessel run on [the Federalist] way," wrote Jefferson in December 1800, "and been trimmed to it, that to put her on her republican tack will require . . . the new establishment of republicanism."[61] Here he seems to suggest that the ship of state would need a new compass. He knew, as well, that it would need a new crew, and he had carefully planned to provide one. By the end of 1801, just nine months into his first term, Jefferson had blunted in one way or another the Federalist influence in sixteen of the eighteen judicial districts—his first priority. The last two were added in 1802. Moreover, he had begun to make inroads in the customs service and the post office. And, by legislative action, he had eliminated scores of Federalist internal revenue officers, dismissed sixteen influential Federalist judges, and discharged a number of his opponents in the army. With less than two years in office, his reformation of both the civil and military establishments was well along. The ship of state had embarked a new crew that would be responsive to its captain's orders.

When viewed in this light, the policies of removal and accommodation are not antithetical. Rather, they are merely two elements of a comprehensive package of reform. Far from being inconsistent, halfhearted, or reluctant, Jefferson's actions were consistent and logical—elements of a coordinated plan to gain control of the essential instruments of government.

As one of his last official acts, Jefferson appointed his secretary of war, Henry Dearborn, to replace Benjamin Lincoln, as collector at Boston—the last of the Federalist holdovers in the nation's major ports. Dearborn, who had managed Jefferson's reform of the military establishment and the creation of the military academy, now became one of the final vehicles of reformation on the civil side. Each step had been one element of a whole conceived to allow the new president to govern effectively.

Jefferson's calculated creation of the United States Military Academy at West Point and his broader reformation of the military establishment were but one element of a much larger effort. Across the board, in both the civil and military establishments, a carefully modulated program of reform had brought those once Federalist instruments of government into consonance with the broad aspirations and goals of Jefferson's new Republican regime.

Notes

1. Theodore J. Crackel, "The Founding of West Point: Jefferson and the Politics of Security," *Armed Forces & Society* 7 (Summer 1981): 529–43. See also Theodore J. Crackel, *Mr. Jefferson's Army: The Political and Social Reform of the Military Establishment, 1801–1809* (New York, 1987), 54–73; and Theodore J. Crackel, *West Point: A Bicentennial History* (Lawrence, Kans., 2001), 29–51.

2. Joseph Gardner Swift, "Memoirs" (unpublished manuscript), Swift Papers, USMA Lib., 36.

3. Cadet Application Papers, 1805–15, Record Group 94, Microfilm Publication 688, National Archives.

4. Crackel, "Jefferson, Politics, and the Army: An Examination of the Military Peace Establishment Act of 1802," *JER* 2 (Spring 1982): 21–38.

5. Crackel, *Mr. Jefferson's Army,* 180.

6. Carl E. Prince, *The Federalists and the Origins of the U.S. Civil Service* (New York, 1977), 20.

7. In this essay I draw frequently on the work of Carl Prince—particularly *The Federalists and the Origins of the U.S. Civil Service.* Prince detailed the political nature of the Federalist civil service and the initial response of Jefferson. Prince's focus, however, was on the Federalists and on how events affected them. Even in an earlier article dealing with Jefferson's removals, Prince focused on the Federalist aristocracy and not on Jefferson's motivation in removing them. (See "The Passing of the Aristocracy: Jefferson's Removal of the Federalists, 1801–1815," *Journal of American History* 57 [December 1970]: 563–75.) Still, Prince's data and observations have been very useful in making my case.

8. Each of these senior officials had the authority to hire some number of assistants or (in the case of the federal attorneys) to contract out work when necessity required it.

9. Nominations to these posts, and Senate actions, are noted throughout the *Senate Executive Journals* of each of the Congresses (1st through 7th) of this period.

10. Elbridge Gerry to TJ, 4 May 1801, TJ Papers, Lib. Cong.

11. Prince, *The Federalists and the Origins of the U.S. Civil Service,* 23.

12. Ibid., 39.

13. Ibid., 93.

14. Joseph Bloomfield to Aaron Burr, 8 April 1801, in *Political Correspondence and Public Papers of Aaron Burr,* 2 vols., ed. Mary-Jo Kline (Princeton, N.J., 1983), 2:556–57.

15. Prince, *The Federalists and the Origins of the U.S. Civil Service,* 146.

16. Ibid., 153–54.

17. Ibid., 184.

18. TJ to John Taylor, 26 November 1798, in Ford, 7:309.

19. Prince, *The Federalists and the Origins of the U.S. Civil Service,* 254–56.

20. The sixth circuit, as the result of an anticipated lighter case load, had only one new circuit judge and filled the other two seats with the district judges from Kentucky and Tennessee. In all, then, there were sixteen new judges appointed to fill the circuit court benches.

21. Gouverneur Morris to Robert R. Livingston, 20 February 1801, in *The Life of Gouverneur Morris. . .,* 2 vols., ed. Jared Sparks (Boston, 1832), 2:153–54.

22. William Branch Giles to TJ, 1 June 1801, TJ Papers, Lib. Cong.

23. *National Intelligencer* (Washington), 18 November 1801.

24. Prince, *The Federalists and the Origins of the U.S. Civil Service,* 245, 251.

25. Ibid., 252.

26. Richard Ellis, *The Jeffersonian Crisis: Courts and Politics in the Young Republic* (New York, 1971), 41.

27. Prince, "The Passing of the Aristocracy", 565.

28. Andrew Pickens to Col. Marinus Willett, 15 August 1801, Pickens Papers, Huntington Library, San Marino, California.

29. Thomas McKean to TJ, 28 July 1801, TJ Papers, Lib. Cong.

30. TJ to Abigail Adams, 13 June 1804, *AJL,* 270.

31. TJ, First Inaugural Address, 4 March 1801, *TJW,* 493–95.

32. TJ, "Anas," 17 May 1801, in Ford, 1:295.

33. Boston *Independent Chronical,* 10 Sept. 1801, quoted in Jerry W. Knudson, "The Jefferson Years: Response by the Press, 1801–1809" (Ph.D. diss., University of Virginia, 1962), 150.

34. TJ, "Anas," 8 March 1801, in Ford, 1:293.

35. Ibid., 295.

36. Ibid. Cilley was replaced in 1802.

37. TJ, First Annual Message, 8 December 1801, *TJW,* 503–8.

38. Manning Dauer, *The Adams Federalists* (Baltimore, 1953), 165.

39. Data concerning appointments made by Jefferson throughout this essay is drawn from the *Senate Executive Journals* of the 7th–10th Congresses. The Judiciary Act of 1801 created twenty-two district courts—one in most states and the Ohio territory, but two in New York, Pennsylvania, Virginia, and Tennessee. Each district court had a judge, an attorney, and a marshal. With the repeal of that act in 1802, the number of districts was reduced to eighteen, and it is in these eighteen districts that Federalist attorneys' and marshals' removal by Jefferson are noted in this essay.

40. TJ to Rush, 24 March 1801, in Ford, 7:31–33.

41. These eleven ports—the only ones important enough to be assigned a collector, a naval officer, and a surveyor—were Portsmouth, New Hampshire; Newburyport, Salem, and Boston in Massachusetts; New York City; Philadelphia; Baltimore; Norfolk, Virginia; Charleston, South Carolina; Savanna, Georgia; and Wilmington, North Carolina.

42. Prince, *The Federalists and the Origins of the U.S. Civil Service,* 156.

43. Ephraim Kirby to TJ, 10 November 1801, Appointment Papers, Record Group 59, National Archives.

44. Wesley Everett Rich, *The History of the United States Post Office to the Year 1829* (Cambridge, Mass., 1924), 128–30.

45. Granger to (displaced postmasters), New York *Evening Post,* 2 March 1802.

46. TJ to Martha Jefferson Randolph, 27 November 1801, in *The Family Letters of Thomas Jefferson,* ed. Edwin Morris Betts and James Adam Bear Jr. (Columbia, Mo., 1966), 214–15.

47. The Peace Establishment bill, for example, was drawn up by Dearborn. Jonathan Williams recalled visiting Dearborn in early December 1801. "I found the Secretary of War fully occupied with his plan for a Peace Establishment," he wrote. "His whole plan was read to me by himself, in private, and I was ordered not to reveal a word to anyone." Williams to James Wilkinson, 8 August 1803, Williams Papers, Lilly Library, Indiana University, Bloomington, Indiana.

48. TJ, First Annual Message, 8 December 1801, *TJW,* 504.

49. I have laid out the details of this elsewhere, so here I will merely outline the case. For a detailed discussion, see Crackel, "Jefferson, Politics, and the Army"; or Crackel, *Mr. Jefferson's Army,* 17–73.

50. Just two months after his inauguration, Jefferson reported to Nathaniel Macon that "the Army is undergoing a chaste reformation." TJ to Macon, 14 May 1801, in L&B, 10:261.

51. On the difficulty of dealing with Jefferson, see Peter S. Onuf, "The Scholars' Jefferson," *WMQ,* 3rd ser., 50 (October 1993): 671–99.

52. Henry Adams, *History of the United States of America during the Administrations of Thomas Jefferson and James Madison,* 9 vols. (New York, 1889–91) 1:200–201, 238.

53. Malone, 4:85.

54. Noble E. Cunningham, *The Jeffersonian Republicans in Power: Party Operations, 1801–1805* (Chapel Hill, N.C., 1963), 70.

55. Prince, "The Passing of the Aristocracy," 565, 575.

56. Forrest McDonald, *The Presidency of Thomas Jefferson* (Lawrence, Kans., 1976), 34.

57. Robert M. Johnstone Jr., *Jefferson and the Presidency: Leadership in the Young Republic* (Ithaca, N.Y., 1977), 113.

58. TJ to Dupont de Nemours, 18 January 1802, *TJW,* 1100.

59. Oliver Wolcott to Roger Griswold, 2 February 1802, quoted in Linda Kerber, *Federalists in Dissent: Imagery and Ideology in Jeffersonian America* (Ithaca, N.Y., 1970), 159.

60. Theodore Sedgwick to Rufus King, 20 February 1802, in *The Life and Correspondence of Rufus King,* 6 vols., ed. Charles R. King (New York, 1894–1900), 4:73.

61. TJ to Robert Livingston, 14 December 1800, in Ford, 7:464–65.

Mr. Jefferson's Academy

An Educational Interpretation

JENNINGS L. WAGONER JR. *and*
CHRISTINE COALWELL MCDONALD

One early August morning in 1821, 200 young West Point cadets marched from their encampment in Boston to Braintree, the home of John Adams. The retired president provided breakfast and then addressed the assembly from the porch of his Massachusetts home. "My young fellow citizens and fellow Soldiers," he began softly, "I rejoice that I live to see so fine a collection of the future defenders of [our] country in pursuit of honour, under the auspices of the national government." He congratulated the young men on the "great Advantages" they possessed "for attaining eminence in Letters and Science as well as Arms. These Advantages," he said, "are a precious deposit which you ought to consider as a Sacred trust for which you are responsible to your Country and to a higher tribunal. These Advantages and the habits you have acquired well qualify you for any course of Life you may choose to pursue." At the end of his brief address, Adams shook hands with each member of the Corps of Cadets.[1]

Reflecting a few days later on the visit of the cadets and the history of the academy, Adams wrote to Jefferson of West Point's growing renown.[2] Jefferson not only shared Adams's admiration of the United States Military Academy, but at the time also had an especially intimate knowledge of the institution. His protégé and future grandson-in-law, Nicholas P. Trist, was then at Monticello enjoying his first summer furlough after having completed three successful years at West Point.

Trist, whose grandmother was an old friend of Jefferson's, had been invited to Monticello for an extended stay in 1817, a year before he entered West Point and several years before his marriage to Jefferson's granddaughter. Trist had considered attending the College of William and Mary, Jefferson's alma mater, but Jefferson encouraged him to consider the military academy and recommended him for an appointment. In the fall of 1818, Trist departed from Monticello for West Point. Although he left the academy after three years to pursue legal studies under Jefferson's direction, he later in life expressed his respect for West Point by declaring that the institution was "confessedly the best in the Union" for the study of the mathematical sciences.[3]

Jefferson's desire that Trist attend West Point is of more than passing interest. Jefferson clearly had a low opinion of the level of education offered by William and Mary, and his own plans to establish the University of Virginia had not yet been sanctioned by the Virginia legislature. Jefferson may have also directed Trist toward West Point out of financial considerations. Left with nothing after his stepfather's death, Trist, like Jefferson, was deeply in debt, and the fact that tuition at the academy was free for those fortunate enough to gain an appointment was no small matter. But there were other factors at work as well. Jefferson, like Adams, had come to respect West Point for its scientific and technical orientation and, as Robert Drexler has noted, he could reasonably expect that the young man's "intellectual horizons would be broadened by exposure to those fields of knowledge" taught at West Point.[4]

The significance of Jefferson's interest in and involvement with West Point goes far beyond his endorsement of the institution to young men such as Trist, however. As president of the United States, Jefferson had supported and signed into law the bill that gave birth to the United States Military Academy in March 1802. In the same year that Adams exchanged accolades with the cadets who had come to pay him respects, Jefferson also received a salute from the academy. Jared Mansfield, the academy's professor of natural and experimental philosophy, informed Jefferson that the faculty and cadets had commissioned Thomas Sully to paint his portrait. Jefferson acknowledged the honor by remarking that "I have ever considered the establishment [West Point] as of major importance to our country and in whatever I could do for it, I viewed myself as performing a duty."[5]

Yet Jefferson's involvement in the founding of West Point has long presented a puzzle to historians. In his efforts to establish a statewide system of education in his native Virginia, Jefferson was deliberate and quite detailed in drafting and modifying his proposals. He presented the legislature with specific bills aimed at instituting reforms at the College of William and Mary and creating a state library in Richmond. He labored for years on the architectural and academic plans for the University of Virginia and wrote hundreds of letters detailing particulars of what became known as "Mr. Jefferson's University."[6]

Jefferson was largely silent, however, on matters pertaining to the education of military officers. There are no bills drafted in his hand, no detailed guides addressing curriculum concerns, no architectural sketches or administrative directives that give us a clear picture of exactly what Jefferson had in mind for his military academy. The intensity and sense of personal identification that characterized many of Jefferson's other educational undertakings are lacking with respect to his role in the establishment of West Point. Trying to explain how and why Jefferson gave support to the founding of the school constitutes a real challenge. Why would Jefferson, a strong republican who repeatedly expressed a fear of standing armies and who extolled the virtues of a volunteer militia drawn from the general population, push for the establishment of a military academy soon after taking office as president?[7]

The most compelling explanation advanced thus far regarding Jefferson's motives in establishing West Point has been put forward by Theodore Crackel. Crackel has demonstrated that Jefferson and his secretary of war, Henry Dearborn, entered office in March of 1801 acutely aware that they had inherited an army composed of Federalist officers who had been appointed during Adams's presidency. They knew as well that the majority of those officers were strongly opposed to Republican (and, they feared, republican) aims and values. Jefferson and Dearborn thus set out to mold an army that would "threaten neither the new Republican regime nor the republic itself." This was to be done, Crackel maintains, by introducing Republicans into the officer ranks at every opportunity and by gaining the favor of moderate Federalists who might in time support the Republican agenda. West Point was to play a crucial role in this reform. The new military academy was to provide an avenue to train and introduce into service sons of the Republican faithful. No longer was "rank," military or civilian, to be determined chiefly by birth and parental status. Way was being made for young men who possessed "virtue and talent"—and to the degree possible, correct political principles.[8]

But the significance of West Point as an element in Jefferson's "chaste reformation" of the military establishment should not eclipse the fact that Jefferson's interest in and support of the academy also needs to be understood as an attempt to give life to a scientific branch of a national university. As odd as it may seem in the context of Jeffersonian aversion to energetic government at the federal level and as out of character as it might appear to those who have overemphasized Jefferson's distrust of a professional military establishment, his advocacy of West Point reflected scientific as well as military ends, politically expedient as well as longer-term republican concerns, and a conviction that a congressionally mandated specialized school of military science could be compatible with private, state, and even a national institution of higher learning.[9]

The developments that led to the creation of West Point need to be understood within the context of Jefferson's unyielding commitment to the vital role of education in the evolving new social order. He was convinced that the future security of his "country" (at first Virginia, and later the fledgling republic) was tied much more directly to the general enlightenment of the population than to its military strength. Jefferson called for a "crusade against ignorance" as he championed the education bills he placed before the Virginia legislature. He wrote to George Washington from Paris in 1786 that "our liberty can never be safe but in the hands of the people themselves." He added, significantly, that "this it is the business of the state to effect, and on a general plan."[10]

In spite of Jefferson's appeals for support from Washington and numerous other Virginia worthies, he was defeated in his efforts to prod the state legislature into providing public support for a comprehensive system of education. Even so, in the years that followed, he continued to look for ways in which education at any and all levels might be advanced in Virginia and throughout the new nation. He became well informed about the educational institutions of Europe during his period of service as minister to France from 1784 through 1789. Before, during, and after his return from France, he studied various educational treatises and engaged in lengthy correspondence concerning educational matters with men of learning on both sides of the Atlantic. While specific details and matters of emphasis in Jefferson's educational thinking shifted over time as he gained awareness of various theories and practices then in vogue—and as he reacted to particular circumstances of the moment—his commitment to a multilayered system of publicly supported education remained constant.[11]

Jefferson's desire to elevate the level of learning available in the United States, especially in terms of the useful sciences, prompted him to consider a number of schemes, both foreign and domestic in origin, in the years before as well as during his presidency. One intriguing proposal that caught Jefferson's attention, at least briefly, was the grandiose plan of Quesnay de Beauprepaire, a former captain in the American army under Lafayette's command. In the mid-1780s, Quesnay set out to establish in Richmond an Academy of Arts and Sciences patterned after the famous French Academy. Complementing the institution in Richmond were to be branches in Baltimore, Philadelphia, and New York, all of which were to be affiliated with the royal societies of London, Paris, Brussels, and other learned bodies of Europe. Under the tutelage of French professors, separate schools were to offer instruction and conduct investigations in a wide array of scientific fields, including civil and military architecture, mineralogy, mathematics, experimental physics, astronomy, chemistry, geography, and foreign languages—fields of study that would in time be included in the curricula of both West Point and the University of Virginia.[12]

Apparently based on conversations the two had while Jefferson was in Paris, Quesnay in his prospectus for the academy listed Jefferson along with Lafayette, Beaumarchais, Condorcet, and numerous other conspicuous French and American celebrities as sponsors of the project. Quesnay managed to raise a considerable amount of money as well as moral support on both sides of the Atlantic for the venture. The cornerstone for the Richmond Academy was laid on June 24, 1786, with great ceremony, but the outbreak of the French Revolution three years later brought an abrupt end to the elaborate scheme before the new building could be put to its intended use. Even before the events following the storming of the Bastille doomed Quesnay's project, however, Jefferson had pulled back from whatever initial support he may have proffered. Determining that there would be little legislative support for the venture, and claiming that European professors might be disappointed in their expectations of America, Jefferson cautioned Quesnay on January 6, 1788, that he feared the undertaking was "too extensive for the poverty of the country." While he wished Quesnay "every possible success" and said that he would "be really happy to see your plan answer your expectations," he made clear his reservations and expressed his desire to remain "absolutely neutral" concerning the future of the project.[13]

However conflicted Jefferson's motives may have been regarding his reluctance to push Quesnay's plan, his reaction a few years later to a proposal from a Genevan, François D'Ivernois, was quite different. D'Ivernois, a man of "considerable distinction for science and patriotism, and that too of the republican kind," informed Jefferson in 1794 that the faculty of the University of Geneva had become dissatisfied with their political environment and would consider transplanting themselves to America if proper arrangements could be made.

Excited by the prospect of luring the faculty of such an esteemed institution to Virginia, Jefferson asked Wilson Cary Nicholas to sound out, privately, trusted members of the state legislature regarding their stance on this proposition. Just over two months later, however, Jefferson had to convey to D'Ivernois his disappointment in having to report that, despite warm support on the part of some legislators, the majority could not be persuaded to back the measure. He detailed three reasons others gave in determining the plan to be impractical. The first was "that our youth, not familiarized but with their mother tongue, were not prepared to receive instructions in any other." Second, some feared "that the expence of the institution would excite uneasiness in their constituents, and endanger it's permanence." In addition, legislators worried "that it's extent was disproportioned to the narrow state of the population with us." Although "the decision rested with others," he wrote, "I should have seen with peculiar satisfaction the establishment of such a mass of science in my country." He assured D'Ivernois, moreover, that his own devotion to "science, and freedom, the first-born daughter of science," was so firm that he would have been tempted to establish a second residence in whatever neighborhood such an institution would have been placed.[14]

Discouraged but not deterred, Jefferson sought President Washington's support for the idea. He had been in communication with Washington since 1786 regarding the general's interest in donating shares of stock in the Potomac and James River canal companies to finance some educational undertaking. Washington had earlier received the stock as a gift from the Virginia legislature and, fearing that he might be criticized for profiting from his service to his countrymen, had been in correspondence with Jefferson, among others, regarding using the gift to establish charity schools or for some other educational project. Jefferson was well aware of Washington's long-standing interest in the creation of a national university. Washington had recommended the creation of such an institution in his message to Congress on January 8, 1790, and had urged Alexander Hamilton, to no avail, to include reference to the national university as he refined the drafts of what became Washington's "Farewell Address" to the nation. In Washington's final message to Congress on December 7, 1796, he again recommended the creation of a national university as well as a military academy.[15]

Jefferson hit upon the idea of using Washington's interest in advancing education along these lines to gain his support for the Geneva project. In a letter to Washington on February 23, 1795, within weeks of his letter of regret to D'Ivernois, he described the Geneva proposal and suggested that Washington use the canal shares to establish the institution as the national university—to be located *near* the capital but *within* the borders of Virginia, because that state would contribute to its support by paying interest on the donated stock. The university, Jefferson assured Washington, would draw students "from all our states" and probably from other parts of the hemisphere as well.

Washington, however, had already been informed of the proposal by Adams, who had also been contacted by D'Ivernois. Washington expressed to Jefferson his lack of enthusiasm for the idea. He noted that it might not be wise to transplant the Geneva professors en masse, because they "might not all be good characters nor all sufficiently acquainted with our language." Moreover, said Washington, their political principles seemed at variance with the leveling party in their own country and might give further support to those who, "without any just cause that I can discover, are continually sounding the bell of aristocracy." Washington also thought it better, if foreign professors were to be attracted to this country, to draw them from several countries rather than all from one. This project, like Quesnay's proposal, was dropped.[16]

Both Jefferson's interest in and his equivocations about these particular plans point to his mounting concerns—and frustrations—regarding the low level of educational and scientific development in the country. Even while duties of state absorbed more and more of his time, he continued to search for ways to implement, in whole or in part, educational undertakings that would sever America's dependence on and secondary status to European citadels of learning.

Jefferson's membership in the American Philosophical Society, the premier scientific organization of the day, enabled him to keep educational concerns and plans under active consideration. In January of 1797, he was elected president of the society and was regularly reelected to the position for the next seventeen years. Jefferson's election as vice president of the United States presented the opportunity to be in Philadelphia, where the society met. He arrived on March 2. The next day he was installed as president of the society and the following day took on the responsibilities of vice president of the nation. For a time, at least, he thought he might enjoy an "honorable and easy" position under Adams and engage in "philosophical evenings" with kindred souls.[17]

Among the concerns that attracted the attention of the American Philosophical Society was the matter of education in the new nation. A little more than a year before Jefferson's election as its president, the society had arranged a contest with a prize of $100 to be awarded to the author of an essay best describing a "system of liberal education and literary instruction, adapted to the genius of the government of the United States." On December 15, 1797, three days after returning from a trip to Monticello, Jefferson convened the meeting of the society at which the winner of the prize was to be announced. Jonathan Williams, secretary of the society (and later Jefferson's choice as the first superintendent of the United States Military Academy), recorded that "none of the Systems of Education then under review appeared . . . so well adapted to the present state of Society in this Country," but that two of the essays had been judged as being of "superior merit." Samuel Knox, a Presbyterian minister from Baltimore, shared the essay prize with Samuel H. Smith, soon to become the editor of the Jeffersonian *National Intelligencer.* Both essayists called for an extensive and uniform system of publicly supported schools reaching from the primary levels to academies and colleges and, at the apex of the system, a national university.[18]

The plans offered by Knox and Smith differed in detail, but the general schemes were similar and the project itself was not new. For several years Benjamin Rush, the Philadelphia physician and signer of the Declaration of Independence, had been advocating a national system of schools and the creation of a national university. Four months before the delegates to the Constitutional Convention assembled in Philadelphia in 1787, Rush had published an article in the *American Museum.* Proclaiming that "THE REVOLUTION IS NOT OVER," Rush contended that a federal university was needed to disseminate knowledge of every kind throughout the country. The university should offer programs in history, the law of nature and nations, civil law, principles of commerce—and gunnery and fortification. In this and later, more detailed proposals, Rush blended patriotism with calls for investigations into the sciences of agriculture, manufacturing, commerce, natural philosophy, and in the practical applications of chemistry. "We shall never restore public credit, regulate our militia, build a navy, or revive our commerce," he wrote, "until we remove the ignorance and prejudices, and change the habits of our citizens." This, he maintained, "can never be done until we inspire them with federal principles." Among the nearly 500 subscribers to the *American Museum* were Washington, Hamilton, Jefferson, James Madison, and Benjamin Franklin.[19]

The essays by Rush, Smith, Knox, and others put forth in the 1790s were echoing ideas that were very much in the air at the time. Particulars of various plans differed, but concern for bringing the people and states of the new union into closer harmony spurred a number of theorists to view publicly supported education—and even the possibility of a national system of education—as being worthy of serious consideration. Essayists and political leaders eager to ensure that the citizens be educated in a systematic fashion directed most of their attention to government policy, but it was mostly via private and local initiatives that schools and colleges gradually spread across the nation. As Frederick Rudolph has emphasized, the leading educational theorists of the period conveyed "a deep sense of a nation being formed, a people's character being shaped." While they hoped that the general diffusion of knowledge would maximize happiness and assist able and deserving young men to attain positions of influence in society and government, they were at bottom clearly more concerned about the future of the nation than with the rise of individuals. These essayists, along with Jefferson, searched for a system of education that would be suitable for coming generations of free and independent citizens intent on maintaining a republican society. They sought educational arrangements that would unite Americans and their diverse state republics into "an empire for liberty" bound together by ties of interest and affection.[20]

As the year 1800 dawned, Jefferson intensified his efforts to refine his thinking about and plans for the advancement of education. On January 18 he wrote to Joseph Priestley, a noted theologian and scientist, of his "wish" to establish a publicly supported university in a more central part of Virginia, a university that would embrace all the sciences and would, above all else, be useful. Seeking Priestley's advice regarding the academic structure of the institution, Jefferson observed that "in an institution meant chiefly for use, some branches of science, formerly esteemed, may now be omitted; so may others now valued in Europe, but useless to us for ages to come."[21]

Jefferson hastily listed courses, chiefly scientific, that struck him as being among the most useful and practical. Yet he implored Priestley to improve on the list and to suggest the most efficient and economical arrangement of studies that would enable the university to bring the greatest extent of knowledge within the reach "of the fewest professors possible." Jefferson's list included botany, chemistry, zoology, anatomy, surgery, medicine, natural philosophy, agriculture, mathematics, astronomy, geography, politics, commerce, history, ethics, law, arts, and fine arts. In another letter several days later, Jefferson noted that he did not mean to imply in his earlier listing that he thought study of languages to be useless. Instead, he noted that the ability to read Latin and Greek authors in the original was a "sublime luxury" and, while not essential to obtaining "eminent degrees of science, nonetheless very useful towards it." He reminded Priestley of his earlier plans for a comprehensive system of education in Virginia and his hope that, when finally implemented, the district colleges could attend to the teaching of "languages, geography, surveying, and other useful things of that grade; and then a single University for the sciences."[22]

Priestley's response, his "Hints Concerning Public Education," was rather general. A point that may have impressed Jefferson, however, was Priestley's recommendation that there be two classes of "public seminaries," one for specialized training in the professions and the other for gentlemen "who are designed for offices of civil and active life." The former institutions would be fewer in number but would require a larger number of more specialized professors, especially in the sciences, than would the liberal arts institutions. In acknowledging Priestley's "thoughts on the plan of an university," Jefferson assured him that "as soon as we can ripen the public disposition we shall bring forward our proposition."[23]

Within weeks of issuing his request to Priestley, Jefferson delighted in a visit at Monticello from Pierre Samuel Du Pont de Nemours, an intimate associate from his days as minister to France. The pair discussed Jefferson's educational aspirations, a subject on which they focused much of their subsequent correspondence. Jefferson asked Du Pont to identify those branches of science "which in the present state of man, and particularly with us, should be introduced into an academy." He emphasized the necessity of arranging and "reducing the important sciences to as few professorships as possible, because of the narrowness of our resources." Du Pont need not consider subjects such as Greek, Latin, "common arithmetic," music, fencing, and dancing, Jefferson said, for they could be learned in other settings. "I should also exclude those which are unimportant," he added, "and those which are acquired by reading alone, without the help of a master, such as ethics."[24]

Although Jefferson made it clear to Du Pont that he was not requesting a treatise on the subject of education, that is exactly what Du Pont developed. Du Pont criticized Europe's universities, which he claimed had become sterile "extinguishers of intelligence" with a reverence for "dead languages" and the "gibberish" of metaphysics. Referencing Jefferson's own plans for Virginia, Du Pont emphasized the importance of publicly supported (as well as private) primary and secondary schools ("colleges") throughout the states. Focusing on the national level, however, Du Pont advocated the creation of a national library, a botanical garden, and a museum that would contain chambers that could accommodate meetings of a national philosophical society. Du Pont applied the term "University" to the whole system, but specified that there should be four independent "special schools" for the higher sciences located in the nation's capital: schools of medicine, mines, social science and legislation, and one of "higher geometry and the sciences that it explains." This latter branch, the School of Transcendental Geometry, should provide a concentrated engineering curriculum, with studies focused on transcendent geometry and the sciences dependent on it such as astronomy, hydrology, navigation, construction and rigging of ships, and "engineering, both civil and military, for the artillery." The engineering professorships, Du Pont asserted, would form "the nucleus of an admirable Philosophic Society" that "will do wonderful things in a country where it will be so tremendously rewarded." Du Pont also observed that, in terms of engineering for military and civil construction, "no nation is in such need of canals as the United States, and most of their ports have no means of exterior defense." Finally, Du Pont envisioned a "General Council of Education" composed of a representative from each state to serve as a coordinating body for this "University of North America." There would be two categories of students: those chosen for ability, who would receive scholarships funded by their states, and others who could attend at their own expense.[25]

At the very time that Jefferson was soliciting advice from Priestley and Du Pont regarding the most advantageous arrangement of university studies that would crown the layered education system he had first envisioned in the 1770s, he was forced by circumstances to contemplate as well proposals from within the Adams administration regarding the founding of a military academy. The idea of establishing a military academy that would prepare officers for the artillery and engineering corps was, of course, by no means novel in 1800. Calls for a military academy dated back to the early days of the Revolutionary War; the idea had been endorsed and encouraged repeatedly by Washington. In 1776 Adams proposed that the Continental Congress form a committee to study a "plan for the Establishment of a military Academy, in the Army." He also wrote to Colonel Henry Knox that "I wish We had a military Academy, and should be obliged to you for a Plan of such an Institution. The expense would be a trifle, no object at all with me."[26]

Congressional inaction killed Adams's plan, but others would follow. Jefferson himself had given close (but unofficial) attention to a 1783 proposal submitted by General Frederick William von Steuben that called for the establishment of three military academies. Steuben had suggested that graduates of the proposed academies might apply for appointments in the regular army but recommended that the large majority should return to civilian life, where they might "diffuse sound military opinion throughout the nation." Jefferson had been intrigued enough by this plan to make private calculations on the range of subject areas and the number and projected salaries of the instructional staff for such institutions. He confided to his notes, however, an important question: "Will it not be better to improve colleges into them?"[27]

A decade passed before Congress again considered the need for a military academy. Jefferson said he objected on constitutional grounds to the creation of a military academy when the idea was twice broached in cabinet meetings in November 1793. He recorded in his "Anas" that "the President said he would not choose to recommend anything against the Constitution." If, however, the constitutionality was merely *"doubtful,"* then Washington, "so impressed with the necessity of this measure," said that "he would refer it to Congress, and let them decide for themselves whether the Constitution authorized it or not."[28]

Although Congress did not heed Washington's plea for a military academy, in the spring of 1795 it did enact a provision that provided for "books, instruments, and apparatus" and the extension of limited instruction to officer candidates stationed at West Point. In 1798, at the urging of Secretary of War James McHenry, Congress took another halting step toward military education by authorizing "four teachers of the arts and sciences necessary for the instruction of the artillerists and engineers." Determined to avoid appointing foreigners (especially Frenchmen) to the post, President Adams, after lengthy consideration, failed to identify a candidate who fully satisfied his expectations.[29]

Meanwhile, Hamilton had been at work developing plans for a "new and enlarged army" and the establishment of a military academy on a more elaborate and comprehensive scale than had yet been envisioned. He proposed creating an academy that would consist of five schools. A two-year School of Fundamentals would lay the foundation with instruction in mathematics and "all the sciences necessary to a perfect knowledge of the different branches of the military art." Upon completion of the basic course, cadets would be sent to one of the more advanced schools for additional training. Those in the School of Engineering and Artillery would continue for two more years in theoretical and field studies; those in the School of Cavalry or School of Infantry would complete one additional year concentrating on riding, fencing, and allied practical and tactical subjects. Cadets appointed to the School of the Navy would spend two additional years that combined advanced theoretical work with shipboard experience. Hamilton forwarded his plan to Secretary McHenry in November of 1799; McHenry in turn sent to Congress the proposal, as well as an estimate of the funds needed to put the plan into operation. Congress, however, adjourned in April 1800 without bringing the matter to the floor.[30]

Congressional inaction did not deter Jefferson from now giving renewed attention of his own to the idea of a military academy. Although creating a military school certainly had not been of primary interest to Jefferson when he sought the advice of Priestley and Du Pont in the early months of 1800, it is equally certain that he was well informed about the details of Hamilton's plan, a proposal "almost the whole" of which he initially had dismissed as being "useless." Jefferson, however, could not fail to have had an interest in the arrangement or placement of sciences related to military arts and other fields of importance related to the security, development, and further expansion of the American empire of liberty. He shared with others a sense of embarrassment and uneasiness over the nation's deficiency of knowledge in engineering and other useful sciences. When in 1788 his countryman Ralph Izard had solicited Jefferson's advice regarding his younger son's desire to become an engineer, Jefferson had to confess to American deficiency and recommended two institutions in France for engineering studies. None of the existing colleges in the United States offered instruction in the application of mathematics, mechanics, physics, and allied sciences necessary for the building of fortifications, bridges, artillery placements, and other essential military undertakings. Attention to matters of military science and military preparedness was all the more a matter of concern in the climate of increasingly fragile relations on the western frontier as well as threats from abroad that marked the closing years of the eighteenth century.[31]

Although the lineage of the military academy project can be traced back at least to 1776, the most proximate proposal was of Hamiltonian design. Jefferson's assumption of the presidency in 1801 made it possible for him to sponsor a more economically feasible plan for a military academy, one that would be directed toward useful national and scientific as well as military ends. Seen in this light, the educational plans of Priestley and Du Pont, and those of the advocates of national systems and a national university—as well as Jefferson's own continuously evolving designs for the advancement of science and enlightened republicanism—all take on new significance.

Jefferson was awash in educational ideas, plans, and proposals as the new century ushering in the Republican "revolution of 1800" dawned. As he would write years later to his nephew, Peter Carr, with regard to renewed efforts that eventually culminated in the founding of the University of Virginia, he had "lost no occasion of making myself acquainted with the organization of the best seminaries in other countries, and with the opinions of the most enlightened individuals" on both sides of the Atlantic. While struck by the "diversity" of the plans, Jefferson considered the proposals and theories he had reviewed over the years to be "the subject of mature reflection, by wise and learned men, who, contemplating local circumstances, have adapted them to the condition of the section of society for which they have been framed." No one of them, Jefferson continued, "if adopted without change, would be suited to the circumstances and pursuits of our country." The value of other proposals and institutional arrangements, he asserted, was their service as examples from which selections might be made "which are good for us," thus enabling the creation of institutions "whose arrangement[s] shall correspond with our own social condition and shall admit of enlargement in proportion to the encouragement [they] may merit and receive."[32]

In this letter, written over a decade after the founding of the academy, Jefferson once again outlined a three-tiered system of education (elementary schools, general schools, and professional schools) and specified a department at the professional level devoted to "Architecture, Military and Naval; Projectiles, Rural Economy, (comprehending Agriculture, Horticulture and Veterinary), Technical Philosophy, the Practice of Medicine, Materia Medica, Pharmacy and Surgery." While he envisioned West Point as an institution for the preparation of officers for the Corps of Engineers, other institutions, including the projected University of Virginia for which he was (once again) developing a founding strategy in 1814, were also to provide scientific and military training to capable leaders of the militia.[33]

Already twice defeated in his efforts to get the Virginia legislature to enact his own comprehensive school plans and frustrated with the lack of support for other educational ventures he had considered, Jefferson had no way of knowing when, if ever, his state might push forward on plans for publicly supported elementary and secondary schools, much less act favorably on plans still in incubation regarding a state university. Up to this point, as his correspondence with Priestley and Du Pont in 1800 reveals, Jefferson had expressed only the hope—not anything approaching a developed plan—that some type of institution of advanced learning might be established sometime in the future somewhere in Virginia. A future that might (or might not) bring into existence the University of Virginia was uncertain and unknowable; the needs and possibilities of the present were more obvious.[34]

Jefferson's inability to predict future developments also helps explain his interest both before and after West Point's founding in Joel Barlow's plans for a national university. Barlow had also corresponded with Jefferson in 1800 regarding his dream of founding a great national institution in Washington. Ideas that were embryonic in 1800 did not take definite shape until several years later. By January 1806, however, four years after West Point's founding, Barlow had developed his scheme into a *Prospectus of a National Institution to be established in the United States.* Although Barlow's 1806 *Prospectus* was more elaborate than Du Pont's earlier plan, both shared the feature of having special schools, including a military academy, that would operate as components of a national university. In Barlow's plan, the military academy then in existence at West Point was to be moved to Washington. Barlow also called for a school of mines, a school of roads and bridges (which was to include studies in navigation, canals, and hydraulic architecture—a subject included at the suggestion of Robert Fulton), a conservatory of useful arts and trades, a museum of natural history, a museum of fine arts, a national library, a *prytaneum* (school of general science), a mint, an observatory, and district colleges scattered throughout the union that would be associated with the national institution in Washington. Barlow's plan also provided for the establishment of a printing press for the production and dissemination of scientific and scholarly researches as well the publication of textbooks for use in elementary schools throughout the country. He maintained that cheap and widely distributed textbooks would "give a uniformity to the moral sentiment, a republican energy to the character, [and] a liberal cast to the mind and manners of the rising and following generations."[35]

Barlow met with Jefferson on February 23, 1806, to discuss the plan and get his endorsement. The next day Jefferson returned Barlow's bill for the establishment of a "National Academy & University at the city of Washington," along with "such alterations as we talked over last night." The alternations, Jefferson assured Barlow, were "chiefly verbal." The president encouraged Barlow by asserting that he had often wished to have a "Philosophical society or academy so organized as that while the central academy should be at the seat of government," affiliated institutions would be spread around the country. Publications from these more distant academies could be presented to the central academy that could, in turn, disseminate the best to the other academies. "In this way," reasoned Jefferson, "all the members wheresoever dispersed might be brought into action, and an useful emulation might arise between the filiated societies." Jefferson closed with the speculation that perhaps "the great societies now existing might incorporate themselves in this way with the National one. But time does not allow me to pursue this idea."[36]

Pennsylvania senator George Logan introduced a bill in March 1806 based on Barlow's *Prospectus,* but after three readings, the bill died in committee. In his next annual message to Congress on December 2, however, Jefferson tried to revive the proposal by encouraging Congress to consider amending the Constitution, if necessary, to allow for federal expenditures in support of a national university and internal improvements. He urged Congress to think of public outlays for education and internal improvements as means whereby sectionalism could be reduced and union cemented "by new and indissoluble ties." He explained that "education is here placed among the articles of public care, not that it would be proposed to take its ordinary branches out of the hands of private enterprise, which manages so much better all the concerns to which it is equal," but rather because "a public institution can alone supply those sciences which, though rarely called for, are yet necessary to complete the circle, all the parts of which contribute to the improvement of the country, and some of them to its preservation."[37]

Once again Congress refused to follow Jefferson's lead. As one of Barlow's biographers would later put the matter, the failure of Congress to pursue the national university scheme proposed by Barlow and endorsed by Jefferson meant that the third president would have to "content himself" with setting up the University of Virginia during his retirement years. Whether the University of Virginia was seen by Jefferson (or should be seen by us) as a mere consolation is debatable. What is more certain is that Jefferson had learned from long experience that "there is a snail-paced gait for the advance of new ideas on the general mind, under which we must acquiesce." To Barlow he observed that "a 40. years' experience of popular assemblies has taught me, that you must give them time for every step you take. If too hard pushed, they baulk, & and the machine retrogrades." Jefferson's hope for congressional attention to education and other domestic needs in the future was tempered by his awareness that legislators, if they acted at all, would probably show a preference for internal improvements. "People generally have more feeling for canals & roads," he lamented, "than education."[38]

Barlow's plan and Jefferson's responsiveness to it before and after West Point's founding suggest a continuing connection between the academy and Jefferson's interest in a multifaceted national educational establishment. At the outset of his administration in 1801, Jefferson saw the creation of a military academy as a modest but attainable and necessary step in the right direction. As a "special school" devoted to military (and civil) applications of science, the military academy at West Point could fit into his larger scheme of establishing publicly supported institutions at various levels and of various types that would bring about the more general diffusion of knowledge, increase harmony between the different sections of the union, advance the application of useful sciences, and foster republican leadership in the military establishment that was essential to the security of the new nation. The haste with which Jefferson moved to establish a military academy composed of men who shared his enthusiasm for scientific advancement, internal improvements, republicanism, and military preparedness becomes all the more understandable when considered against this background. Here was a Federalist plan that could be converted into Republican uses.

Jefferson's designs for West Point can be discerned even more fully in his choice of Jonathan Williams as the founding superintendent of the academy. Williams, a moderate Federalist, had little military experience beyond having translated a French treatise on artillery. Appointed by Adams as a major in the Second Regiment of Artillerists and Engineers in February 1801, Williams had been in uniform less than three months when notified that Jefferson had selected him to serve as inspector of fortifications and officer in charge of the Corps of Engineers that was to constitute a military academy at West Point. He had, however, been known to Jefferson since their time together in Paris in the 1780s, when he lived with and served as the research assistant of his granduncle, Benjamin Franklin. On their return voyage from Europe in 1785, Franklin and Williams had conducted experiments on the relationship between water temperature and ocean currents. Williams extended his research on later voyages and in 1799 published his findings as a book to aid in navigation. He also contributed essays to the *Transactions* of the American Philosophical Society and was serving as its secretary when Jefferson became its president. Correspondence between Williams and Jefferson touched on various scientific topics, including Jefferson's improved plow design and methods each had used to calculate the heights of mountains along the Blue Ridge of Virginia. After receiving from Williams a copy of his *Memoir on the use of the Thermometer in Navigation* and his translation of Heinrich Otto Von Scheel's *Treatise on Artillery,* Jefferson acknowledged that he would "be very happy to see the corps of which he is a member profit by his example and pursue the line of information he has so well pointed out." By selecting Williams, Jefferson not only entrusted West Point to the care of a man with at least moderately acceptable political views; he also made a practical-minded scientist its leader.[39]

Official provisions and expectations for the new school were modest. As initially established by the 1802 Military Peace Establishment Act, the academy was not created to train officers for all branches of the regular army or the militia, or even the nucleus of a general officer corps. Instead, the military academy aimed to prepare a small number of cadets for duty in a narrow branch of technical service, the Corps of Engineers, which by law was limited to twenty members. The law left open the question of curriculum, directing only that "the necessary books, implements and apparatus for the use and benefit of the said institution" should be provided "at the public expense." Williams testified to the lack of direction given by the administration when in 1803 he confided to Major W. W. Burrows that, other than instructions to use a specific mathematics text, "I have not received from the Secretary of War, one word descriptive of the plan of the institution and the Education expected."[40]

It soon became obvious that Williams's aspirations for the United States Military Academy were far greater than the resources available. When he sent a request to the administration for books and equipment via his second in command, Major Decius Wadsworth, Williams instructed him to keep in mind that "we should consider ourselves happy in the deposition of Government, not only to establish, but to nourish our Institution." Supplies not needed immediately, he said, soon "will be, after the Corps is full and tolerably advanced." Williams thought it desirable to have the American ministers to England and France seek the opinion of "the most eminent professional Men in London and Paris" and purchase for the academy "every Book of merit that is extant, so far as is connected with the Profession." In addition, he told Wadsworth to impress upon Dearborn the "absolute necessity of a drawing master" and to drop a "hint or two about a French teacher."[41]

In his own correspondence with Dearborn, Williams had earlier assured the secretary of war that he was endeavoring to economize by seeking mathematical instruments "of the cheapest sort" and confessed his fear that, "considering the infant state of the Institution, you will probably think the list too extensive." But Williams pressed on. "If you will please to take into view the important national Establishment to which I hope it will in due time increase," he wrote, "you will doubtless consider it rather below than above what a proper apparatus ought to be."[42]

Jefferson personally reviewed the initial request for books and implements drawn up by Williams, made comments in the margins that included additional recommendations, and via Dearborn returned the list to Williams with instructions for him to determine which books and instruments could be purchased in New York or Philadelphia and which could only be purchased in Europe. Williams was to be reimbursed for any volumes in his own library that he would place in the academy's collection. Dearborn directed Williams "to purchase or cause to be purchased such Books and Instruments as may be obtained and the bill will be paid."[43]

However much Jefferson and Dearborn may have shared Williams's vision and ambitions for the academy, budgetary constraints limited the purchase of books and supplies. When in one instance Williams attempted to get approval to buy an entire set of the *Encyclopedie Raisonee* for $80, he was rebuffed by Dearborn with the rationale that "improvements in the Sciences are so rapidly advancing" that the *Encyclopedie* would soon be obsolescent and therefore useless. Dearborn considered it necessary to remind Williams that, in light of "the present state of the Academy funds" appropriated by Congress, future spending should not "exceed what may be *necessary.*"

Although one might argue, as has Theodore Crackel, that Dearborn's denial of Williams's request for the *Encyclopedie* is evidence that the administration "resisted efforts to increase the school's emphasis on science," another explanation—financial exigency—is equally plausible. Concern for economy was by no means limited to purchases of books. Cadets were not given provisions for uniforms; after all, Dearborn reminded Williams, "these young gentlemen are receiving their education at the expense of the United States, and may, or may not continue in service, after having obtained them."[44]

In spite of the administration's stringent financial policies and the vagaries of the act of establishment, Williams, who was promoted to lieutenant colonel in July 1802, endeavored to do whatever he could within the constraints of his official—and limited—powers to bring a semblance of order and scientific orientation to the academy. Within four days of his arrival at West Point, he had investigated the source of a conflict between a junior officer and the only civilian instructor at the academy, Professor George Baron. The inquiry resulted in the dismissal of the civilian.

A few weeks later, Dearborn commissioned William A. Barron and Jared Mansfield as captains in the Corps of Engineers and ordered them to West Point as mathematics instructors. Barron had been a classmate of John Quincy Adams at Harvard and had tutored mathematics there. Mansfield, an acquaintance of Jefferson, had attended Yale, served there as mathematics instructor, and had published a study of the motion of bodies in free space. His *Essays, Mathematical and Physical,* published in 1801, dealt with problems in algebra, geometry, calculus, and nautical astronomy and included a chapter on gunnery and fundamental ballistics problems. Mansfield was the first scientist to consider the gyroscopic phenomenon in ballistics; previous investigators had studied projectiles without considering the effect of the medium through which they passed. A year after the appointments of Barron and Mansfield, Francis de Masson joined the faculty to teach topographical drawing and French, thus introducing the cadets to the language that at the time was the gateway to the sciences of the military profession.[45]

Williams's desire to transmit to the cadets a spirit of scientific inquiry and an awareness of the broad horizons their new profession offered was perhaps best exemplified by his establishment of the United States Military Philosophical Society. "Our guiding star," Williams wrote, "is not a little mathematical School, but a great national establishment. . . . We must always have it in view that our Officers are to be men of Science, and as such will by their acquirements be entitled to the notice of learned societies." On November 12, 1802, Williams presented the idea of forming a scientific society to the officers of the Corps of Engineers. The officers voted the society into existence and a week later elected Williams to the presidency. Wadsworth, second in command at the academy, was elected vice president.[46]

Within a month the society adopted a constitution that made the officers and cadets of the Corps of Engineers members by right and the nucleus of the governing body. The constitution further provided that "any gentleman, provided he be a citizen of the United States, whether a military man or not," was eligible for membership. The society, patterned on the American Philosophical Society, was designed to supplement the educational and scientific activities of the Corps of Engineers.[47]

Williams immediately solicited Jefferson's sponsorship of the United States Military Philosophical Society. Explaining that its purpose was to preserve the elements of military science that veterans of the Revolution and travelers may have acquired, Williams invited Jefferson, as president of the United States, to become the society's "perpetual Patron." Jefferson's response was clearly supportive. Describing himself as "A friend of Science in all of its useful Branches, and believing that of the Engineer of great utility, I sincerely approve of the Institution of a Society for its Improvement," he wrote. He recognized that the society's membership would be small at the outset, but reasoned that as scientific inquiry was "directly in the line of their profession, and entitled to all their time" the officers and cadets would soon give ample evidence of the society's value. While stating that "it is not probable that I may be able to render it any service," he accepted "the Patronage you are pleased to propose" and again noted the "the perfect coincidence" of the society's objects "with the legal duties" of its members. Jefferson concluded his note of acceptance by stating that sponsorship of the society was "consistent with the duties which I owe" to the military academy.[48]

Jefferson's involvement with the society came as especially welcome news to Wadsworth, who was on assignment at Fort Nelson when word came of his election to the vice presidency and Jefferson's acceptance of the offer to become patron of the organization. Wadsworth confided to Williams that he had "entertained serious [d]oubts" as to Jefferson's intentions regarding the academy. He explained his anxiety and now his relief to Williams by noting that he "was apprehensive that the Plan of a Corps of Engineers was *reluctantly* adopted to satisfy a national wish, which had been strongly manifested for some years past, of seeing a military school in this country: that deprived almost entirely of countenance of support it would be left to languish untill Experience of its inutility would justify therein in renouncing it." Jefferson's "cordial disposition" toward the academy had now changed his mind, and his patronage was deemed by Wadsworth as "of more consequence than any thing else in Relation to the Society." Mansfield also expressed his pleasure in having the support of Jefferson and Dearborn, for he was "persuaded," he informed Williams, "that we shall have the whole weight of their influence in favor of arrangements which you have projected."[49]

With Jefferson on board as patron, the United States Military Philosophical Society appeared to be off to an auspicious beginning. A conflict over command between Williams and the ranking officer of the Corps of Artillerists during the summer of 1803, however, provoked Williams's resignation before the society could make headway. Although Williams had been appointed superintendent of West Point, his authority was limited to command over officers and cadets in the Corps of Engineers. The issue of command authority dated back to the Revolutionary War, when all engineers in the employ of the American army were foreigners. Based on that circumstance, the tradition evolved whereby engineers were seen as staff officers without the authority to command troops. Although circumstances had changed by the time Williams had become the officer in charge of the Corps of Engineers and superintendent, the policy had not. Williams bristled when confronted with the fact that officers in other corps did not recognize his presumed authority.

He appealed directly to Secretary Dearborn in Washington when returning to West Point following an inspection tour of coastal fortifications in Wilmington, North Carolina. Dearborn explained that the policy of limited command adhered to "the general practice during our Revolutionary War & in present Corps from its establishment." He could not mollify Williams, however, who viewed the situation as humiliating and disgraceful. Reluctantly, Dearborn accepted his resignation.[50]

To "exonerate" himself "of all responsibility" as academy superintendent, Williams notified Dearborn that he had requested Professor Barron to inventory books and instruments. Barron's inventory provides insight into the status of the fledgling academy's library. Barron listed over seventy "books, maps and charts, belonging to the Military Academy at West Point." Five of the books concerned artillery, five focused on engineering and science, nine dealt with fortifications and architecture, and thirteen related to geography, astronomy, and navigation. Fifteen books concentrated on mathematics and surveying, while three concerned military science. About 40 percent of the books were in French, including almost all of the texts on engineering, tactics, and architecture. The inclusion on the list of Franklin's *Miscellanies, Moral and Instructive,* as well as Williams's copy of Bernard Forest de Belidor's *Architecture Hydraulique, ou 'art de condaire, d'Elever, et de Menager les Eaux Pur*

Les Differents Bensions Delavie, suggest that some of the volumes had indeed come from the superintendent's own collection.[51]

Following his resignation in June 1803, Williams remained a private citizen for 22 months before accepting reappointment in the spring of 1805—even though the command issue had not been completely resolved and would cause him to resign once again in 1812. During this interlude, the academy went through a period of near ruin. Under the ineffective commands of first Barron and then Wadsworth, discipline and morale declined. The United States Military Philosophical Society did not meet. In the fall of 1804, Lieutenant Alexander Macomb gave Williams a description of conditions at the academy. "Morals and knowledge thrive little and courts-martial and flogging prevail," he reported. It had become a place "of ignorance & illness" instead of a seat of knowledge. "Never was West Point so much in want of you as at this moment." This reality, Macomb acknowledged, was difficult to face. "I know it must be as painful to you," he wrote, "as it is to me."[52]

Agitation for Williams's return by the Corps of Engineers along with a softening of positions and expressions of compromise extended by both Williams and the administration led to his reinstatement on April 19, 1805. Upon resuming command, Williams immediately undertook to resurrect the military philosophical society. Writing to Jefferson about his intentions, he informed the president that he wanted to extend the society's influence and political standing by inviting into membership "the most distinguished characters in our country." Unsure which congressmen might be considered most scientifically oriented and not wanting to offend any by omission, he proposed including all United States senators and representatives. Jefferson responded with caution, offering his opinion "that if you appoint all the members of the legislature to be members of the institution, it will gratify no particular member" and would not cause any of them to feel any more interest in the institution than they might at present. Jefferson recommended the "judicious selection of a few friends of science or lovers of the military art." Those so honored, Jefferson reasoned, would be inspired "with the desire of actively patronizing" the society's interests.[53]

Williams heeded Jefferson's advice and waited until Congress was back in session in November before extending membership to sixty-seven well-known dignitaries that fall. The expanded society roster now included Federalists such as Nicholas Fish, Robert Troup, John Langdon, and Nicholas Gilman, along with Virginia Republicans William Branch Giles, Meriwether

Lewis, and Secretary of State James Madison. Among other distinguished citizens whose names were added at that or later meetings were John Quincy Adams, Henry Knox, Albert Gallatin, James Monroe, John Marshall, DeWitt Clinton, Joel Barlow, Benjamin Latrobe, Charles Cotesworth Pinckney, Stephen Decatur, Robert Fulton, Eli Whitney, and Bushrod Washington.

Commodore William Bainbridge responded to his invitation by noting that he regretted that such a society had not been earlier instituted and pledged "all the services in my power to promote the views and objects of the Corps." Most invitees responded to their election with similar expressions of support, exactly as Williams had hoped. Senator John Taylor of South Carolina, for example, captured the dominant spirit when he described himself as "Sensible of the importance & necessity of Military Science in every nation, especially in our own Country, at the present period." He said that he was "happy to perceive, that a spirit of inquiry and enterprise is awake." An academy "founded on a basis like yours, & supported by so Honourable a body as the Corps of Engineers, will undoubtedly be of great benefit to society," he affirmed. Taylor pledged that his "influence however small, & effects however feeble, will on all occasions, cheerfully be exerted in its favour." The link that bound Taylor, Bainbridge, and the rest to the United States Military Philosophical Society—and thus the academy—was their common interest in and support of military preparedness, the advancement of engineering sciences, and western exploration. Each member received an engraved certificate bearing the society's motto, *Scientia in Bello Pax,* translated by Williams as "Science in War is the Guarantee of Peace.[54]

As membership expanded to more than 200 over the next few years, meetings of the society occasionally were held away from West Point in Washington, D.C., and New York City. By 1807 the military philosophical society had become international in scope and, according to several scholars of West Point, was seen as a "center of scientific activity in America."[55]

While it would be easy to exaggerate the significance of the society during its relatively brief lifetime (it was discontinued after 1813), its intended reach suggests something about the Jeffersonian vision for the academy. The scope of its mission can be judged at least in part by Williams's expansive definition of science as related to military concerns. "Science," he contended, "is in its own nature so diffuse, that it is almost impossible to designate any dividing lines." He noted that "astronomy, geography and mathematics run into each other at every step. Chymistry and mineralogy are inseparable. The laws of motion, mechanics and projectiles are also interwoven, and in some way or other (although the extreme points may be distant) the gradations become insensible. Military science embraces all these branches." Certainly Jefferson had a similar view of the interconnectedness of scientific inquiry.[56]

Topics addressed at society meetings also attest to the breadth of knowledge considered appropriate for discussion. Williams, for example, read papers describing the falls at Louisville, construction of a floating battery, experiments pertaining to the performance of muskets with barrels of varying lengths, and observations of a solar eclipse. Lieutenant Alden Partridge, a recent graduate, who in 1807 was appointed assistant to the professor of mathematics, presented the results of meteorological observations and experiments in artillery fire. That same year, Barron's replacement as professor of mathematics, the Swiss-born Ferdinand R. Hassler, outlined for the society the need for a coastal survey of the United States. When Hassler introduced analytic trigonometry into his West Point course, he became the first instructor in the country to teach the subject. In 1810 this pioneer resigned his position to become the first superintendent of the United States Coast Survey and professor of mathematics and natural philosophy at Union College.[57]

Another important object of the society was the creation of an impressive collection of scientific texts and instruments. Williams and Hassler, as well as other members of the faculty, sold portions of their own libraries to the academy and made the books that they retained available to members of the group. As more and more titles were acquired by the military philosophical society, West Point became the site of "the most extensive grouping of scientific, engineering and mathematical treatises in the United States" during the early decades of the nineteenth century.[58]

As impressive as these ambitious undertakings were in some respects, West Point struggled during the years of Jefferson's presidency. Unable to appreciate fully the political sophistication of Jefferson's congressional maneuverings on behalf of the academy, Williams complained that the administration neglected the institution and campaigned repeatedly for its relocation to the nation's capital. In fact, one of motives both men shared in enlisting so many legislators and men of scientific and military prominence as members of the society was their hope that they would use their influence to help resituate the academy in Washington. Both men wanted it to become the national school of engineering along lines that earlier had been proposed by Du Pont and later reflected in the plan of Barlow. A move to the nation's capital would place the academy directly under the watchful—and generous—eyes of Jefferson and Congress. Williams anticipated this possibility when he drew up the constitution for the United States Military Philosophical Society with the proviso that its location would be "wherever the Military Academy shall be established."[59]

In January of 1803, Dearborn indicated a possible move by the president to bring the Corps of Engineers to Washington, but stated that it would require "an amendment in the law to authorize such a measure." He noted that "it is not considered practicable or expedient to effect the removal immediately, but if legally authorized, preparations will be made as soon as convenient to do it." He thought it was "doubtful" that it could be accomplished during the present year.[60]

Although other sites from time to time were discussed as possible locations for the academy—Baltimore, Fredericktown, Harpers Ferry, and eventually even Staten Island—Dearborn reassured Williams two years later that "whenever a new site for the Academy is established, it will be in this City." Even though Jefferson and members of his cabinet had indicated their support for moving the school to Washington, Williams remained concerned. He expressed his fears to Dearborn in the summer of 1805 by noting that Jefferson's possible retirement at the end of his first term was cause for alarm. He called for a redoubling of their efforts to bring the institution "to its highest state of perfection before it should be abandoned to its fate." Williams again expressed his belief that only by locating the academy near the president might it become a truly scientific institution "sufficiently extensive to embrace every branch of physics."[61]

Although Jefferson remained in office for a second term, Williams's anxiety was not without basis. He realized that Jefferson's patronage was essential to the success of their plans. Dearborn had informed Williams that only financial considerations kept the president from relocating the academy to Washington. That year passed, however, as did the next, without specific action on the removal project. During this period, Jefferson threw his support behind Barlow's larger project of a national university, but congressional refusal to take up that issue along with presidential concern for constitutional as well as financial limitations may well explain Jefferson's inability to move ahead with Williams's proposal.[62]

Williams tried again in 1807 to secure the academy's relocation. As the possibility of war increased, he wrote to Secretary of the Treasury Gallatin and urged him to use his influence to have the academy moved to Washington. He outlined a plan that he thought would mesh nicely with Gallatin's interest in federally supported national improvements. Williams's proposal called for a faculty of seven full-time instructors as well as a several "honorary professors." The permanent faculty would be composed of members of the Corps of Engineers, while honorary professors would be given short-term appointments to provide lectures and demonstrations on theoretical and practical scientific topics. Williams identified Benjamin Latrobe as an "honorary professor" of civil and military architecture and Adam Seybert for a similar post in chemistry and mineralogy. Both men were ready to accept their appointments, Williams noted, provided that the academy would be relocated in Washington.[63]

Jefferson himself made another concerted effort to effect the academy's removal in 1808. Recognizing "that the scale on which the military academy at West Point was originally established, is become too limited," he directed Williams to "consider the subject" and make recommendations to Congress. Accordingly, Williams prepared a report on "the Progress and Present State of the Military Academy, with some suggested alternations." Williams rehearsed the struggles of the academy and candidly stated that, if Congress had given the president power to appoint instructors and superintend the internal affairs of the academy, "we should, at this day, have a greater number of well instructed young officers than we can boast of." He contended that, despite the restraints imposed upon the institution by its 1802 act of incorporation, the academy had "progressed beyond what could have been expected from its means." Like Jefferson, he had grand designs for the institution, which, he noted, "as it now stands, is like a foundling, barely existing among the mountains, and nurtured at a distance, out of sight, and almost unknown to its legitimate parents."[64]

Removal to Washington was not the only remedy suggested by Williams. He proposed that "the military academy be placed under the direction of the President of the United States in all that does or can relate to it, any thing contained in any former law to the contrary notwithstanding." He called for an expansion of the number of cadets to include civilians as well as military personnel, an increase in faculty positions, and an expansion of the curriculum to include additional work in French, German, chemistry, mineralogy, mathematics, nautical astronomy, geography, navigation and engineering as part of a four year curriculum. His intent was to make the United States Military Academy a great national scientific institution.[65]

In transmitting Williams's report to Congress, Jefferson stated that "the idea suggested by him of removing the institution to this place" was worthy of attention. "Beside the advantage of placing it under the immediate eye of the government," Jefferson advised, a relocated academy would "render its benefits common to the naval department, and will furnish opportunities of selecting on better information, the characters most qualified to filfil the duties which the public service may call for." Jefferson assured Williams while the bill was before Congress that "the state and interests in the Military Academy will not be forgotten," and he was true to his word. When Williams sent to Jefferson a transcription of an unsigned paper regarding militias in the belief that the document could be useful in swaying members of Congress to favor the new plan, Jefferson informed him that he had taken the liberty of having "a sufficient number of copies printed to lay one on the desk of every member without the least indication of the quarter from whence they came."[66]

Congress, however, was persuaded by neither Jefferson's overt nor covert efforts in behalf of Williams's plan. Many in Congress had no enthusiasm for establishing a national engineering school in Washington and certainly had reservations about giving to the president the extensive powers that Williams had proposed. The bill died, and with it perished the dream of a national university with an affiliated military academy located in the nation's capital.

After Jefferson retired from the presidency, he received a letter from his successor. President James Madison wanted to understand a comment that Du Pont had made in a recent communication. "What does he mean," Madison asked Jefferson, "by his desire 'to contribute' to the execution of his project for Education?" Jefferson informed Madison that at one time he had "conceived a hope that Virginia would establish an University" and that Du Pont, at his behest, had written "an elaborate treatise" on the subject. "After I saw that establishment to be desperate," Jefferson noted, he "gave up the view of making it the legatary of my library." He then "conceived the hope, and so mentioned to Dupont, that Congress might establish one at Washington." Du Pont's inquiry, Jefferson concluded, was an expression of his desire "to contribute to the execution of his *plan*" perhaps by "becoming President, or a professor."[67]

Madison would in the years to come declare his allegiance to the project. Upon accepting his role as presidential patron of the United States Military Philosophical Society, Madison informed Williams that "the advantage of the Military Academy, of fixing it at the seat of Govt seems obvious, yet a different bias with some, seconded by peculiarities of opinion in others, may retard it [but] not prevent the change."[68]

Although Madison took up the cause, during his administration congressional critics haggled over appropriations for West Point and debated even the continued existence of the academy itself. William Eustis, Madison's secretary of war, thought the militia was adequate to the nation's needs and saw West Point as a nest for dangerous professional officers. Although he was in time removed from office by Madison, by the eve of the War of 1812, the academy had reached a desperate situation. Faced with war and led by Madison, Congress did authorize a plan of reorganization for the academy in April of 1812, a plan that enlarged the faculty and increased the number of cadets to 250. The academy was still operating at a level beneath the better colleges, but brighter days were ahead. West Point would indeed have an illustrious future, but that future would have to wait until Alden Partridge, Joseph Swift, Sylvanus Thayer, and other men who had been exposed to the vision shared by Jefferson and Williams could build on the foundation that had been laid with the Military Peace Establishment Act of 1802.[69]

There is abundant evidence to point to the important role that the Corps of Engineers played in extending Jefferson's "empire of liberty" into the western territories. The achievements of West Point graduates in exploration, mapping, building canals, bridges, roads, and railways were unrivaled. Francis Wayland, president of Brown University, cited West Point in his 1850 report to that institution's trustees by noting that, "although there are more than 120 colleges in the United States, the West Point Academy has done more to build up the system of internal improvements in the United States than all the colleges combined." West Point never became the scientific branch of a national university as envisioned by Jefferson, Williams, Du Pont, Barlow, and others, but it did establish itself as the first school of engineering in the country and, by the 1820s, was recognized by Harvard reformer George Ticknor as having standards of intellectual discipline that would "cast a reproach on any of the colleges in the country." As Henry Adams—the great-grandson of Jefferson's Federalist predecessor—later wrote, West Point had introduced "a new and scientific character into American life."[70]

Notes

1. John Adams, "Address delivered before the cadets of the U.S.M.A. & citizens of Boston," (14) August 1821, John Adams Papers, USMA Lib. For an account of the event, see David McCullough, *John Adams* (New York, 2001), 635.

2. Adams to TJ, 20 August 1821, *AJL*, 573–74.

3. For Jefferson's recommendation of the academy to Trist, see Elizabeth Trist to Nicholas Trist, 28 November 1818, Trist Papers, University of North Carolina at Chapel Hill Library, Microfilm Reel 1. For Trist's account of academics at West Point, see Trist to James Madison, 1 February 1827, Nicholas P. Trist Papers, Virginia Historical Society. See also Robert Arthur Brent, "Nicholas P. Trist: Biography of a Disobedient Diplomat" (Ph.D. diss., University of Virginia, 1950), 22–23.

4. Robert W. Drexler, *Guilty of Making Peace: A Biography of Nicholas P. Trist* (Lanham, Md., 1991), 21–27. On the precarious financial state of Trist, see Thomas Mann Randolph to Peachy Gilmer, n.d., Thomas Mann Randolph Personal Papers, Letters to the Gilmer Family, 1804–1818, Personal Papers Collection: 18760, item 425, Library of Virginia, Richmond. On Jefferson's efforts to secure appointments for several young men who, like Trist, had been "left without any resource but in himself," see TJ to Jonathan Williams, 23 February 1809, TJ Papers, Lib. Cong.; Williams to TJ, 17 September 1810, ibid. See also Henry Dearborn to Williams, 24 December 1801, War Department Letters Relating to the United States Military Academy 1801–1838, USMA Lib.; TJ to Albert Gallatin, 22 February 1809, Gallatin Papers, New-York Historical Society (hereafter NYHS); E. Trist to N. Trist, 28 November 1818, Trist Papers, University of North Carolina at Chapel Hill Library, Microfilm Reel 1.

5. "An Act Fixing the Military Peace Establishment of the United States," 16 March 1802, *Annals of Congress,* 7th Congress, 1st Session, 1801–1802, 2 *U.S. Statutes,* 1312 (hereafter *Annals*). Jared Mansfield to TJ, 26 January 1821, Jared Mansfield Papers, USMA Lib.; TJ to Mansfield, 13 February 1821, TJ Papers, Lib. Cong.

6. Jefferson's "Bill for the More General Diffusion of Knowledge," "Bill for Amending the Constitution of the College of William and Mary," and "Bill for Establishing a Public Library" may be found in the Appendix to Roy J. Honeywell, *The Educational Work of Thomas Jefferson* (Cambridge, Mass., 1931), 199–210. On his plans for the University of Virginia, see especially (Nathaniel F. Cabell, comp.), *Early History of the University of Virginia as Contained in the Letters of Thomas Jefferson and Joseph C. Cabell* (Richmond, 1856).

7. On Jefferson's shifting reasoning vis-à-vis the constitutionality of establishing the United States Military Academy and his position on the relationship between state militias and a professional army corps, see the companion essays in this volume by David Mayer ("'Necessary and Proper': West Point and Jefferson's Constitutionalism") and Elizabeth D. Samet ("Great Men and Embryo-Caesars: John Adams, Thomas Jefferson, and the Figure in Arms"). See also Leonard D. White, *The Jeffersonians: A Study in Administrative History, 1801–1809* (New York, 1961), 262; Malone, 5:510.

8. See Theodore J. Crackel, *Mr. Jefferson's Army: Political and Social Reform of the Military Establishment, 1801–1809* (New York, 1987), 59–62, and Crackel, "The Founding of West Point: Jefferson and the Politics of Security," *Armed Forces and Society* 7 (Summer 1981): 529–43, and his essay in this volume. Reference to "natural aristocrats" as men of "virtue and talent" is contained in TJ to Adams, 28 October 1813, *AJL*, 387–92.

9. In framing his argument, Crackel dismisses as "unpersuasive" rationales, other than the republicanization of the officer corps, that have been advanced to explain Jefferson's interest in the establishing the academy. We take exception in particular to his rejection of Jefferson's interest in West Point as a "national academy that emphasized science" and its utility as a institution that would "produce graduates who would use their knowledge for the benefit of society." Our argument tracks closely with the assertion of Henry Adams, who maintained that "Great as the influence of this new establishment was upon the army, its bearing on the general edu-

cation of the people was still greater, for the government thus assumed the charge of introducing the first systematic study of science in the United States." See Henry Adams, *History of the United States of America during the Administrations of Thomas Jefferson* (New York, 1986), 205. See also Malone, 5:510; Stephen Ambrose, *Duty, Honor, Country: A History of West Point* (Baltimore, 1966), 15–18.

10. TJ to George Wythe, 13 August 1786, *TJP* 10:243–45; TJ to George Washington, 4 January 178(6) (misdated 1785), ibid., 9:150–52. See also TJ to James Madison, 20 December 1787, ibid., 12:442.

11. For a consideration of sources of Jefferson's ideas on education, see Honeywell, *Educational Work,* chapter 11; Joseph Kett, "Education," in *Thomas Jefferson: A Reference Biography,* ed. Merrill D. Peterson (New York, 1986), 233–51.

12. Herbert B. Adams, *Thomas Jefferson and the University of Virginia* (Washington, D.C., 1888), 21–30; Philip Alexander Bruce, *History of the University of Virginia, 1819–1919,* 5 vols. (New York, 1920), 1:55–60; Honeywell, *Educational Work,* 56–58.

13. TJ to Quesnay de Beaurepaire, 6 January 1788, *TJP* 12:499–500. Bruce (*History of the University of Virginia,* 1:59) speculates that Jefferson's coolness toward the project was occasioned by the fact that he was already contemplating plans for a university "in the shadow of Monticello." Both Bruce and Honeywell (*Educational Work,* 57) credit Quesnay's plan with having influenced Jefferson's plans for the University of Virginia to have separate schools and a bias toward the sciences, but the direct influence is questionable. Jefferson would have been exposed to these ideas by his familiarity with French educational institutions in any case.

14. TJ to Wilson Cary Nicholas, 23 November 1794, *TJP* 28:208–9. Jefferson reminded Nicholas that "the colleges of Edinburgh and Geneva, as seminaries of science, are considered as the two eyes of Europe; while Great Britain and America give preference to the former, and all other countries to the latter." TJ to Francois D'Ivernois, 6 February 1795, ibid., 262–64. Adams (*Jefferson and the University of Virginia,* 45) views this overture as "the historical origin of his [Jefferson's] project for a cosmopolitan university, to be equipped with the best scientific talent that Europe could afford."

15. TJ to Washington, 4 January 178(6), *TJP* 9:150–52. See Joseph J. Ellis, *Founding Brothers: The Revolutionary Generation* (New York, 2001), 154.

16. TJ to Washington, 23 February 1795, *TJP* 28:275–78, emphasis added; Washington to TJ, 15 March 1795, *TJP* 28:306–8. Contrary to the popular view that Washington gave his Potomac shares to the institution that became George Washington University, his shares remained vested in the Commonwealth of Virginia until 1832, when they were transferred to Washington's survivors and eventually lost their value. The James River shares, however, went to Liberty Hall Academy in Lexington, Virginia, which became Washington College and today, Washington and Lee University. See Elmer L. Keysar, *Bricks without Straw: The Evolution of George Washington University* (New York, 1970), and Neil M. Shawen, "Thomas Jefferson and a 'National' University: The Hidden Agenda for Virginia," *Virginia Magazine of History and Biography* 92 (July 1984): 323; Shawen, "The Casting of a Lengthened Shadow: Thomas Jefferson's Role in Determining the Site for a State University in Virginia" (Ed.D. diss., George Washington University, 1980), 400.

17. Gilbert Chinard, "Jefferson and the American Philosophical Society," *Proceedings of the American Philosophical Society* 87 (July 1943): 267; TJ to Elbridge Gerry, 13 May 1797, *TJP* 29:362; TJ to Benjamin Rush, 22 January 1797, ibid., 275.

18. Minutes, 15 December 1797, *Early Proceedings of the American Philosophical Society . . . from 1744 to 1838* (Philadelphia, 1884), 265; Merle M. Odgers, "Education and the American Philosophical Society," *Proceedings of the American Philosophical Society* 87 (July 1943): 12–24; William

Edward Hershey, "A Study of Plans for a System of National Education as Submitted to the American Philosophical Society for Promoting Useful Knowledge—1797," MS, American Philosophical Society, Philadelphia; Jonathan Williams, Secretary of the American Philosophical Society, 17 December 1798, in *Remarks on Education,* Samuel Harrison Smith (Philadelphia, 1798), [i–ii]. The essays by Knox and Smith are most conveniently found in Frederick Rudolph, ed., *Essays on Education in the Early Republic* (Cambridge, Mass., 1965). It is interesting to note that Jefferson, on behalf of the Board of Visitors of Central College (later to become the University of Virginia), offered a professorship to Knox in 1818, but Knox declined the position.

19. Benjamin Rush, "Address to the People of the United States," *The American Museum* (January 1787), 9–11; Rush, "Plan for a Federal University," ibid. (December 1788), 444. See also David Madsen, *The National University: Enduring Dream of the USA* (Detroit, Mich., 1966), 16–19. James Madison and Charles Pinckney were among the framers of the Constitution who advocated specifying that Congress had authority to establish a national university. When a vote was taken on 14 September 1787, four states backed the proposal—Pennsylvania, North and South Carolina, and Virginia—but six were opposed: New Hampshire, Massachusetts, New Jersey, Delaware, Maryland, and Georgia. Connecticut was divided, with Roger Sherman opposing the motion and William Samuel Johnson supporting it. It is interesting to speculate whether the clause would have been inserted had the delegates been able to anticipate the restrictions imposed by the later adoption of the Tenth Amendment. See Madsen, *The National University,* 21–24.

20. See Richard D. Brown, "The Idea of an Informed Citizenry in the Early Republic," in *Devising Liberty: Preserving and Creating Freedom in the New American Republic,* ed. David T. Konig (Stanford, Calif., 1995), 141–77; Rudolph, *Essays,* xi. Compare Allan Oscar Hansen, *Liberalism and American Education in the Eighteenth Century* (1926; New York, 1977) and Rush Welter, *Popular Education and Democratic Thought in America* (New York, 1962), 336–41. On Jefferson's "nationalism" and his hopes for an expanding and consensual union of free republics held together by ties of interests and affection, see Peter S. Onuf, *Jefferson's Empire: The Language of American Nationhood* (Charlottesville, Va., 2000), 2, 12, chapters 2–4.

21. TJ to Joseph Priestley, 18 January 1800, *TJW,* 1070–71.

22. Ibid.; TJ to Priestley, 27 January 1800, ibid., 1072–73.

23. Priestley to TJ, 8 May 1800, *The Correspondence of Jefferson and Dupont de Nemours,* comp. Gilbert Chinard (1931; New York, 1979), 15–18; TJ to Priestley, 11 August 1800, TJ Papers, Lib. Cong.

24. TJ to Du Pont de Nemours, 12 April 1800, *Correspondence of Jefferson and Dupont de Nemours,* 11–12.

25. Pierre Samuel Du Pont de Nemours, *National Education in the United States of America,* trans. Bessie Gardner Du Pont (1812; Newark, Del., 1923), 121–61.

26. L. H. Butterfield, ed., *Diary and Autobiography of John Adams,* 4 vols. (Cambridge, Mass., 1961), 3:467, 441–42. See the accompanying essay by Don Higginbotham, "Military Education before West Point." See also Edgar Denton III, "The Formative Years of the United States Military Academy" (Ph.D. diss., Syracuse University, 1964), 1–26.

27. On Steuben's plan for "Military Academies and Manufacturies," 16 April 1783, see John M. Palmer, *Washington, Lincoln, Wilson: Three War Statesmen* (Garden City, N.Y., 1930), 62–65. Palmer (ibid., 64) contends that Steuben's military academies were to serve as "normal schools" to develop trained officers and instructors for a well-regulated militia." For Jefferson's notes, see TJ, "Memo on Military Academies," 23 November 17(8)3 (misdated 1793), TJ Papers, Lib. Cong. For Washington's "Sentiments on a Peace Establishment," see Washington to Hamilton, 2 May

1783, in *The Writings of George Washington,* 39 vols., ed. John C. Fitzpatrick (Washington, D.C., 1931–44), 26:374–98.

28. See TJ, Notes of a Cabinet Meeting on the President's Address to Congress, 23 November 1793, *TJP* 27:428.

29. Denton, "The Formative Years of the United States Military Academy," 19–21.

30. Hamilton to James McHenry, 23 November 1799, *AHP* 24:69–75.

31. In asking Priestley for his ideas on education on 18 January 1800 (*TJW,* 1070), Jefferson had referred to the Hamilton/McHenry plan as containing branches of science that were "useless to us for ages to come." On French engineering schools, see Ralph Izard to TJ, 10 November 1787, *TJP* 10:338–40; TJ to Izard, 17 July 1788, *TJP* 13:372–73. The prospectus sent by Jefferson has not been preserved among his papers, but Joseph Swift reported serving in "the company of artillery of Captain George Izard," during the summer of 1802. George Izard was the son of Ralph Izard, the United States senator from South Carolina. Swift further reported that "Captain Izard had been educated at the Military School of Metz, in France; and at the Experimental School of Metz, he was esteemed to be an accomplished officer." See Joseph G. Swift, *The Memoirs of Gen. Joseph Gardner Swift* (Worcester, Mass., 1890), 35. See also editor's note regarding Sarsfield to TJ, 28 May 1788, *TJP* 13:211n1: "Sarsfield enclosed two copies of the prospectus of an engineering school, one of them for Ralph Izard, but neither has been found and the school has not been identified, though it was probably the Ecole des Ponts et Chaussées." On the French system of engineering education, see Peter Michael Molloy, "Technical Education and the Young Republic: West Point as America's *Ecole Polytechnique,* 1802–1833" (Ph.D. diss., Brown University, 1975); Janis Langins, "The *Ecole Polytechnique* and the French Revolution: Merit, Militarization, and Mathematics," *Llull* 13 (1990): 93–105.

32. TJ to Peter Carr, 7 September 1814, *TJW,* 1346–52.

33. Ibid.

34. In 1796 the Virginia General Assembly had again considered Jefferson's comprehensive educational plan. The Assembly adopted a grotesquely watered-down version only, a measure that merely authorized local officials to determine whether or not to tax inhabitants for the support of primary schools. The act's voluntary character made it essentially worthless in practice.

35. Joel Barlow to TJ, 15 September 1800, TJ Papers, Lib. Cong.; "Further Extracts from Mr. Barlow's Pamphlet," *National Intelligencer,* 26 November 1806.

36. Barlow to TJ, 23 February 1806, TJ Papers, Lib. Cong.; TJ to Barlow, 24 February 1806, *TJW,* 1160. See also James Woodress, *A Yankee's Odyssey: The Life of Joel Barlow* (New York, 1958), 241–43; Charles Burr Todd, *Life and Letters of Joel Barlow, LL.D.: Poet, Statesman, Philosopher* (New York, 1886), 208–9; Carla Mulford, "Joel Barlow," *American National Biography,* 24 vols., ed. John A. Garraty and Mark C. Carnes (New York, 1999), 2:166–68. Barlow's *Prospectus,* initially published in the *National Intelligencer* (1 August, 24 November, and 26 November 1806), can be found in William K. Bottorff and Arthur Ford, eds., *The Works of Joel Barlow,* 2 vols. (Gainesville, Fl., 1970).

37. TJ, Sixth Annual Message, 2 December 1806, *TJW,* 530–31; Honeywell, *Educational Work,* 62–64.

38. Woodress, *A Yankee's Odyssey,* 243; TJ to Joel Barlow, 10 December 1807, TJ Papers, Lib. Cong.

39. On Williams, see Dorothy S. Zuersher, "Benjamin Franklin, Jonathan Williams, and the United States Military Academy" (Ph.D. diss., University of North Carolina at Greensboro, 1974), 60–82. For correspondence on mountain measurements and Jefferson's mould-board plow, see TJ to Williams, 3 July 1796, *TJP* 29:139–40. The two books Williams sent Jefferson were Henri Othon von Scheel, *A Treatise of Artillery,* trans. Jonathan Williams (Philadelphia, 1800) and

Jonathan Williams, *Thermometrical Navigation* (Philadelphia, 1799). See Williams to TJ, 7 March 1801, TJ Papers, Lib. Cong.; TJ to Williams, 14 March 1801, ibid.; E. Millicent Sowerby, comp., *Catalogue of the Library of Thomas Jefferson,* 5 vols. (Washington, D.C., 1952–59), 1:311, 525. That Jefferson was intent on privileging political and scientific qualifications over military expertise is further attested to in his appointment of Robert Livingston as his secretary of the navy. "Republicanism is so rare in those parts which possess nautical skill, that I cannot find it allied there to the other qualifications," he explained to Livingston. "Tho' you are not a nautical by profession, yet your residence and your mechanical science qualify you as well as a gentleman can possibly be, and sufficiently to enable you to choose under-agents perfectly qualified, and to superintend their conduct." TJ to Robert R. Livingston, 14 December 1800, TJ Papers, Lib. Cong.

40. *Annals,* 1312; Denton, "The Formative Years of the United States Military Academy," 24–28; Zuersher, "Benjamin Franklin, Jonathan Williams, and the United States Military Academy," 89–95, quotation at 94. Dearborn to Williams, 24 March 1806 (as cited in Crackel, *Mr. Jefferson's Army,* 59).

41. Williams to Major Decius Wadsworth, 13 May 1802, Williams Papers, USMA Lib.

42. Williams to Henry Dearborn, 14 February 1802, ibid.

43. Dearborn to Williams, 31 May 1802, ibid.; Dearborn to Williams, 9 July 1802, ibid.

44. Williams to Dearborn, 14 February 1802, ibid.; Williams to Wadsworth, 13 May 1802, ibid. Dearborn to Williams, 24 March 1806, Records of the Office of the Secretary of War, Letters Sent—Military Affairs, II, 446, National Archives, Washington, D.C. (hereafter LSMA) as quoted by Zuersher, "Benjamin Franklin, Jonathan Williams, and the United States Military Academy," 108; Williams to Dearborn, 9 August 1802; Dearborn to Williams, 5 June 1805, USMA Lib. Compare Crackel, *Mr. Jefferson's Army,* 59.; Dearborn to Williams, 28 October 1805, LSMA, II, 392; compare Zuersher, "Benjamin Franklin, Jonathan Williams, and the United States Military Academy," 108; Molloy, "Technical Education and the Young Republic," 289.

45. Denton, "The Formative Years of the United States Military Academy," 32–35; Zuersher, "Benjamin Franklin, Jonathan Williams, and the United States Military Academy," 94–95; Ambrose, *Duty, Honor, Country,* 25–26; Swift, *Memoirs,* 40. After his dismissal from his teaching post at West Point, George Baron went on to become founder in 1804 of the *Mathematical Correspondent,* the first specialized scientific journal in the United States. See George H. Daniels, *American Science in the Age of Jackson* (New York, 1968), 15.

46. Papers of the United States Military Philosophical Society, NYHS (hereafter Papers, USMPS).

47. Constitution of the United States Military Philosophical Society, 12 November 1802, TJ Papers, Lib. Cong.; Williams to TJ, 12 December 1803, ibid. See Sidney Forman, "The United States Military Philosophical Society, 1802–1813: Scientia in Bello Pax," *WMQ,* 3rd ser., 2 (July 1945): 273–85; Sidney Forman, *West Point: A History of the United States Military Academy* (New York, 1950), 20–35; Arthur P. Wade, "A Military Offspring of the American Philosophical Society," *Military Affairs* 38 (October 1974): 103–7. In 1807 the Society's constitution was amended to permit membership of non-Americans.

48. Williams to TJ, 12 December 1802, TJ Papers, Lib. Cong.; TJ to Williams, 25 December 1802, ibid.

49. Decius Wadsworth to Williams, 17 January 1803, Williams Papers, USMA Lib.; Jared Mansfield to Williams, 31 January 1803, ibid. Jefferson and Dearborn were "duly elected" as members of the United States Philosophical Society at a meeting held on 4 July 1803.

50. See Williams, "Report on Circumstances Regarding his Resigning from the Corps of Engineers," m.s., USMA Lib.; Williams to Joseph Swift, 9 October 1812, ibid. Compare Zuersher,

"Benjamin Franklin, Jonathan Williams, and the United States Military Academy," 105–7; Denton, "The Formative Years of the United States Military Academy," 34; Forman, *West Point*, 26–29; Ambrose, *Duty, Honor, Country*, 31–32. The ranking officer of the Corps of Artillerists with whom Williams was in conflict was George Izard, the son of Ralph Izard; see n. 30.

51. "Inventory of Books, Maps and Charts, belonging to the Military Academy at West Point," Williams Papers, USMA Lib. See also Alan C. Aimone, "Genesis of the U.S. Military Academy Library," unpublished manuscript in authors' possession. As to Jefferson's contribution to the early library, an examination of Sowerby in comparison to the 1803 USMA Lib. inventory indicates that he probably suggested titles dealing with mathematics, geography, astronomy, and surveying with little or no input as to military science and artillery titles. Molloy, "Technical Education and the Young Republic," 287–88; Forman, *West Point*, 281; Joe Albree, Dabid C. Arney, and V. Frederick Rickey, *A Station Favorable to the Pursuits of Science: Primary Materials in the History of Mathematics at the United States Military Academy* (Providence, R.I., 2000).

52. Alex Macomb to Williams, 8 October 1804, Williams Papers, USMA Lib. Compare Denton, "The Formative Years of the United States Military Academy," 43.

53. Williams to TJ, 18 June 1805, USMPS Papers, USMA Lib.; TJ to Williams, 14 July 1805, TJ Papers, Lib. Cong.

54. Minutes, 4 November 1805, Papers, USMPS; John Taylor to Williams, 29 January 1806, ibid.; William Bainbridge to Williams, 16 October 1807, as quoted in Denton, "The Formative Years of the United States Military Academy," 47–48. Williams authored the society's motto and solicited advice from Jefferson, Barlow, and others regarding the seal. See Williams to TJ, 6 February 1806, Papers, USMPS; TJ to Williams, 23 February 1806, ibid.; Barlow to TJ, 12 February 1806, ibid. For an analysis of strains between Federalists and Republicans over the meaning of science, see Linda K. Kerber, *Federalists in Dissent: Imagery and Ideology in Jeffersonian America* (Ithaca, N.Y., 1970), chapter 3.

55. Forman (*West Point*, 31) notes that "by 1807 the society was of national importance." See also Ambrose, *Duty, Honor, Country*, 32.

56. Williams, "Address to the USMPS," 30 January 1808, as quoted in Zuersher, "Benjamin Franklin, Jonathan Williams, and the United States Military Academy," 99–101.

57. Ibid.; Minutes of the United States Military Philosophical Society, NYHS; Forman, *West Point*, 29; Forman, "United States Military Philosophical Society," 278–79. Ambrose, *Duty, Honor, Country*, 30–31. Barron was dismissed from West Point after being charged with "suffering prostitutes to be the companions of his quarters and table—(testimony does not look into the chamber), thereby setting an example injurious to the morals of youth and disgraceful to the institution." See Williams to Swift, 11 February 1807, USMA Lib.; Ambrose, *Duty, Honor, Country*, 32; Denton, "The Formative Years of the United States Military Academy," 54.

58. Molloy, "Technical Education and the Young Republic," 287–88; Forman, "The United States Military Philosophical Society," 281.

59. Constitution of the United States Military Philosophical Society, TJ Papers, Lib. Cong.

60. Dearborn to Williams, 13 January 1803, Williams Papers, USMA Lib.; Molloy, "Technical Education and the Young Republic," 317, 325.

61. Dearborn to Williams, 19 June 1805, USMA Lib.; Williams to Dearborn, 8 June 1805, USMA Lib. Compare Molloy, "Technical Education and the Young Republic," 317.

62. See TJ, Sixth Annual Message, 2 December 1806, *TJW*, 529–30. TJ to Gallatin, November 14, 1806, Albert Gallatin Papers, NYHS. Jefferson's draft notes for the address to Gallatin contain the notation "The university, this proposition will pass the states in the winter of 1807.8. & Congress will not meet, & consequently cannot act on it till the winter of 1808.9."

63. Williams to Gallatin, 19 September 1807, Williams Papers, USMA Lib.; Molloy, "Technical Education and the Young Republic," 319.

64. Williams to Dearborn, Report to Congress, 18 March 1808, *Annals,* 2807–12; compare Molloy, "Technical Education and the Young Republic," 319–26; TJ, Special Message to Congress, 18 March 1808, in L&B, 3:471–72.

65. Williams to Dearborn, Report to Congress, 18 March 1808, *Annals,* 2807–12.

66. TJ, Special Message to Congress, 18 March 1808, in L&B, 3:471–72; TJ to Williams, 28 October 1808, TJ Papers, Lib. Cong.; Williams to TJ, 31 October 1808, ibid.; TJ to Williams, 23 November 1808, ibid.

67. James Madison to TJ, 6 October 1809, in James Morton Smith, ed., *The Republic of Letters: The Correspondence between Thomas Jefferson and James Madison 1776–1826,* 3 vols. (New York, 1995), 3:1603; TJ to Madison, 9 October 1809, ibid., 1604. For Jefferson's offer of his library to a university in Virginia, if one were established by the state legislature, see TJ to Littleton Waller Tazewell, 5 January 1805, *TJW,* 1152–53.

68. Madison to Williams, 15 July 1809, Papers, USMPS.

69. Molloy, "Technical Education and the Young Republic," 326–28; Ambrose, *Duty, Honor, Country,* 33–37.

70. William H. Goetzmann, *Army Exploration in the American West 1803–1863,* (New Haven, Conn.: 1959). Henry Adams, *History of the United States of America During the Administrations of James Madison* (New York, 1986), 1341–42; Wayland and Ticknor as quoted in R. Ernest Dupuy, *Sylvanus Thayer: Father of Technology in the United States* (West Point, N.Y., 1958), 14–15. Wayland's "Report to the Corporation of Brown University" can be found in Richard Hofstadter and Wilson Smith, eds., *American Higher Education: A Documentary History* (Chicago, 1961).

Developing "Republican Machines"

West Point and the Struggle to Render the Officer Corps Safe for America, 1802–33

SAMUEL J. WATSON

The United States Military Academy endured a troubled childhood. Indeed, many of the questions that tried the early academy—the quest for practical utility, the balance between moral, physical, and intellectual discipline and democracy—still persist, and should always persist, for they reflect central tensions over the nature, production, and employment of expertise, power, and authority in American society.[1] Yet their expression has changed, and substantially for the better: today West Point addresses these complex issues through a process of calmly reasoned discussion, rather than the acrimonious disputes over the personal rights of officers and cadets common before 1820.

This essay seeks the significance of the early military academy in contingency and evolution, process and outcome. Connecting intent, process, and outcome is essential in evaluating the qualities actually fostered at early West Point and assessing its effectiveness as an instrument of Jefferson's intent and American national policy, both during and after his presidency. To do so, this essay addresses the missions West Point graduates were called on to perform, the visions of the early superintendents and the problems faced by the academy during its first decade and a half, the outcome of the early academy's evolution under the superintendency of Sylvanus Thayer between 1817 and 1833, and West Point's long-term impact on army and nation during the nineteenth century, relating the careers of the academy's graduates to the learning and socialization environment created by its pedagogy and discipline.

This essay also attempts to suggest the degree to which problems and solutions were the results of actions by specific individuals, particularly those at West Point, and more particularly the superintendents. Every successful revolution must develop means to control the armed force that helped win the revolutionary struggle, and one of the basic dilemmas every American faced was to reconcile the culture's drive toward liberal individualism with the need for institutions to temper conflict and further the common welfare—to balance individual liberty with collective obligation and order. Doing so had proven a severe test for the officers and aspiring gentlemen of the Continental army and remained difficult for the officers and civilian politicians of the early republic, who strove to reconcile the often rigid demands of republican selflessness and virtue with the republican zeal (especially common among aspiring gentlemen) for personal independence and the increasingly competitive, opportunistic individualism of an expanding commercial society.[2]

Ultimately, West Point would contribute to the reconciliation of individual and community through the self-discipline and self-regulation of the sort of "republican machines" sought by Benjamin Rush—men who joined in the Enlightenment quest for cosmopolitan knowledge, purposeful rationality, system, moderation, and justice to pursue careers not just as military officers and scientists but also as agents of the fledgling national center, fusing technical knowledge, mental and military discipline, cosmopolitan gentility, and republican dedication. Graduates possessing these qualities would provide broad-minded leadership conducive to the development of ordered liberty on the disordered frontiers of the expanding nation. If enlightened republican government was to be the science of politics and society, West Point alumni were, in fact, among its leading figures, an administrative and executive cadre more closely akin to a national—meaning both nationally oriented and nationwide—managerial class than any other American social or occupational group prior to the Civil War.[3]

Given his closely related interests in science, education, and republican government, it seems likely that Jefferson recognized that the military academy could serve several related purposes. Although neither Meriwether Lewis nor William Clark were graduates, expeditions like theirs must have highlighted the public utility of an institution that could train scientists and engineers, their sense of purpose made more focused and reliable by imbibing a sense of responsibility to the nation through federally sponsored education, facilitating further, more readily planned and sustained explorations of western lands for national rather than local or private benefit. Expansionist efforts like these would help sustain the rough equality of access to land and opportunity Jeffersonians considered essential to the Republic's future. Indeed, the very idea of a national university implied the creation of a national center that would go beyond specifically military training, and perhaps beyond scientific or academic education, to socialize aspiring public servants in a broader—national—civil vision of their future utility and accountability to the public, not unlike today's vision of "leaders of character to serve the nation."[4]

The military academy served all these purposes. By the time the early academy had matured in the 1820s and 1830s, it was producing not just narrowly focused engineers, scientists, and technicians but well-drilled company officers and cosmopolitan technocrats as well. These men provided a sound base of technical knowledge as well as the genteel manners necessary to work harmoniously with civilian leaders, familiarity with comrades and attitudes from across the nation, and the internalized self-discipline fostered by the precepts of duty, honor, and country. Equipped with these qualities, graduates and officers could act as public administrators and local representatives of the federal government in the nation's expanding borderlands, while serving as civil engineers surveying and constructing its transportation infrastructure.[5]

In the early republic, rhetoric about the people and the militia notwithstanding, it was the socially and politically reliable military agency of the federal government—the increasingly professional, meaning both capable and above all accountable, regular or standing army—that explored much of the West, secured New Orleans (both in 1804 and, in large part, 1815), held the Mississippi River and Louisiana Territory, arrested Aaron Burr and other filibusters, kept peace with Spain, seized Florida, crushed Tecumseh's Indian confederacy, expropriated native lands throughout the southeast, designed the fortifications that defended American ports during the War of 1812, and surveyed the routes and supervised the construction of many of the nation's early roads, canals, and railroads. (Like the volunteers of the Civil War, the militia forces so vaunted by politicians usually acted under the direction of regular officers.) In doing so, the regular army, led largely by academy graduates, proved crucial to realizing Jefferson's vision of an agrarian society providing for future generations through territorial expansion. In the process, the West

Point–educated officer corps became the closest thing to a national administrative—and executive—cadre in the early and mid-nineteenth-century United States.[6]

These developments appeared unlikely in 1802, 1810, or even 1815. The early academy's progress was hampered by limited funding, the need to employ the few experienced engineers building fortifications, and the difficulty of coordinating plans and actions given the sluggishness of communications during the first decade of the nineteenth century. Yet officials held high hopes for the institution. Academy archivist Sidney Forman once observed that Colonel Jonathan Williams, the chief engineer, inspector of fortifications, and first superintendent, wanted cadets to develop "a spirit of scientific inquiry, a willingness to continue their studies after graduation, and a comprehension of the broad horizon of their profession in a new, expanding country."

Writing to Jefferson in 1807, Williams conveyed his hope that the president would receive "the applauses of a grateful country for having established a national academy on such an extensive and advantageous scale, as to ensure, that whatever future armies their justice, safety & honor may require shall be officered by men well educated in every branch of military Science." Williams always stressed that the Corps of Engineers and the academy should serve national ends, especially those of defense (which he identified largely with the construction of a modern system of coastal fortifications). He cautioned Major Decius Wadsworth to "never lose sight of our leading *star,* which is not a little Mathematical School, but a great national establishment." Its mission, he said, was "to turn out characters which, in the course of time, shall equal any in Europe. . . . Could we arrive at such a state . . . we may defy foreign Invaders of all nations."[7]

One of Williams's chief innovations was the United States Military Philosophical Society, which he established with high hopes in 1802. Yet the society's limits—particularly the average attendance of a mere nine officers, faculty members, and cadets at its meetings—illustrate a dichotomy that plagued the early academy. While some cadets came to West Point with extensive college experience and were able to proceed quickly by tutorial and self-study, the majority were substantially less prepared or mature. Many languished or fell by the wayside and left the academy and the army. Like the Military Philosophical Society, the early academy catered to a self-selecting elite.[8]

This did not bother Williams, who saw the Corps of Engineers as a technocratic elite akin to the French Corps du Génie educated at the École Polytechnique. Such exalted hopes both reflected and intensified Williams's concern for forging connections with the nation's elite, and redoubled his desire to move the academy to Washington, where he believed a more cosmopolitan audience would produce funds for a more advanced institution, a vision that made him reluctant to request money for more permanent facilities at West Point. Williams's elevated concept of the Corps of Engineers as an elite within the army also led to his resignation when he was denied the authority to command troops in 1803, to his acceptance of reappointment in 1805, and to his second and final resignation in 1812, when again he was denied command authority. Faced with an apparently decrepit academy, Williams sent his son, Cadet Alexander J. Williams, away from West Point to Dartmouth. In these instances Williams's example was damaging, implicitly sanctioning the resignations of junior engineer officers—which were common before 1812—and an elitism that spurred divisions among officers by encouraging an overly narrow vision of military education and professionalism.[9]

Williams was not solely to blame for the academy's problems, for he was constantly called away to oversee coastal fortifications and was unable to attend consistently to the routine of cadet education. Perhaps because of its interest in moving the academy to Washington, the Jefferson administration proved slow to press Congress for increased appropriations or statutory reform. Yet Williams persevered in putting forth plans for a more exalted academy. As early as 1802, he tried to establish a standardized curriculum, but Congress took little action to provide the necessary instructors or funding. By 1808 Williams had become despondent. His report that year was chiefly a call for more professors (there were still only three), a recommendation not accepted until 1812, and a proposal that Congress grant the president wide discretion over the academy's faculty, facilities, and curriculum—a degree of autonomy the legislature was unwilling to accept. Despite Williams's efforts and the buildup of American forces beginning in 1808, no additional legislation passed until 1812.[10]

By 1810 the academy was suffering from confusion of mission and purpose, leading to disorder and extended absences without leave among the cadets. Hoping to improve instruction and discipline but too busy with fortification duty to stay at West Point himself, Williams sent his protégé, Captain Joseph Swift, to take command in 1807 and unsuccessfully sought Lieutenant Colonel Jared Mansfield's return for that purpose in 1809. Lieutenant

Alden Partridge (class of 1806) took Swift's place as acting superintendent when the latter was called to fortification duty in 1808. Having failed in his quest to move the academy to Washington, Williams set his sights on New York City. But desperation over the academy's uncertain prospects led him to ponder resignation before he was able to send Captain Charles Gratiot (class of 1806) and Lieutenant Sylvanus Thayer (class of 1808) to help Partridge supervise the institution.

Yet dissension among officers continually plagued Williams's efforts. Gratiot was instructed to support Partridge, who had become the senior professor by virtue of several resignations, in the latter's execution of "the rules established for the particular administration of academical superintendence," but Partridge took the loss of his other functions badly and sought a leave of absence. Indeed, Partridge's behavior in 1810 prefigured both Williams's resignation in 1812 and his own reactions to the staff, faculty, secretary of war, and president during the years that followed. Partridge advised Williams about "the conditions upon which I am willing to continue my duties at the Academy" and demanded that, despite Gratiot's seniority, "all Academy regulations, and also the cadets, be exclusively and in every respect under my direction." Williams had set a precedent for such demands with his own resignation when he was refused command authority in 1803, but he did not accept such overt insubordination within the Corps of Engineers, and Partridge was forced to claim illness—a gentleman's agreement to smooth over conflict, but also a dereliction of duty on both officers' parts—in order to secure the leave he sought.[11]

Attention from civil authorities increased during 1810. That April President James Madison's secretary of war, William Eustis, promulgated new curricular and disciplinary regulations designed by Williams, Gratiot, Thayer, and Partridge. These established minimal entrance qualifications, including "good moral character," "a sound constitution," and being "well-versed in the English language" and composition, and required that cadets appear promptly and do four years service in return for their appointments. Even so, cadets were still allowed to progress through the academy at their own pace, graduating in anywhere from six months' to six years' time. Indeed, Eustis did much to hinder the academy, appointing only six cadets in 1809 and 1810, and none in 1811, and cutting the salaries of the civilian instructors by a third (which led two of the three to resign). Eager to get future officers into the field to gain experience, he commissioned cadets from West Point, contrary to the new regulations, without their passing graduation exams. Eustis also spoke of requiring graduates to do service and gain experience as enlisted men before being commissioned, an idea he was persuaded to drop.[12]

The secretary's actions proceeded partly from Republican suspicions of abstraction, expense, and aristocracy, and partly from the need to train more infantry and artillery officers to help drill the large forces raised in Jefferson's 1808 military buildup, an expansion anticipated to continue should tensions with Britain not diminish. In December 1810 President Madison presented Williams's latest recommendations to Congress—the first mention of the academy any president made in an annual message. His address suggested a quest to train combat arms commanders rather than the school of fortress design envisioned by Williams, referring to "military science," "military instruction," and "the elementary principles of the art of war." The curriculum changed with the times, retreating from hopes that West Point might form a scientific elite at a time when trained engineers were busy supervising fortification construction. Mathematics, surveying, and "artificer's work" aside, engineering (including fortification design and construction, which had been part of the curriculum in 1809) per se was not included in the 1810 curriculum; graduates were instead to attain a "perfect" knowledge of the drill movements of infantry and artillery.[13]

Cadets now received formal command and administrative experience. There was to be a cadet adjutant and officer of the day, offices that appeared first in Partridge's "Academy Orders" in 1809, along with a provision for cadets to lead and instruct drill. Yet Eustis undermined the institution's discipline and raison d'etre by reassigning those dismissed from the academy to other duties in the army; he even commissioned them as officers. The 1810 regulations, and the stipulations of the law of 1812 that drew on them, were only sporadically enforced before 1817, though this surely resulted in part from the turmoil that accompanied a poorly planned mobilization for war.[14]

Williams resigned for a final time in 1812, when he was denied command over troops in New York harbor. He acted prematurely and, in fact, insubordinately, writing to his successor Joseph Swift "that the condition upon which I alone accepted my Commission having failed I of course became absolved from all obligation," and "that as my resignation was on the ground of failure in the contract, acceptance in the usual way was not required." Yet Williams knew the terms of his service—he had already been denied command authority over troops—and quit when he was unable to change them.

Officers are not usually permitted to resign during wartime, but it is hardly surprising that Eustis was happy to have a valid reason to let the self-centered engineer go.[15]

Leading army historian William Skelton observes that "in many respects, Williams's career epitomizes the amateurism of military leadership in the early national period." Similarly, Skelton suggests that it is tempting to see the Corps of Engineers and auxiliary institutions like the United States Military Philosophical Society as the nucleus of a professional culture in the pre–War of 1812 officer corps, but observes that doing so would be an exaggeration. Skelton credits Williams for inspiring the officers of the corps to a sense of their profession, but he recognizes that neither the military philosophical society nor the academy achieved institutional momentum independent of, or sustainable without, Williams's inconsistent stimulus. Williams's conduct as superintendent displayed none of the persistence later shown by Sylvanus Thayer, who remained in the army for more than half a century, well after he left the superintendency for other duties. Williams's resignations set a damaging example that would reverberate in the behavior of his protégés for another decade. Williams once told Swift that "duty must be paramount to every other consideration," but Williams, Swift, and Swift's protégé, Partridge, would each conclude their academy and army careers by resigning when they subordinated duty to self-centered conceptions of their rights as individuals.[16]

Yet the careers of many other early graduates tell a different story, one of dedication to the pursuit of military science and inspiration to serve, for several made the army their career, providing unprecedented continuity in the leadership of the technical branches to which they belonged. Walker Armistead, for example, was a member of the class of 1803, who, from 1818 to 1821, succeeded Swift as chief engineer before commanding an artillery regiment until his death in 1845. Gratiot also served as chief engineer (1828–38), as did the class of 1805's Joseph G. Totten (1838–63), the Corps of Engineers' representative on the board that planned the "Third System" of American coastal defense fortifications between 1818 and the Civil War. John Anderson (class of 1807) and John J. Abert (class of 1811) provided leadership for the army's topographical engineers until 1861; George Bomford, a class of 1805 graduate, whose appointment as a cadet Swift claimed to have secured, earned distinction as the inventor of the "Columbiad" shell-firing gun and as the army's chief of ordnance from 1821 until his death in 1848.

Other engineer officers went on to serve very effectively in all theaters of the War of 1812, and all but Partridge (who remained at the academy throughout the war) received honors or promotions. Alexander Macomb (a cadet at West Point in 1801, although not a graduate), who Williams sought to take command of the corps he had just abandoned, left the engineers to serve in a variety of important roles as staff officer and field commander, returning to command the corps between 1821 and 1828 before concluding his career as commanding general of the army from 1828 until his death in 1841. Williams's value as a source of inspiration is evident in the engineer officers' pleas that he return after his first resignation, in their 1804 petition for his reappointment and Totten's subsequent return to the Corps of Engineers, and in the graduation of fifteen cadets in 1806, after only ten had graduated from 1802 to 1805. Key graduates of the Williams era—Swift, Partridge, Thayer, Rene DeRussy (superintendent after Thayer, to 1838), Gratiot, and Totten—carried forth Williams's sense of "the national importance of a military academy," and would eventually make his vision a reality.[17]

Swift was the first of Williams's protégés and the first graduate of the United States Military Academy; he named his first son after Williams and another for Williams's son Alexander, who was killed in the defense of Fort Erie in 1814. He came from the same upper-middle-class, moderately genteel—and moderately Federalist—background as Williams. He responded eagerly to the opportunity to associate himself with the cosmopolitan learning of the Corps of Engineers and the rapid military advancement and social connections it offered; his service as a government engineer encouraged him to adopt an enduring and essentially nonpartisan nationalism.

Swift felt the same responsibility for national defense and scientific development as Williams did. In fact, Swift's 1808 proposal for reforming the academy was more comprehensive, detailed, and positive than Williams's report of that year. Swift outlined a scheme for grouping and instructing cadets by graduating class, suggested a minimum of three years' instruction, and sought to separate the duties of superintendent from those of the chief engineer so that each could concentrate and specialize in his work. But the core of Swift's proposals was a more socially attuned and ethically informed curriculum, the first real alternative to Williams's scientific-technical vision of education presented by anyone connected with the academy. Swift advocated hiring a professor of history and geography to take on duties later assigned to the chaplain (first appointed in 1813); he added ethical instruction to the chaplain's responsibilities in 1814. He stressed the need for a more liberal education and sought to include socialization in genteel manners in order to prepare future officers for effective interaction with the elites of the local communities where they would be assigned, a lesson from his own experiences dealing with local leaders while directing fortification construction in North Carolina and New York City.[18]

In 1815, with the war at an end, it appeared that many sons of the elite—to whom Swift, like most early national leaders, looked for the government's officers—were eager to resign from the army in order to enter civilian colleges, where they could gain the liberal education expected of gentlemen. Swift hoped to prevent the erosion of the officer corps' social prestige and its potential for gaining acceptance in American political culture. He added liberal arts to the curriculum to provide for more genteel socialization, hoping to rejoin the authority of science, social respectability, and military professionalism along cosmopolitan, moderate Federalist lines acceptable to the Republicans who had become increasingly nationally minded because of the war.

Like Williams, Swift proposed that instruction be given in riding and fencing; he soon added dancing, and his letters to acting superintendent Partridge stressed that cadets be able to communicate clearly in writing. "The handwriting & spelling of the cadets must be attended to," he observed; "keeping the books clean to be examined every Saturday morning" was so important that "neglect or carelessness [was] to be punished by arrest or confinement." Swift's intent was supported by Secretary of War William H. Crawford and sanctioned in the 1816 regulations, which observed that "the study of the English grammar is deemed indispensable" and mandated that new cadets be able to "read distinctly and pronounce correctly; to write a fair legible hand." These qualities would enhance both the officer's social prestige and his ability to communicate orders amid the chaos of battle.[19]

A moderate Federalist in an age of religious revivals, Swift also expressed greater concern for cadets' spiritual lives. He secured the appointment of the first chaplain, an Episcopalian (as were all the pre–Civil War chaplains), in 1813. Swift's understanding of the way moderate religiosity, genteel manners and decorum, and learned discourse on current and cosmopolitan subjects helped officers to maintain social respectability among civilian elites came together in this office. The position included duties as the first professor of history—a subject that came to include world, American, and Revolutionary War topics under the 1816 regulations, as well as geography—which was to include the government and economy of foreign nations—and ethics, which included "natural and political law." All these subjects were combined in a course that had so much to cover that it was easily criticized for superficiality. Yet, at least one hundred instructional hours, the equivalent of two or more semesters today, were eventually devoted to the course. This was the first explicit effort at ethical development at West Point, which needed instruction in moral philosophy more than most civilian colleges, given the widespread popular mistrust of standing armies and military professionalism that still existed in 1815.[20]

Swift also anticipated Partridge's desire to diffuse military science to the militia, proposing to open West Point to some aspiring militia officers and supporting the creation of a separate, probably state-run academy for others. Yet Swift refused to undermine the national military academy, the unifying influence of which he considered increasingly important as sectional tensions grew after 1819; four decades later, just before the *Dred Scott* decision in 1857, Swift referred to the academy as "the only national institution in the Union, save the supreme court," an attitude that permeates graduates' papers.[21]

Swift thus displayed the broadest vision of any superintendent before Thayer. He also put his money where his mouth was, using his New York City connections (cultivated during his time there as director of the local fortifications) to secure a loan to sustain the academy when Congress failed to provide funds for 1815. Swift faced the same dilemmas as Williams, however, and his efforts addressed many of the same problems. Like Williams, Swift found it physically impossible to superintend the academy while inspecting and supervising the construction of coastal fortifications up and down the eastern seaboard, and he never remained at the academy long enough to foster anything more than a temporary improvement in the lax cadet discipline. Swift agreed with Williams that the academy would wither in the isolation of West Point and repeatedly tried to move it to Washington or New York to enhance the publicity they assumed would bring greater recognition and appropriations. Yet the politicking necessary to pursue this objective, along with the centralization of the army's staff departments in Washington after the war, kept Swift in the capital when he was not engaged in supervising coastal defenses, so he only visited West Point intermittently.[22]

Thus the two first chief engineers, who as the intermediaries between the president and secretary of war and the senior officer actually at the academy were the men most responsible for its development, shared mental reservations about the existing institution's potential and focused their energies on transforming it instead of attending to daily operations. However "visionary" in today's sense of the word, this lack of attention to detail seriously constrained the improvement of the academy as it actually existed and must be considered one of the principal reasons for its early difficulties.

Neither Williams nor Swift provided the consistent, hands-on direction expected of their successors. Their social and political connections, and the consciousness of publicity and influence these fostered, led them to pursue an ideal, while actual conditions remained in flux until new civilian leaders, Secretary of War John C. Calhoun and President James Monroe, forced change on the academy. Under the administrative circumstances of the early republic, in which the limits of technology and the heavy burdens borne by an insufficient number of executive personnel made long-distance communication and supervision difficult, officials were selected with the expectation that they could operate autonomously to fulfill executive branch intent while adhering to law. The constitutional self-constraint and administrative incapacity of the Jefferson and Madison administrations deserve some of the blame for the controversies and indecision that wracked the academy, but Williams and Swift deserve full shares as well.

Extreme rights-consciousness—the desire to be honored by others, to be recognized as a gentleman among equals having no superior authorized to alter existing duty relationships chosen by the individual officer—drove both Williams and Swift to resign rather than continue in the service of their country. Swift's cosmopolitanism and admiration for French engineers ran head-on into his nationalism and personal pride when President Monroe appointed a Frenchman, Simon Bernard, to serve on the board planning coastal fortifications in 1818. Although Bernard had no command authority over American officers, he was given the honorary rank of brigadier general, one higher than any held by American engineers. Swift believed that the appointment showed a lack of confidence in his competence, bringing his authority as chief engineer into question. While he initially determined to "adopt a mild and steady course of duty" and directed the American engineers to follow Bernard's guidance, he soon chafed at the Frenchman's influence and resigned. Swift disapproved of "concert[ing] to interfere with the public service," however, and refused to organize or endorse a mass resignation protesting Bernard's appointment. Thus, despite his Federalism, his vacillation concerning Partridge, and his resignation, Swift remained faithful to a publicly apolitical, or at least antipartisan, stance and counseled other officers to follow his example.

This, perhaps, was his most significant contribution to the officer corps' professional culture—one that presaged Thayer's affirmation of duty to country as the officer's paramount obligation.[23]

Swift's greatest practical failing was allowing Partridge to remain as superintendent from 1815 until mid-1817. Partridge became embroiled in vindictive controversies with the faculty; he failed to restrict the entry of new cadets to those who met legal standards, to clearly classify the cadets according to a four-year program, to hold graduation exams, and to certify cadets competent for graduation—all measures mandated by law or regulation, including regulations Partridge issued himself. Swift allowed Partridge to remain at West Point despite repeated and explicit instructions by Presidents Madison and Monroe and Secretaries of War Crawford and Calhoun to replace him; he maintained that none of the other engineers wanted the job (which was true, but irrelevant in the face of direct orders) and that replacing Partridge "could not be just to his official rights." Jealous of his own authority, Swift took advantage of the divided attention and uncertainty of the executive branch to remain in Washington until ordered to take up the superintendency in person in the fall of 1816; even then he delayed his departure and returned to Washington as soon as he was able. Ordered to assign Thayer as superintendent during the spring of 1817, he continued to delay, obstructing the president's intent.[24]

The resulting lack of guidance allowed controversies among the staff and faculty to deteriorate into acrimonious personal disputes, indiscipline, and insubordination; it also spurred the alienation, mutiny, and resignation of Partridge, a valuable officer who had carried the chief engineers' weight for the better part of a decade. Most historians agree that Partridge was an honest, well-intentioned individual with a deep regard for the welfare of the academy. But, as with Swift and Williams, the intensity of Partridge's hopes blinded him to alternative viewpoints—particularly those of his superiors. Much as his concern for the cadets eventually led to a familiarity that bred insubordination, his idiosyncrasy, capricious behavior, and micromanagement betrayed an inability to focus and prioritize.[25]

Partridge did have a vision of sorts, though its supposedly military (rather than academic) character may have been as much a product of limited funding and his personal disputes with the faculty as of his military interests per se. A "military" approach may have been the one most appropriate to the wartime years, when teenagers were being rushed through the academy in a year and needed little more than practice in discipline and drill, but Partridge proved unable to adjust his vision or behavior to suit the new circumstances of the postwar era. Although he proposed a wide variety of reforms very much like those presented by Swift, Williams, and Thayer, his arbitrary, unfocused intervention in matters beyond his competence, such as classroom instruction, led to inconsistency in instruction and administration.

Partridge's fundamental problem was that he refused to trust the operations of the academy to anyone else. Whether because of long service or personal temperament, he came to believe that he alone knew what was best for the academy—that he was indispensable to its successful development. Thus, although he gradually went beyond his wartime emphasis on military training to advocate a liberal arts education in the humanities, his reluctance to accept that he could neither run the entire academy nor intervene at will to teach every subject as he saw fit produced continuing confusion and dissension. It is unlikely that the academy would have survived intensified congressional scrutiny had these conditions persisted.[26]

Never a role model for Jeffersonian aspirations—whether cosmopolitan, egalitarian, or democratic—Partridge's later association with popular democracy and the citizen-soldier tradition gained recognition because it suited the emergence of Jacksonian egalitarianism and democracy. Between 1810 and 1818, however, Partridge's sense of duty and obligation became consumed in his jealous assertion of personal rights. His supporters among the cadets—whose demonstrations he encouraged, as if command were a popularity contest—lauded him for "that independence of spirit which every American soldier should possess." But Partridge's "independence" was that of the gentleman owing no superior, not the soldier subordinate to elected representatives. Neither Jefferson, the army, nor the nation could accept so egotistical an independence in men sworn to sacrifice their self-interest to defend the Republic.[27]

Williams, Swift, and Partridge each employed this gentry language of rights, closely connected to that of personal independence and honor. Echoed by all the major players at West Point prior to Thayer, this ultimately aristocratic value system was a common source of dissension in the early national army (as it had been in the Continental one) before Thayer's academy socialized its junior officers in concepts of duty, honor, and integrity rooted in disinterested personal accountability and obligation rather than the self-centered personal "independence" of citizens and gentlemen. Williams used this language when demanding command authority, the civilian professors referred to it in their letters against Partridge to Madison and Monroe, and Partridge made it the core of his claim to seize command from Thayer in July 1817. Three years later, Partridge wrote to the president, justifying his conduct in exactly these terms: it was "an act of which I shall feel proud as long as I live. By doing it, I taught an *Ephemeral Upstart* that my rights were not to be trampled on by usurped authority." Despite his conviction by court-martial, Partridge remained unwilling to accept that the "upstart" Thayer was the president's choice, armed with orders from the president and the chief engineer—hardly those of a "usurped authority."[28]

In claiming the prerogative to resist constitutionally sanctioned orders, Partridge undermined the principle of military subordination to civil authority and could have precipitated a constitutional crisis. Instead of stressing his vision for the academy or his long experience at West Point, Partridge chose to make a rigid and self-interested stand. He appealed to the public over his superiors' heads by publishing a pamphlet in New York City; yet his argument for retaining the command depended on a complex, legalistic, and absolute conception of rights that ultimately had little resonance for the average American civilian or, apparently, the vast majority of congressmen.

Partridge's later popularity as a critic of West Point "aristocracy" derived from a different, though equally resentful, approach that suited the emergence of Jacksonian egalitarianism by emphasizing social equality rather than personal status. In Partridge's case, like those of Williams and Swift, the rights normally acclaimed in the citizen proved subordinate to the demands for accountability that citizens made of their servants in arms. To be entrusted to perform republican service the soldier would have to prove himself more disinterested, more self-sacrificing, and more subordinate to public standards than the republican citizen, a dichotomy that only increased as the citizenry became more individualistic during the nineteenth century. This dichotomy—only superficially a paradox—still exists today. Recognizing and accepting it remains a crucial step in the professional socialization of every cadet and officer.

Appointed superintendent in 1817, Thayer immediately "commenced a system of reformation" that would, he said, "regulate and harmonize the whole machine of instruction" by enforcing standards already on the books. He vowed to "persevere until I produce that state of Military Discipline which is as indispensable in an institution of this sort as in a regular Army." Thayer lacked Swift's rank and connections and was not officially concerned with coastal defense or directing the Corps of Engineers, but he had far more support from the Department of War (now under a reformist secretary who shared Thayer's predilections for system and regularity) than any superintendent to date. Most of the reforms Thayer implemented had already been mandated between 1812 and 1816. Yet, as historian Marcus Cunliffe once observed, "there is no doubt that the high reputation of the Academy dates from Thayer's superintendency," for it was Thayer who finally brought the reforms into effect.[29]

While Thayer's accomplishments have often been detailed, their consequences require some elaboration, making a fitting conclusion to the story of early West Point, given his initial training, education, and socialization in Jefferson's academy. Like most early nineteenth-century pedagogues, Thayer believed that the purpose of higher learning was less the teaching of specific disciplines than the inculcation of "mental discipline," a quality particularly essential for what Swift had called "a corps of instructed administrative officers [to serve] . . . as a nucleus upon which may be predicated any force."[30] Thayer worked steadily to foster an unprecedented uniformity, stability, and predictability—a composite quality graduates labeled "regularity"—as in the terms "regular army," and "regular officers"—in West Point's operations and graduates. Indeed, he began an effort to shape and transform individuals matched only by those who oversaw the early republic's penitentiaries.[31]

Understandably hesitant to take on the superintendency, Thayer succeeded because he was self-sacrificing enough to stick with the assignment for sixteen years—as long as all his predecessors combined. Socialization at Thayer's academy sought to habituate cadets to the principles enshrined since 1898 in the West Point motto—"Duty, Honor, Country." These words articulated essential prerequisites for the creation of a capable military profession accountable to civil authority and republican values. Duty meant committing oneself to serving others and accepting subordination to constitutionally authorized command. Honor now meant performing one's duties with selfless integrity more than being "honored," acknowledged, or rewarded. Country provided the focal point that concentrated and legitimated graduates' efforts to perform their duties.

Disciplinary problems persisted, but the institution of uniform standards, fairly enforced, and the gradual evolution of an honor code that encouraged personal accountability produced a balance of discipline and character development crucial to the professional ethic of responsible service. Through four years of socialization in these principles, working with comrades from around the country toward a common goal under the mentorship of experienced officers who had undergone the same process as cadets themselves, graduates imbibed a strong sense of their duty to serve the nation responsibly and accountably. This was the moral and emotional basis for their professional commitment—an early version of today's professional military ethic.

In the process, the Corps of Cadets, the source of the vast majority of new officers during Thayer's sixteen-year tenure, began to develop a distinct identity and camaraderie, with their own rituals and symbols as novitiate professionals serving the nation. Cadets began to speak of themselves publicly and privately as "children of the Union," of West Point as "the National School," "the school of the Union," a "school for national feeling," and a "school of Union." They contributed significant portions of their meager salaries to the construction of monuments to Thaddeus Kościuszko, to fellow cadets, and to soldiers slain by the Seminole Indians. They routinely referred to military officership as a profession and to the Corps of Cadets, the officer corps, and the army as "bands of brothers" sworn to serve the nation. Most important, they served far longer than their pre-1820 predecessors, providing the commitment and stability that made ongoing professional development possible.[32]

The basic "Thayer system" principles of thorough preparation, rigorous testing, and equal treatment continue to support the Jeffersonian objective of a meritocracy dedicated to public service even today. Although the social and political connections that pervaded the early republic led to a disproportionate presence of the sons of the elite at West Point, the rigorous enforcement of academic standards under the Thayer system meant that rich and well-connected youths frequently flunked out and were refused reinstatement. In addition, the academy accepted a substantial number of cadets from middling or even impoverished backgrounds. To quote one otherwise critical historian, the military academy "probably came closer to producing the aristocracy of talent espoused by Jefferson and Adams than any other educational [or, it should be added, public] institution in the antebellum United States."[33]

Merit was determined by constant, standardized, and systematic ("regular") evaluation; competition under conditions of legally mandated equality and clearly delineated lines of specialized expertise and functional authority habituated aspiring officers to public performance, subordination to legally constituted hierarchies of authority, and accountability to public expectations and values. In effect, socialization under Thayer encouraged officers to view their duty positions as offices, and their perquisites as privileges—which could be withdrawn—rather than as "rights." Officers still disputed the rights due to specific ranks and specific offices, but they increasingly demonstrated an understanding that these "rights" were inherent in the duties of specific offices, rather than the individuals temporarily holding them. This sense of selfless public duty was essential for efficiency and accountability, not only in public administration but in republican government and society as a whole.[34]

The constant, meticulous, and comparatively impersonal attention to assessment, combined with the army's growing fiscal and political accountability and 1843 legislation formalizing the congressionally apportioned system of cadet appointments (an informal practice since 1828, and probably before), enabled the military academy to answer Jacksonian critics on their own terms of equal opportunity and democracy, for every state, section, and party knew that its interests were represented.[35] The beginning of instruction in civil engineering during the early 1820s helped to answer public demands for practical utility in a time of international peace, helping to convince Congress to maintain the academy as the army's principal source of officers and the army as the nation's ultimate defense on land, as Jefferson had suggested in his first inaugural decades before.

To paraphrase administrative historian Leonard White, Thayer's military academy fostered the first organized professional body in the nation's service—the first national bureaucracy, in the positive sense of an institution organized both hierarchically, to ensure subordination and accountability, and along lines of functional specialization, to ensure accountability and efficiency in the performance of specific duties. West Point graduated leaders whose sense of duty and accountability to national objectives proved indispensable to national growth and, during the Civil War era, to reunification. Allied with values of system, instrumental rationality, and order, the practice of specialization, organization, and "regularity" became a hallmark of the army officer corps. The new ethic enhanced the army's engineering, logistical, and administrative capabilities while socializing officers to respond to the ideal and practical demands of civilian supremacy with laudable accountability despite the complex dilemmas they constantly faced in their duties on the nation's borders and frontiers.[36]

Thayer's academy successfully joined scientific and republican education in an incubator of meritocracy, an inculcator of accountability, and a national training center for engineers, explorers, artillerists, administrators, and future militia officers. After a generation of difficulty, West Point produced the most nationally focused social and occupational body in the early republic, an officer corps that undertook all the roles mentioned above, along with those of coastal and interior surveys, river and harbor improvement, and road, railroad, and canal design and construction. This corps also provided the leadership and junior cadre of the army's technical branches, including the ordnance officers who designed and tested new weapons and munitions and oversaw the national arsenals and armories where the "American system of manufactures," employing interchangeable parts, was first developed. The graduates who left the army usually went on to careers as engineers and educators—particularly in math, science, and engineering—as well as lawyers, editors, politicians, and federal civil servants—especially the agents assigned to conduct federal relations with the Indians in the territories.[37]

The habits of mental discipline and accountability that became the heart of the academy's socialization process under Thayer proved invaluable, and probably indispensable, to administering and supplying the nation's largest, most centralized, yet most specialized and farthest-flung full-time organization. The army that graduates maintained was the strongest and most autonomous federal presence on the nation's frontiers, the only willing and capable force available to restrain private incursions from the United States into neighboring countries and to keep some degree of peace between whites and Indians. As such, Jefferson's academy ultimately proved one of the most—or, perhaps, one of the few—successful efforts in the early republic at creating a new, nationally oriented social body, a triumph of the nationalist visions and "comprehensive programs" so often under fire during the years between the Revolution and the Civil War, and so often neglected by historians.[38]

Not all of the consequences were so positive. Army officers, by 1830 overwhelmingly West Point graduates, were in the forefront of the design and construction of the early national transportation infrastructure and the forced expulsion of the Native Americans across the Mississippi, crucial stages in the nation's economic growth and the so-called Market Revolution that spurred the advance of the plantation economy and slavery into the Indian lands. Two generations after the establishment of the academy, these graduates would lead the advance of American empire into Texas, the Southwest, and California. Their administrative abilities enabled the United States to project its power into central Mexico without facing the guerrilla warfare that extensive foraging for supplies might have stirred among the Mexican people had the army been unable to rely on West Point–educated logisticians and officers socialized in self-discipline and accountability.

West Point graduates had much the same impact in the Civil War—brought on in large part by tensions over the disposition of the western "empire for liberty" they did so much to win—in which corruption and inefficiency, largely resulting from the vastly multiplied scale of operations and the influx of volunteer administrators without academy socialization, did not prevent the eventual formation of one of the world's most effective systems of supply to support the projection of one of its most powerful military forces, led almost exclusively by West Point graduates at the senior level. This army destroyed the Confederacy that questioned majoritarian democracy and threatened the national union that loyal West Pointers considered, to quote William Tecumseh Sherman, the starting-point for the welfare of "all future generations."[39]

West Point and the officers it graduated were leading actors in the evolution, for good and ill, of the American nation during the nineteenth century. That they did so with a distinct, academy- and experience-shaped interpretation of Jefferson's protean values, tightening the bonds of the national union and furthering the process many historians refer to as the political, social, economic, and cultural "incorporation of America," was no anomaly. West Pointers served the nation's elected representatives, both in conquering the Native Americans and in crushing slavery. Transformed by its own processes of socialization and the decades of national and nationalist republicanism that followed Jefferson's presidency, Thomas Jefferson's military academy ultimately fostered the nationalism and national power wielded by its graduates against the classical "small republics" of Jefferson's South. Yet they acted in the cause of individual liberty as well as majoritarian democracy and national and international order, pursuing an Enlightenment vision of liberalism that saw the American union as the torchbearer of hopes for a new order of peace and prosperity—as a truer, more comprehensive "empire of liberty" than Jefferson had ever imagined.[40]

Achieving the liberal world order envisioned by the Enlightenment statesmen who founded the American republic requires immense and constant effort on many fronts, effort that often poses hard choices amid moral dilemmas. The quest for peace and happiness in a disordered world demands the alliance of motivation with application, combining the ideal of obligation with its systematic practice to produce what cadets and graduates still know as duty. In the midst of violence and chaos, the practice of duty requires specialization, cooperation, and discipline on the parts of soldiers and public servants who possess both the motive and the ability to act on the first principles enunciated in Jefferson's Declaration of Independence. West Point's education in the principles and practice of dutiful service to the community continues to carry this vision forward, so long as American nationalism continues to embody the Enlightenment ideals of liberty and justice.

Socialization in nationalism and scientific-technical disciplines, combined with the hierarchical institutional discipline intended to assure subordination and accountability to the constitutionally sanctioned authority of the central government, has encouraged army officers to see themselves as the objective representatives of that government, pursuing national order and harmony at its direction even when that direction took paths we might deem undemocratic, intolerant, or unjust. In this they have reflected, but also influenced, the perpetually shifting balances between liberty, democracy, and order in American life: the balances between democratic majoritarianism, republican community, and liberal individualism, between the pursuit of a liberty whose content is always contested and the illiberal means sometimes believed necessary to secure its blessings.[41]

Notes

1. See Daniel H. Calhoun, *Professional Lives in America: Structure and Aspiration, 1750–1850* (Cambridge, Mass., 1965); Samuel Haber, *The Quest for Authority and Honor in the American Professions, 1750–1900* (Chicago, 1991); Gerald L. Geison, ed., *Professions and Professional Ideologies in America* (Chapel Hill, N.C., 1983); and Maxwell Bloomfield, *American Lawyers in a Changing Society, 1776–1876* (Cambridge, Mass., 1976) for larger historical perspectives on the demands for accountability that go with the public trust placed in the professions. See Daniel H. Calhoun, *The Intelligence of a People* (Princeton, 1973), 35–70, and George H. Daniels, *Science in American Society: A Social History* (New York, 1971), 126–205, concerning parallel dilemmas in American science and education in the transition from colonies to nation, and Burton J. Bledstein, *The Culture of Professionalism: The Middle Class and the Development of Higher Education in America* (New York, 1976) on these dilemmas during the nineteenth century.

2. See Charles Royster, *A Revolutionary People at War: The Continental Army and American Character, 1775–1783* (Chapel Hill, N.C., 1979), on the turbulence—disputes, duels, and resignations—produced by an exaggerated sense of honor among American officers during the Revolution. For the post-Revolutionary context, see Richard Kohn, *Eagle and Sword: The Beginnings of the Military Establishment in America* (New York, 1975). This self-centered sense of honor was

also present among civilian politicians in the decades following the Revolution; see Joanne B. Freeman, *Affairs of Honor: National Politics in the New Republic* (New Haven, Conn., 2001).

3. Rush, "Of the Mode of Education Proper in a Republic," in *Selected Writings of Benjamin Rush*, ed. Dagobert D. Runes (New York, 1947), 92. See Steven C. Bullock, *Revolutionary Brotherhood: Freemasonry and the Transformation of the American Social Order, 1730–1840* (Chapel Hill, N.C., 1996), particularly chapters 5 and 8, for an examination of the links between cosmopolitan learning, ambition, gentility, respectability, and nonsectarian nationalism among the Freemasons, links that were commonly present among Continental army and later officers. The principal sources for officers' military careers are Francis B. Heitman, comp., *Historical Registry and Dictionary of the United States Army, from Its Organization, September 29, 1789 to March 2, 1903*, 2 vols. (Washington, D.C., 1903); Charles K. Gardner, comp., *A Dictionary of the Officers of the Army of the United States* (New York, 1860); Thomas H. S. Hamersly, comp., *Complete Army Register of the United States, for One Hundred Years (1779 to 1879)* (Washington, D.C., 1880); William A. Gordon, comp., *A Compilation of Registers of the Army of the United States, from 1815 to 1837* (Washington, D.C., 1837); and George W. Cullum, comp., *Biographical Register of the Officers and Graduates of the United States Military Academy at West Point, from Its Establishment, in 1802, to 1890* (Boston, 1891), vols. 1–2.

4. The following works are particularly essential to understanding early republican and Jeffersonian visions of society, federation, union, and nation, and the very real presence and activism of the nation-state therein: Drew R. McCoy, *The Elusive Republic: Political Economy in Jeffersonian America* (Chapel Hill, N.C., 1980); John Lauritz Larson, *Internal Improvement: National Public Works and the Promise of Popular Government in the Early United States* (Chapel Hill, N.C., 2001); James E. Lewis Jr., *The American Union and the Problem of Neighborhood: The United States and the Collapse of the Spanish Empire, 1783–1829* (Chapel Hill, N.C., 1998); and Peter S. Onuf and Nicholas G. Onuf, *Federal Union, Modern World: The Law of Nations in an Age of Revolutions, 1776–1814* (Madison, Wis., 1993).

5. My generalizations about the officer corps are based on the research for Watson, "Professionalism, Social Attitudes, and Civil-Military Accountability: The U.S. Army Officer Corps, 1815–1846" (Ph.D. diss., Rice University, 1996) and my forthcoming book on the army officer corps in the borderlands of the early republic (University Press of Kansas, 2005). The best source on the army officer corps as a social and occupational group is William B. Skelton, *An American Profession of Arms: The Army Officer Corps, 1784–1861* (Lawrence, Kans., 1992).

6. For the engineers' wartime accomplishments, see George W. Cullum, *Campaigns of the War of 1812–15, against Great Britain . . . with Brief Biographies of the American Engineers* (New York, 1879). The most comprehensive account of American land operations is in Robert S. Quimby, *The U.S. Army in the War of 1812: An Operational and Command Study*, 2 vols. (East Lansing, Mich., 1997). The role officers played in establishing a federal presence in the borderlands is detailed in Samuel J. Watson, "The Uncertain Road to Manifest Destiny: Army Officers and the Course of American Territorial Expansionism, 1815–1846," in *Manifest Destiny and Empire: American Antebellum Expansionism*, ed. Christopher Morris and Sam Haynes (College Station, Tex., 1997). They were at least equally active in doing so before 1815, when the civil bureaucracy was less developed; my book on the army officer corps in the borderlands of the early republic will address both periods. See Skelton, *An American Profession of Arms*, 137–39, for the growing predominance of West Point graduates in the officer corps between 1815 and 1860.

7. Sidney Forman, *West Point: A History of the United States Military Academy* (New York, 1950), 24; Williams to TJ, 12 June 1807, TJ Papers, Lib. Cong.; Williams to Wadsworth, 13 May

1802, Williams Papers, USMA Lib. (original in the Jonathan Williams Papers, Lilly Library, Indiana University).

8. Papers of the Military Philosophical Society, 1789–1813, microfilm, USMA Lib. The standard works on the society are Sidney Forman, "The United States Military Philosophical Society, 1802–1813," *WMQ*, 3rd ser., 2 (July 1945): 273–85, and Arthur P. Wade, "A Military Offspring of the American Philosophical Society," *Military Affairs* 38 (October 1974): 103–7. Written explicitly in quest of the germs of American military professionalism, these works exaggerate the society's effect on cadets, American military expertise, and American military professionalism. See Theodore J. Crackel, *West Point: A Bicentennial History* (Lawrence, Kans., 2002); George S. Pappas, *To the Point: The United States Military Academy, 1802–1902* (Westport, Conn., 1993); and Watson, "Professionalism, Social Attitudes, and Civil-Military Accountability," chapter 3, for details regarding the early academy.

9. Forman, *West Point*, 32; Thomas Elliott Shaughnessy, "Beginnings of National Professional Military Education in America, 1775–1825" (Ed.D. diss., Johns Hopkins University, 1956), 132. See Theodore J. Crackel, *The Illustrated History of West Point* (New York, 1991), 85, for a critique of the society, of Williams's ambitions for command, and of Williams's lack of attention to detail at West Point. See James L. Morrison, *"The Best School": West Point, 1833–1866* (Kent, Ohio, 1998); Matthew Moten, *The Delafield Commission and the American Military Profession* (College Station, Tex., 2000); and Samuel J. Watson, "Knowledge, Interest, and the Limits of Military Professionalism: The Discourse on American Coastal Defense, 1815–1860," *War in History* 5 (Fall 1998): 280–307, for critiques of elitism and mental rigidity in the Corps of Engineers and the army, which Morrison and Moten attribute largely to the engineering emphasis at West Point. See Williams to TJ, 17 September 1810, TJ Papers, Lib. Cong., for Williams's complaints against West Point as a post, and Williams, Engineer Orders, 20 June 1803, Williams Papers, USMA Lib., explaining his reasons for resigning to the Corps of Engineers.

10. Williams, 14 March 1808, in the *Annals of Congress*, Tenth Congress, First Session, 1807–1808, part 2, 2808–12 (available at http://www.memory.loc.gov). The 18 March 1808 message that transmitted Williams's report was the sole mention of the military academy in a major message from Jefferson to Congress; see James D. Richardson, *A Compilation of the Messages and Papers of the Presidents*, 10 vols. (New York, 1896–1904), 1:433. Jefferson observed that "the scale on which the Military Academy . . . was originally established is become too limited to furnish the number of well-instructed subjects in the different branches of the artillery and engineering which the public service calls for. The want of such characters . . . will be increased with the enlargement of our plans of military preparation." (Indeed, about four times as many cadets were appointed in 1808 as in any previous year.) Jefferson endorsed Williams's call for moving the academy to Washington, "under the immediate eye of the government," apparently because this would make it easier to match graduates to duties, but simply commended the report "for the consideration of Congress," perhaps because he tended to see Congress as the initiator of legislation. (Jefferson did not mention or repeat William's call for enhancing the president's executive authority.) See Skelton, *An American Profession of Arms*, 102 and 387, n. 50, for Williams's efforts to stimulate congressional action; he later provided a draft for what became the law of April 1812.

11. Pappas, *To the Point*, 57, 63–64; Williams to Madison, 13 June 1810, in J. C. A. Stagg, et al., eds., *The Papers of James Madison: Presidential Series*, 4 vols. to date (Charlottesville, Va., 1984–), 2:378–79. See State of New York, *Public Papers of Daniel D. Tompkins, Governor of New York, 1807–1817, Military*, 3 vols. (Albany, N.Y., 1898–1902), 2:217, 273, 300–301, 306–9, and 336, regarding efforts to move the academy to Long Island. In March 1809 Williams intimated that

only Partridge's presence had enabled him to maintain discipline: "If I had not been well assisted by Lieut. A. Partridge I should not have been able to have got through in the Government of the young men" (Williams to Mansfield, March 1809, quoted in Pappas, *To the Point,* 63). Partridge's "Academy Orders" of 31 March 1809 (approved by Williams, USMA Lib.) demanded "the strictest attendance" and "the utmost order" and prohibited the unauthorized discharge of firearms, "unnecessary noise" on parade, and "disorderly meetings . . . and all meetings for interfering with the regulations or discipline of the institution," indications of significant tumult.

12. "Regulations relative to the Military Academy at West Point," 30 April 1810, enclosed in Eustis to Williams, 18 May 1810, USMA Lib. See James Ripley Jacobs, *The Beginning of the U.S. Army, 1783–1812* (Princeton, N.J., 1947), chapters 13–14, for a critical assessment of Eustis's tenure as secretary of war; see Pappas, *To the Point,* 55–58, and Crackel, *West Point,* 70–71, for balanced synopses and evaluations of Eustis's actions and intent concerning West Point.

13. Madison, 5 December 1810, in Richardson, *Messages and Papers of the Presidents,* 2:471–72. Madison did not again address the academy in a state message until 1815. (The 1811 message contains an implied reference; ibid., 479.)

14. Partridge, Academy Orders, 31 March 1809, USMA Lib.; Pappas, *To the Point,* 57–58; "Internal Regulations for the Military Academy," compiled by Partridge and approved by Williams, 25 May 1810, file W-88, Office of the Secretary of War, Letters Received, Record Group 107, National Archives; "An act making further provision for the Corps of Engineers," 29 April 1812, *Statutes at Large,* Twelfth Congress, First Session, 720–21 (http://www.memory.loc.gov). Among the many indications that regulations went unenforced, see Swift to Secretary of War James Monroe, 25 April 1815, concerning cadets' timely arrival at West Point; Swift to the secretary of war, 30 December 1815, noting that cadets had not been examined before admission, and lacked the required qualifications; and Adjutant General Daniel Parker to Swift, 5 September 1816, regarding uniforms (all in the Swift Papers, USMA Lib.).

15. Joseph G. Swift, *The Memoirs of General Joseph G. Swift,* ed. Harrison Ellery (Worcester, Mass., 1890), 106; Williams to Swift, 24 July 1812, Swift Papers, USMA Lib. Nineteenth-century armies did not usually permit officers in "staff" or technical branches to hold commands over combat arms (infantry, artillery, and cavalry) units. In the United States, this tendency was intensified by the desire to prevent European officers—like the engineers employed during the Revolution—from commanding American troops. See Secretary of War Henry Dearborn to Wadsworth, 21 June 1803, in War Department, Letters Relating to the Corps of Engineers (Buell Collection), National Archives, Record Group 107, M417, roll 1: "Engineers should devote their time & attention exclusively to the theory & practice of their profession, by which means we may avoid the unpleasant necessity of employing Foreigners as Engineers." See Pappas, *To the Point,* 64–65; Williams to Eustis (copy sent to Swift), 8 May 1809; and Williams to Swift, 9 October 1812, Swift Papers, USMA Lib., for elaborations of Williams's perspective.

16. Skelton, *An American Profession of Arms,* 99, 104; Williams to Swift, 26 August 1805, Swift Papers, USMA Lib. (concerning Swift's request for a furlough).

17. Memorial enclosed in Alexander Macomb to Swift, 24 December 1804, Swift Papers, USMA Lib.; Williams to Jared Mansfield, 12 June 1807, TJ Papers, Lib. Cong. See Macomb to Williams, 8 October 1804, Williams Papers, USMA Lib., for a plea that Williams return lest the academy collapse, and Macomb to Williams, 10 December 1808, enclosure to Williams to Dearborn, 27 December 1808, file W-362, Office of the Secretary of War, Letters Received, Record Group 107, National Archives, for Macomb's own plan for the academy.

18. Swift, "Sketch of a Plan for the conducting of a Military Academy," January 1808, and Swift to Secretary of War James Monroe, 28 December 1814, Swift Papers, USMA Lib.

19. Swift to the War Department, 25 April and 11 May 1815, and to Partridge, 16 October 1813, Swift Papers, USMA Lib.; Regulations, 2 July 1816, USMA Lib.

20. Theodore J. Crackel and Robert A. Doughty, "The History of History at West Point," in *West Point: Two Centuries and Beyond,* ed. Lance A. Betros (Abilene, Tex.: McWhiney Foundation Press, 2004).

21. Swift, *Memoirs of General Joseph G. Swift,* 126, 276; Williams to Swift, 9 October 1812, Swift Papers, USMA Lib.

22. Swift, *Memoirs of General Joseph G. Swift,* 139–40; Crackel, *West Point,* 73. Partridge's "Orders" of 1 April 1814 (USMA Lib.) suggest that the academy had definitely faltered in the caliber of both instruction and cadets, filling all instructional time with mathematics and drawing and warning against such juvenile acts as "scuffling," not paying debts, "wantonly" damaging quarters, and throwing "water or any thing else out of the windows."

23. Swift, *Memoirs of General Joseph G. Swift,* 142–46 (first quotation on 146) and 179 (second quotation); Joseph H. Harrison, "Simon Bernard, the American System, and the Ghost of the French Alliance," in *America, the Middle Period: Essays in Honor of Bernard Mayo,* ed. John B. Boles (Charlottesville, Va., 1973), 145–67. See Watson, "Professionalism, Social Attitudes, and Civil-Military Accountability," chapters 2, 3, and 9, on the dissension produced by the genteel, quasi-aristocratic consciousness of rights among early national officers and cadets, its gradual decline (due in large part to Thayer-era socialization), and its persistence in moderated form during the 1820s and beyond. The decline of this dissension is one of the principal themes of Skelton, *An American Profession of Arms.*

24. Edgar Denton, "The Formative Years of the United States Military Academy, 1775–1833" (Ph.D. diss., Syracuse University, 1964), 123, 144–45, 160; "Regulations," 2 July 1816, USMA Lib.; Swift to the secretary of war, 30 December 1815, and to Acting Secretary of War George Graham, 5 January 1817, Swift Papers, USMA Lib.; Swift, *Memoirs of General Joseph G. Swift,* 141 (written 31 December 1816); Pappas, *To the Point,* 86–90; Crackel, *West Point,* 77–80. Swift's draft regulations, dated 22 May 1816, are enclosed in Crawford to Swift, 1 July 1816, *Annals of Congress,* Fourteenth Congress, Second Session, 2439–43 (http://www.memory.loc.gov). When Swift was ordered to West Point as superintendent that November, he sought to retain Partridge at the academy as instructor of tactics, but the acting secretary of war refused, "because the resignation of Capt. Partridge [presumably from the superintendency] has been accepted under the impression, that his connection with the Academy was to cease" (George S. Graham to Swift, 21 January 1817, Swift Papers, USMA Lib.).

25. Peter M. Molloy, "Technical Education and the Young Republic: West Point as America's Ecole Polytechnique, 1802–1833" (Ph.D. diss., Brown University, 1975), 365. See Forman, *West Point,* 39, for additional praise (along with extensive criticism), and Marcus Cunliffe, *Soldiers and Civilians: The Martial Spirit in America, 1775–1865* (Boston, 1968), 257–60, for "The Case for Partridge" from the larger perspective of democracy and the citizen-soldier tradition. Cunliffe is referring to the Partridge of the 1830s, however, not defending the insubordination of the 1810s.

26. The reputedly "military" quality of Partridge's vision may be traced largely to the "Recollections of the Cadet Life of George D. Ramsay," in Cullum, *Biographical Register,* 3:621–22, which is quoted in virtually every history, often with little further evidence.

27. Swift, *Memoirs of General Joseph G. Swift,* 170; memorial of the "Majority of the Corps of Cadets" to Colonel Henry Atkinson, 7 April 1816, cited in Stephen F. Ambrose, *Duty, Honor, Country: A History of West Point* (Baltimore, 1966), 55.

28. Partridge to Swift, 11 November 1816 and 31 August 1817, quotation from Partridge to Monroe, 20 November 1820 (emphasis in original), quoted in Lester A. Webb, *Captain Alden*

Partridge and the United States Military Academy, 1806–1833 (Northport, Ala., 1965), 98, 119–20, 154. See also Mansfield to Madison, 26 March 1810, in Stagg, et al., eds., *The Papers of James Madison: Presidential Series,* 2:287. See Christopher Duffy, *The Military Experience in the Age of Reason* (New York, 1988), 79, on the pervasiveness of this sense of honor among the eighteenth-century European officers American regulars looked to as examples.

29. Thayer to Josiah Moulton, 17 October 1817, Thayer Papers, USMA Lib.; Cunliffe, *Soldiers and Civilians,* 157.

30. Swift, diary, 10 March 1814, in Swift, *Memoirs of General Joseph G. Swift,* 125. See Thayer to a major general Armstrong, 11 March 1822, USMA Lib., for Thayer's critique of the academy's operations before his arrival, "prior to which there was but little system or regularity." See Patricia Cline Cohen, *A Calculating People: The Spread of Numeracy in Early America* (Chicago, 1982), chapter 4, for the role mathematics was expected to play in disciplining the minds of republican citizens, and chapter 5 for its role in state formation and administration. Thayer's intent is often summarized as the creation of a school for civil engineers (essentially Peter Molloy's view, and that of James W. Kershner, "Sylvanus Thayer: A Biography" (Ph.D. diss., West Virginia University, 1975), but Thayer initially resisted the introduction of civil engineering, and it was not actually incorporated into the curriculum until the early 1820s, at the initiative of civilian officials (Crackel, *West Point,* 96–98).

31. See "Rules and Regulations for the Government of the Military Academy at West Point," *American State Papers: Military Affairs* (hereafter cited as *ASP:MA*) 2:77–79 (http://www.memory.loc.gov), and "Regulations of the United States' Military Academy at West Point," *ASP:MA* 2:648–57, for the 1820 and 1824 regulations. The next complete edition was published in 1832, suggesting Thayer's success and satisfaction with the disciplinary scheme in place by the mid-1820s. See Rodney Hessinger, "'The Most Powerful Instrument of College Discipline': Student Disorder and the Growth of Meritocracy in the Colleges of the Early Republic," *History of Education Quarterly* 29 (Fall 1999): 237–62, for similar but less successful efforts in civilian colleges.

32. Quotations from Cadet Joseph Ritner, *An Oration Delivered before the Corps of Cadets of the United States Military Academy at West Point, on the Fifty-third Anniversary of American Independence* (Newburgh, N.Y., 1829); Cadet Benjamin Alvord, *Address before the Dialectic Society of the Corps of Cadets, in Commemoration of the Gallant Conduct of the Nine Graduates of the Military Academy, and Other Officers of the United States Army, Who Fell in the Battles which Took Place in Florida* (New York, 1839); and other Dialectic Society speeches. See Skelton, *An American Profession of Arms,* 137–39, for the growing predominance of West Point graduates in the officer corps between 1815 and 1860, and figure 11.1 and tables 11.1–11.4 (pp. 216, 182–83, 194, and 213), for extensive data on the growing length of officers' careers, despite very slow promotion. Skelton provides the most extensive account of officer socialization and the officer corps' subculture; see also Watson, "Professionalism, Social Attitudes, and Civil-Military Accountability," chapter 9, which focuses on cadet socialization at West Point and officer interaction in garrison.

33. Quotation from Morrison, *"The Best School,"* 152–53. Pre–Civil War officers came disproportionately from urban areas and elite or "upper middle class" backgrounds, and very much so from professional and office-holding families, who can properly be considered elites from the standpoint of gentility and social and political power. West Point did serve as a means of social mobility for a number of poor youths, but most of these were the sons of downwardly mobile professional and erstwhile office-holding families from urban and commercial centers—meaning parents with social and political connections to Washington—who sought security and status for their sons through military commissions. See Skelton, *An American Profession of Arms,* 140–41, 158–61 (tables 9.4 and 9.5) for comparisons with the civilian population. The general

group profile is much akin to that of the civil officers examined in Sidney H. Aronson, *Status and Kinship in the Higher Civil Service: Standards of Selection in the Administrations of John Adams, Thomas Jefferson, and Andrew Jackson* (Cambridge, Mass., 1964). Indeed, Skelton points out that more than a quarter of the officers on the 1830 army register were related to men who had served or were serving in high offices, nearly four-fifths of those in civil life. Perhaps more significant than social origins per se, scholars generally agree that West Point socialized aspiring officers as gentlemen on the European, or at least English, model; I would extend this analysis, as Cunliffe implies (p. 171), to suggest that West Pointers played a role in the "aristocratic revival" of the 1850s described by Richard L. Bushman in *The Refinement of America, 1750–1850: Persons, Houses, Cities* (New York, 1993), and the shift from "boundlessness to consolidation" observed by John Higham (*From Boundlessness to Consolidation: The Transformation of American Culture, 1848–1860* [Ann Arbor, Mich., 1969]).

34. See Samuel Watson, "How the Army Became Accepted: West Point Socialization, Military Accountability, and the State during the Jacksonian Era," *American Nineteenth-Century History* 6 (forthcoming in 2005) for elaboration.

35. See Crackel, *West Point,* 115, for the congressional system of appointment. Representative documents in the debate over "West Point aristocracy" include "Americanus" (Alden Partridge), *The Military Academy Unmasked, or, Corruption and Military Despotism Exposed* (Washington, D.C., 1830); "Exhibit No. 1, Register of Cadets to December 31, 1829," communicated to the House of Representatives, 15 March 1830, *ASP:MA* 4: 308–31, listing cadets who were the sons of federal officers and congressmen; "Justitia," *Letter to the Honorable Mr. Hawes, in Reply to His Strictures on the Graduates of the Military Academy* (New York, 1836), responding to congressional criticism; and Report of the House Committee on Military Affairs, 1844, Twenty-eighth Congress, First Session, House Report no. 476, 15–16, listing the occupations of cadets' fathers to argue that they came from a broad background. See Cunliffe, *Soldiers and Civilians,* 105–11, 162–66, for a balanced view of both the limits of the Jacksonian attacks and the persistence of a strong socially elite presence in the Corps of Cadets and the officer corps. Like Crackel, John G. Cawelti, *Apostles of the Self-made Man: Changing Concepts of Success in America* (Chicago, 1965), 26, maintains that Jefferson sought a new institutional framework to foster a disinterested element in society, one without allegiances to existing class (meaning gentry, or more specifically Federalist) interests. Cawelti argues that this effort failed; I would maintain that West Point did foster a new social-occupational formation.

36. Leonard White, *The Jeffersonians: A Study in Administrative History, 1801–1829* (New York, 1959), 259. For the development and extent of system and regularity, see Keith W. Hoskin and Richard H. Macve, "The Genesis of Accountability: The West Point Connections," *Accounting, Organizations, and Society* 13 (1988), 37–73; Charles F. O'Connell, "The U.S. Army and the Origins of Modern Management, 1818–1860" (Ph.D. diss., Ohio State University, 1982); Merritt Roe Smith, *Harpers Ferry Armory and the New Technology: The Challenge of Change* (Ithaca, N.Y., 1977); Merritt Roe Smith, "Army Ordnance and the 'American System' of Manufacturing, 1815–61," in *Military Enterprise and Technological Change: Perspectives on the American Experience,* ed. Merritt Roe Smith (Cambridge, Mass., 1991); and Samuel J. Watson, "Thomas Sidney Jesup: Soldier, Bureaucrat, Gentleman Democrat," in *The Human Tradition in Antebellum America,* ed. Michael A. Morrison (Wilmington, Del., 2000).

37. The introduction of civil engineering into the military academy curriculum in the early 1820s was indispensable to the implementation of the General Survey Act of 1824, which provided dozens of government engineers to road, railroad, and canal surveys, and from the late 1820s to the design and construction of the Baltimore and Ohio and many other railroads. For

a survey of officers and exploration, see William H. Goetzmann, *Army Exploration in the American West* (New Haven, Conn., 1957); for officers and internal improvements, see Forest G. Hill, *Roads, Rails, and Waterways: The Army Engineers and Early Transportation* (Norman, Okla., 1957) and Robert P. Wettemann, "'To the Public Prosperity': The U.S. Army and the Market Revolution, 1815–1844" (Ph.D. diss., Texas A&M University, 2001); for the ordnance, see Smith, *Harpers Ferry Armory and the New Technology,* and Smith, "Army Ordnance and the 'American System' of Manufacturing." Wettemann also discusses the tensions between state and society, center and periphery, over national economic (in this case infrastructural) planning and direction during the National Republican and Jacksonian periods. For graduates' careers outside the army, see Cullum, comp., *Biographical Register;* United States Military Academy, *The Centennial of the United States Military Academy at West Point, New York,* 2 vols. (Washington, D.C., 1904); R. Ernest Dupuy, *Men of West Point: The First 150 Years of the United States Military Academy* (New York, 1951); and Dale E. Hruby, "The Civilian Careers of West Point Graduates, Classes of 1802–1833" (M.A. thesis, Columbia University, 1965).

38. Watson, "Professionalism, Social Attitudes, and Civil-Military Accountability," chapter 8; Erna Risch, *Quartermaster Support of the Army, 1775–1939* (revised ed., Washington, D.C. 1988); Cynthia Ann Miller, "The United States Army Logistics Complex, 1818–1845: A Case Study of the Northern Frontier" (Ph.D. diss., Syracuse University, 1991); and Chester L. Kieffer, *Maligned General: A Biography of Thomas S. Jesup* (San Rafael, Calif., 1979).

39. Sherman quoted in Henry Steele Commager, ed., *The Blue and the Grey: The Story of the Civil War as Told by Participants,* 2 vols. (Indianapolis, Ind., 1950), 2:929. The inadequacy of American logistics is a common theme in general histories of the war with Mexico, but even the most superficial comparison with the experience of the War of 1812 shows a profound, perhaps decisive improvement. Indeed, the logistical capability developed during the 1820s and 1830s was a prerequisite for the success of Winfield Scott's strategy of conciliating the Mexican people to ease the peace process once he had won a military victory against the armed forces of the Mexican government; see Timothy D. Johnson, *Winfield Scott and the Quest for Military Glory* (Lawrence, Kans., 1998), 179–81, 186–88, 192–94, 207–9.

40. Alan Trachtenberg, *The Incorporation of America: Culture and Society in the Gilded Age* (New York, 1982). See also J. David Greenstone, *The Lincoln Persuasion: Remaking American Liberalism* (Princeton, N.J., 1993). Further insights can be found in Robert H. Wiebe, *The Opening of American Society, from the Adoption of the Constitution to the Eve of Disunion* (New York, 1984); Thomas R. Hietala, *Manifest Design: Anxious Aggrandizement in Late Jacksonian America* (Ithaca, N.Y., 1985); and Major L. Wilson, *Space, Time and Freedom: The Quest for Nationality and the Irrepressible Conflict, 1815–1861* (Westport, Conn., 1974). The standard narrative history of the Army during the early republic, Francis Paul Prucha's *The Sword of the Republic: The United States Army on the Frontier, 1783–1846* (New York, 1969), uses "Agents of Empire" as the title for its chapter on the officer corps.

41. See Lewis, *The American Union and the Problem of Neighborhood;* Onuf and Onuf, *Federal Union, Modern World;* Peter S. Onuf, *Jefferson's Empire: The Language of American Nationhood* (Charlottesville, Va., 2000), chapter 2; and Robert W. Tucker and David C. Hendrickson, *Empire of Liberty: The Statecraft of Thomas Jefferson* (New York, 1990) "on the issue of the [American] nation's proper role in the world" (p. 256) in the era of the early republic. Whatever Jefferson's intentions, his establishment of the military academy put a powerful instrument in the hands of those claiming to pursue Jeffersonian ideals in the world arena.

West Point's Lost Founder

Jefferson Remembered, Forgotten, and Reconsidered

ROBERT M. S. MCDONALD

Before the commandant stood a worried cadet, unjustly accused of disregarding orders and disparaging the memories of Thomas Jefferson and John Adams. Both men had died on July 4, 1826—exactly fifty years after the ratification of the Declaration of Independence, which Jefferson drafted and Adams championed, and exactly twenty-four years after the official commencement of operations at the United States Military Academy, which Jefferson established and Adams supported. When officers at West Point heard the startling news—a coincidence that young mathematicians at Jefferson's other school, the University of Virginia, would calculate the odds against to be more than 1.7 billion to one—they decided that the academy should pay its respects. The cadet, as sergeant of the guard, had been directed to see to it that his peers fire two guns, from reveille to retreat, in quick succession every fifteen minutes. Instead of the regular issue of two clear shots, however, Major William J. Worth, the commandant, had heard haphazard gunfire. "Shortly after morning parade I was sent for in great haste by the Commandant," the cadet later remembered. "I denied disobeying the order, and insisted that the guns were discharged at proper intervals." Worth dismissed the cadet who, "to avoid any further trouble . . . loaded and touched them off myself, watch in hand." Yet "again I was sent for, and rated soundly for failure. What it all meant I could not understand, but the Major went with me to the guard-tent, and just as I touched off the gun, before its echoes died away," another shot thundered in the distance. "The cause," he then realized, "was the blasting of rocks" around nearby Fort Putnam, which Worth "had heard, but which I had not." After Worth "apologized before the whole guard for his unjust censure" and ordered an end to the blasting, the tribute to Jefferson and Adams continued.[1] Such a demonstration of solicitude for the third president's memory would not again occur at West Point for nearly a century.

Jefferson wrote not only the Declaration of Independence but also the Virginia Statute for Religious Freedom and his 1787 *Notes on the State of Virginia,* an encyclopedic collection of information on his native land's flora, fauna, politics, and culture.[2] He served in colonial Virginia's House of Burgesses, the Continental Congress, and the Virginia House of Delegates; he was his state's governor and his nation's minister to France, secretary of state, vice president, and president. He was a noted architect, spirited violinist, ardent farmer, and a leading scientist. He knew seven languages, doubled the nation's territory through the Louisiana Purchase, dispatched Lewis and Clark on their voyage of discovery, introduced pasta and ice cream to the American palate, and fathered the University of Virginia.[3] He was, in short, a true polymath, a Renaissance man whose interests spanned wide and probed deep.

Among his many accomplishments, however, Jefferson's 1802 founding of the United States Military Academy is, and has been, often overlooked. Such was not the case in the early years of West Point—as the incident between Worth and the cadet makes clear. Jefferson was held up as the academy's founder, patron, and creator. His name was recognized and his memory was perpetuated. Beginning in the 1830s, however, new considerations made a connection with Jefferson seem less attractive to the army officers at West Point. At the centennial celebrations of the academy's birth, it was not Jefferson but George Washington who was described as founder. Only in the past half century, in fact, as a new era of footnotes and scholarly professionalism came to guide the academy's view of itself, did Jefferson reemerge. The new question was not whether Jefferson had a role in the creation of West Point—for certainly, he did—but what he did to foster the academy and why, as he wrote in 1821, he considered it "of major importance to our country."[4]

Even so, the die had been cast. Jefferson had been divorced from West Point in the minds of many of its graduates and the public. Buildings had been named, statues erected, and a myth created that characterized as wasted time the years prior to the installation of Sylvanus Thayer as superintendent of the academy. The result was neglect, on the part of some, and ignorance, on the part of others, of Jefferson's contributions.

Despite lapses in historical memory, the fact that the military academy owes its existence to Jefferson is beyond refutation. Plans for a national institution charged with military education had been advanced since the time of the American Revolution. Colonel Henry Knox suggested it, Treasury Secretary Alexander Hamilton supported it, French-American Lieutenant Colonel Ann Louise de Tousard drew up ambitious plans for it, and Presidents George Washington and John Adams asked Congress to establish it.[5] But their various proposals either languished or amounted to little until 1802, when President Jefferson won congressional authorization for the establishment of the military academy. It commenced operations officially on July 4 of that year, the twenty-sixth anniversary of American independence.[6]

The early academy was a small institution with only a handful of faculty and cadets. Even so, it received a good deal of attention from the busy president, who corresponded with West Point professors and Jonathan Williams, its first superintendent; served as honorary leader of the United States Military Philosophical Society, a West Point scientific organization and booster group; and, in 1808, called for the academy's dramatic enlargement. On April 12 of that year, Congress heeded Jefferson's call and increased the authorized enrollment to 256 cadets.[7] Although years elapsed before the academy succeeded in its efforts to attract this number of qualified students, the fact that Jefferson supported an academy of this size suggests much about his commitment to the institution. In the census of 1810, the federal government counted 7.2 million Americans. As a percentage of the population, the academy envisioned by Jefferson was more than twice as large as West Point in 2000, when about 4,000 cadets prepared for the defense of a nation of about 281 million people.

His support did not go unnoticed. In 1821, more than a decade after Jefferson's retirement as commander in chief, mathematics professor Jared Mansfield wrote to Jefferson in behalf of Superintendent Thayer, the faculty, and the cadets. "Impressed with a high sense of the great services you have rendered the nation, and this institution, with which they are connected, originated under your patronage, and presidency," Mansfield informed Jefferson, they were "anxious for some special, and appropriate memorial of your person which may descend to posterity. They have already in the Academy Library the portraits of the great Washington, the Founder of Our Republic, and Col. [Jonathan] Williams, the first chief of the Mil[itary] Academy, and they wish to add yours to the number, as being alike the Founders, and Patrons of both." Jefferson agreed to stand for the portrait, which noted Philadelphia artist Thomas Sully traveled to Monticello to sketch and then paint in the spring of the following year. Sully's 8½- by 5½-foot "Thomas Jefferson" depicts the academy's founder on the verge of his seventy-ninth birthday. Still vigorous in mind and body, at six foot three inches, he towers over many of his contemporaries and stands, like the column beside him, as an enduring pillar of strength. He wears a black coat, knee breeches, and the fur-lined bear skin topcoat given to him in 1798 by Thaddeus Kościuszko, the Polish officer whose Continental army service during the War for Independence included a tour of duty constructing fortifications at West Point.[8] In his left hand Jefferson holds a parchment scroll—perhaps his 1802 law establishing the United States Military Academy. Sully's portrait, the prize of a collection that has hung for nearly two centuries in buildings that have housed the Cadet Library, would be the first and—for the better part of two centuries—final major monument at West Point to the man to whom the military academy owes its existence.

What explains ignorance of Jefferson's role in the years leading up the Civil War? The reasons are both political and personal. What first must be understood is the devotion of West Point officers to Superintendent Thayer—to him, to his superintendency, and to its significance. Thayer's reign as West Point's chief was successful and long—the longest, in fact, of any superintendent before or since. But both his arrival and departure were clouded in controversy. The turbulent 1817 transfer of power from Alden Partridge to Thayer—so turbulent, in fact, that for a while Partridge refused to step aside—perhaps has led chroniclers of West Point's past to depreciate the contributions of Partridge and his predecessors to underscore the legitimacy of Thayer's appointment and the contributions of his tenure by taking an unfairly critical stance on the Jeffersonian institution that he inherited.[9] Thayer's 1833 resignation, after a conflict with President Andrew Jackson, also may have had a negative impact on Jefferson's fame as founder. Like Thayer, many antebellum West Pointers, including the ones who wrote the academy's history, found themselves at odds with Jackson's party and allied themselves with its Whig opponents. They had little reason to exalt the political symbols of Jacksonian Democrats, the most prominent of which was Thomas Jefferson.

Democrats appropriated Jefferson despite the fact that the party of Jackson was hardly the party of Jefferson. Jefferson—and James Madison also—disliked the hero of the Battle of New Orleans. After an 1824 visit to Monticello, Daniel Webster reported that Jefferson said that he felt "much alarmed at the prospect of seeing General Jackson, president." Jackson had "very little respect for laws or constitutions," Jefferson told Webster, and he impulsively sacrificed means to ends. All things considered, Jackson was "a *dangerous man.*"[10] Nonetheless, according to historian Merrill D. Peterson, "to Jacksonian Democrats, and to their conservative antagonists in the Federalist tradition as well, Jefferson and Jackson explained each other, one the originator, the other the executor of democracy, both sainted or satanical according to preference. . . . So tight," Peterson writes, "was the association of these three elements—the Jefferson symbol, democracy, and the Democratic Party—that one scarcely existed in the public mind apart from the others and attempts to disengage them met with fleeting success."[11]

Thayer's dispute with Jackson must be understood in this context. When, in 1833, New York Cadet H. Ariel Norris planted in the middle of the parade ground a "hickory pole," he took a stand not only for Jackson—widely known as "Old Hickory"—but also for Jefferson and the Revolutionary tradition, which had used liberty poles to protest the British imperial regime. As West Point faculty member Ethan Allen Hitchcock later remembered, "Norris had acquired his political tendencies and habits among the lower class of the people in the city of New York." He also had taken a stand against Thayer, whose disciplinary system had been described as oppressive by Cadet Andrew Jackson Donelson, the nephew of Jackson and close friend of classmate (and future grandson-in-law of Jefferson) Nicholas P. Trist, who, like him, in 1818 entered West Point shortly after Thayer's installation as superintendent.

Thayer understood the impropriety of the existence of this symbol of partisanship and insubordination—and physical obstacle—on the parade ground. He ordered the removal of the hickory pole as well as the removal of Norris. Norris appealed the decision, so Thayer sent Hitchcock to Washington to explain the situation. Hitchcock met with Jackson to state his case, but almost immediately, according to Hitchcock, Jackson "became excited, and spoke of the 'tyranny' of Colonel Thayer and, rising from his chair, he stalked before me, swinging his arms as if in a rage and speaking of the case of Norris. . . . 'Why,' said he, 'the autocrat of the Russias couldn't exercise more power!'" Hitchcock stood his ground. Jackson dismissed him and sent for a general. The general later reported to Hitchcock that Jackson had ordered two other generals to conduct an examination of the system of discipline at West Point. Their report recommended no changes and, for three or four months, all was quiet. But then another instance arose where Jackson interfered with Thayer—Norris's case had not been the first. Thayer, indignant, resigned as superintendent in 1833.[12]

The principled departure of Thayer helped to solidify his reputation as a hero of the academy. It also helped to galvanize some army officers in their opposition to Jacksonian Democrats.[13] A case in point is Dennis Hart Mahan, an 1824 graduate of the academy who in 1830 returned as engineering professor, a position he retained for forty years. Mahan exhibited deep admiration for Thayer and deep mistrust of Jacksonian democracy, in part because of Thayer's battle with Jackson and subsequent resignation. The episode so much distressed Mahan that as soon as Jackson left office, he proposed to restore Thayer as superintendent. The plan failed and Thayer never returned, but Mahan remained. He became one of the most influential faculty members in the history of the academy.[14]

Like Mahan, Winfield Scott became involved in Thayer's superintendency. As a major general he presided over the 1817 court martial that found Partridge guilty of disobedience and mutiny for refusing to vacate his West Point post; he also presided over the academy's 1831 Board of Visitors, which, among other measures, called on the government to give Thayer a raise. Although not an academy graduate, he became a consummate academy insider. He spent summers at West Point and, when he finally died in 1866, was buried there. His political leanings mirrored those of Mahan and many others connected with the army. He grew to despise Jackson, with whom he had a series of disputes, and by 1852, after triumphant leadership in the Mexican War and promotion to lieutenant general, became so advanced in his partisanship that he stood as the Whig presidential candidate. Early in life, Scott considered himself an ardent Republican; Jefferson, in fact, interviewed him and awarded his army commission. But then he developed a friendship with Federalist writer Washington Irving, an admiration for Hamilton (who he described as "eminently qualified to be considered great among the greatest of any age or country"), and a highly critical understanding of Jefferson. A friend who had heard Scott speak of Jefferson "a hundred times" maintained that Scott believed he harbored "contempt for the military character." The third president was not only "highly ambitious," Scott later wrote, but also highly resentful, for "in the presence of Washington" he recoiled from a "painful sense of inferiority." While Washington had donned a uniform in the fight for independence, Jefferson had not, a fact that Scott believed led him to oppose Revolutionary War veteran Hamilton's plans for national finance, resign his cabinet post, and embrace states' rights principles that yielded the "first fruits" of the secessionist, rebellious impulses that led to the Civil War.[15]

Robert E. Lee, the academy's eighth superintendent, did not share Scott's nationalism. But Lee, who was born a Federalist and matured as a Whig, did embrace Scott's politics. As a cadet, he borrowed from West Point's library a volume of Hamilton's correspondence no fewer than nine times. The main political constant for Lee he inherited from his family: a hatred of Jefferson.[16] The feud between Jefferson and the Lees dated all the way back to 1809, when his father, General Henry ("Light-Horse Harry") Lee, landed in debtor's prison as a result of business dealings gone bad. The elder Lee, who blamed his financial condition on Jefferson's embargo of foreign trade, spent much of his prison term putting together his *Memoirs of the War in the Southern Department of the United States,* which he published in 1812. The *Memoirs* made Jefferson's supposed "timidity and impotence" as Revolutionary War governor of Virginia a case study in the supposed need for energetic government by officials with coercive authority. Jefferson did not respond publicly to Henry Lee's assertions, but in private he derided the tract as "a tissue of errors from beginning to end," a "parody" based on "rumors," and a book so "ridiculous that it is almost ridiculous seriously to notice it."[17]

There the matter rested—and the feud persisted—until 1826, when a younger Henry Lee, who had inherited not only his father's name but also the rights to his book, prepared a revision of the *Memoirs.* He received an invitation by Jefferson to visit him at Monticello and examine documents relating to his performance as governor. Robert Lee's half brother accepted the offer, but when he arrived at Monticello in June he found Jefferson on his deathbed. "There he was extended," he remembered, "feeble, prostrate; but the fine and clear expression of his countenance not at all obscured. At the first glance he recognized me, and his hand and voice at once saluted me. The energy of his grasp, and the spirit of his conversation, were such as to make me hope he would yet rally—and that the superiority of mind over matter . . . would preserve him yet longer." Jefferson never recovered, however, and Lee never did see his papers.[18] But he departed with a changed heart. When he revised his father's *Memoirs,* he not only softened the most damning passages but also reprinted a letter that Jefferson had written to him. After British troops captured Richmond in 1781, Jefferson recounted, he rode his horse through the countryside in pursuit of new recruits for the militia. The weary animal collapsed beneath him, he said, so he walked with the saddle on his shoulders to a nearby farm, where he borrowed an unbroken colt and continued the journey.[19]

The détente between Jefferson and the Lees did not last for long. Three years after Jefferson's death, his grandson published a collection of his correspondence that reopened old wounds, for it included an 1815 letter to James Monroe that disparaged Light-Horse Harry Lee's *Memoirs* as "a historical novel for the amusement of credulous and uninquisitive readers." It also contained a 1796 note to Washington in which Jefferson described Lee as "an intriguer" and a "miserable tergiversator, who ought indeed to have been of more truth or less trusted by his country."[20] For Light-Horse Harry Lee's sons, including Robert, the recent West Point graduate, these were fighting words. The young men, according to Robert E. Lee biographer Douglas Southall Freeman, "became more confirmed in their opposition to the party of Jefferson," which by then meant the party of Jackson. Henry Lee published in 1832 another printed attack on Jefferson, and seven years later Charles Carter Lee enlarged their father's work, heaping onto Jefferson even more opprobrium. Not to be left out, in 1869 Robert E. Lee, who had otherwise renounced all things bellicose, reissued his father's *Memoirs*—a final shot in a family feud that had lasted for more than half a century.[21]

The Civil War gripped America not long after the conclusion of Lee's superintendency, and Lee was not the only officer to trade his army blues for the gray uniform of the Confederacy. West Point graduate and Confederate General P. G. T. Beauregard, who on April 12, 1861, ordered the shelling of Fort Sumter, had been relieved as the academy's superintendent only two and one-half months earlier. Wade Hampton Gibbes, an 1860 graduate, fired one of the first Confederate shots. Cadets from southern states that had already seceded had been trickling out of West Point for several months; now, however, the number of resignations appeared more like a flood. By May, only twenty-one of the eighty-six southern cadets remained. The rest would join a Confederate officer corps that eventually included 296 academy graduates, 151 of whom, like Thomas J. "Stonewall" Jackson, became the generals of Confederate president Jefferson Davis, yet another West Point alumnus.[22]

Meanwhile, for most of the Civil War, Alexander Hamilton Bowman served as superintendent, an unenviable position in no small part because of the heavy criticism directed at West Point. Secretary of War Simon Cameron submitted to Congress a report that dwelled on the "extraordinary treachery" of academy graduates, a symptom, he suggested, of "a radical defect in the system of education itself." Other northern critics, including many of Congress's radical Republicans, also depicted West Point as a nursery of secessionism. In addition, they characterized the graduates who remained in the Union army as too southern in their views on slavery and emancipation, too theoretical in their tactics, and too timid in their efforts to engage the enemy. "Their caution," wrote one critic, "is educated until it is hardly distinguishable from cowardice." When, in December 1861, Michigan senator Zachariah Chandler called for the closing of the academy, several of his colleagues concurred.[23]

Bowman faced a crisis. West Point's enemies aimed at its destruction, many of his faculty (most in Union blue) had marched south, and—thanks not only to resignations but also to Secretary Cameron's decision to graduate and commission the first two classes—the Corps of Cadets stood depleted.[24] Given this context, it is not surprising that Jefferson's reputation as founder of the military academy continued to slip from public memory. Alexander Hamilton Bowman made no effort to promote his institution through a closer association with his namesake's nemesis. Like the academy, Jefferson had also been described as too southern, too theoretical, and too timid. These criticisms, which originated during his own lifetime (and Henry Lee was not the first to levy them), still reverberated during the Civil War years, when Jefferson's reputation plummeted.

Although the embattled reputations of both West Point and Jefferson during the Civil War combined to discourage the resurrection of Jefferson's image as West Point's founder, the 1902 centennial celebration of its founding provided a clear opportunity to recognize the third president. Yet the academy snubbed Jefferson on its birthday. The massive two-volume *Centennial of the United States Military Academy at West Point,* a collection of speeches, banquet toasts, and histories marking the occasion, mentions his name only twice. In an essay on the academy's origins, Edward S. Holden, the West Point librarian, called attention to Secretary of State Jefferson's doubts, in 1793, about the constitutionality of a national military school. He did not, however, point toward Jefferson's support for the academy in 1802; instead, he wrote that "by the act of Congress . . . the Military Academy was instituted." He gave Jefferson only a single positive nod, and that came in the middle of a long list of benefactors: "Knox, Hamilton, Adams, Jefferson, Monroe, McHenry, Steuben, Huntington, Pickering, Duportail, and other patriots of the Revolution were the authors of the various systems of military education for the new country. . . . In this group two names stand preeminent—Knox and Hamilton."

During the Revolution, Holden pointed out, Henry Knox "was the first proposer and the steady advocate of a military school of the very type of our own. To Hamilton the Academy and the Army owe a well-considered plan for military education that, in its main features, has sufficed for the needs of the century just passed." Holden's tepid recognition excepted, all celebrants of the centennial seem to have ignored Jefferson's support for the early military academy. Many continued to fix their attention on later years, heralding Thayer as the academy's father, and some, such as the author of the brief history of the academy that soon began to appear in *Bugle Notes,* an annually issued collection of information, trivial and otherwise, for cadets' memorization, concurred with Holden's unequivocal assertion that "Its founder is Washington." No one thought to mention that Washington, in 1802, was dead.[25]

Jefferson's banishment from the West Point pantheon one hundred years after the academy's birth cannot be written off solely as conformity to what, by that time, was fairly well-established tradition. The centennial fixed the date of the founding with precision. Jefferson was president in 1802, and the bill supporting the establishment of the academy came not from Congress but from him. As Henry Dearborn, Jefferson's secretary of war, in 1801 wrote to General James Wilkinson, "the President has decided on the immediate establishment of a military school at West Point."[26] In all likelihood, historians of the academy ignored Jefferson in 1902 for two other reasons. The first was a body of scholarship on diplomacy that attacked Jefferson's defense policies; the second was the fact that the chief proponents of this neo-Hamiltonian assessment were influential men with powerful West Point connections.

As in the Civil War, nearly all of Jefferson's detractors considered themselves members of the Republican Party; unlike the Civil War, when a good number of West Pointers allied themselves with Democrats, in 1902 the "big stick" policy of President Theodore Roosevelt won admiration, if not active political participation, from the majority of army officers.[27] Perhaps the most prominent neo-Hamiltonian was Roosevelt himself, a former army officer, veteran of the Spanish-American War, and prolific author. Others included his secretary of war, Elihu Root, and Alfred Thayer Mahan, son of popular West Point Professor Dennis Hart Mahan. Each, echoing the contentions of previous generations, directed sharp criticisms toward Jefferson.[28]

While Roosevelt praised "Hamilton's wonderful genius," he portrayed Jefferson as a conniving, impractical, and self-deluding ideologue. The third president was "unscrupulous," a "pacificist" who established a "tradition of timid avoidance of all physical danger." "I have always regarded Jefferson," Roosevelt affirmed in 1915, as "one of the most mischievous enemies of democracy, one of the very weakest we have ever had in public life." Jefferson's prepresidential policy pronouncements would have been "so wholly absurd in practice," Roosevelt wrote, "that it was out of the question to apply them at all to the actual running of the government. Jefferson could write or speak—and could feel too—the most high-sounding sentiments; but once it came to actions he was absolutely at sea." After his inauguration, Roosevelt maintained, Jefferson "had to fall back on . . . Federalist theories. Almost the only important point on which he allowed himself free scope was that of the national defenses." His foolishness on this matter, according to Roosevelt, "worked very serious harm to the country." The twenty-sixth president blamed Jefferson for the War of 1812: "Ever since the Federalist party had gone out of power in 1800, the nation's ability to maintain order at home and enforce respect abroad had steadily dwindled; and twelve years of Doctrinaire Democracy had left us impotent for attack and almost as feeble for defense." Jefferson, he wrote, "was perhaps the most incapable Executive that ever filled the presidential chair; being almost purely a visionary, he was utterly unable to grapple with the slightest actual danger."[29]

The worst of Jefferson's defense measures, Roosevelt thought, was his plan for "an enormous force of very worthless gun-boats—a scheme," he wrote, "whose wisdom was about on a par with some of that statesman's political and military theories." Roosevelt's blast at Jefferson's proudest naval project—based on the assumption that an American oceangoing navy, which could never match the strength of Britain's, would draw the nation into an unwinnable naval war and should be replaced by small, agile, and economical defensive craft piloted by citizen-sailors—was echoed by that other prominent neo-Hamiltonian, Alfred Thayer Mahan.[30] Mahan's important book on *The Influence of Sea Power upon History* argued for a large, formidable navy of large, formidable ships.[31] To correspondents, Mahan expressed his disdain for Jefferson and his "seductive cheap gunboat policy," which ensured "a minimum of military usefulness at a maximum of pecuniary outlay," as well as for the politicians who, he thought, adhered to the Jeffersonian tradition. "The Democrats still have both feet in the tomb of Jefferson," he informed his sister in 1894. "The future of the country," he confided, "rests with the Republicans."[32]

Despite the efforts of neo-Hamiltonian detractors, Jefferson's reputation among West Pointers and citizens in general improved during the next fifty years, thanks in no small part to the efforts of Franklin Roosevelt. Although his cousin and presidential predecessor helped to lead the neo-Hamiltonians, the younger Roosevelt cast himself as a neo-Jeffersonian. In the early decades of the century, Americans had resurrected Jefferson because of their newfound awareness of him as a family man, educator, westward expansionist, and everyman's favorite political theorist. Then, in the midst of the Great Depression and World War II, Roosevelt sculpted Jefferson's image as a political experimenter and advocate of liberty. In 1943 he dedicated the Jefferson Memorial, complete with sanitized, New Dealish Jefferson quotations inscribed on walls that encircled an incongruous statuary caricature that resulted from the merger of the body made famous by Sully's full-length West Point portrait with a head inspired by another portrait by Rembrandt Peale.[33]

Even before Roosevelt's campaign to renovate Jefferson's image, however, West Point fashioned a humble monument to his memory. His name joined those of a handful of notables inscribed onto the stone walls of the 1910 administration and headquarters building. According to a pamphlet published shortly after the building's completion, Jefferson deserved recognition as the president "during whose administration . . . the Military Academy was founded." Thayer, described as "Father of the Military Academy," and James Monroe, "under whose administration the Military Academy developed and was encouraged," were similarly honored. (Washington received special treatment, for his personal coat of arms appeared high on the courtyard's east wall—directly across from the seal of the United States.) The academy's new headquarters, together with its new barracks, chapel, gymnasium, and equestrian facilities, constituted a major $5.5 million construction project authorized in 1902 and completed a decade later. Aspects of the initiative generated considerable controversy and sometimes pitted Superintendent Albert L. Mills against the permanent faculty members who constituted the Academic Board. Although both Mills and his sometimes rancorous professors solicited goodwill from the Theodore Roosevelt administration, Jefferson's inclusion within the headquarters pantheon demonstrated that the willful disregard for his contributions seen at the centennial did not endure.[34]

So did the naming in Jefferson's honor of the avenue that linked the library with the superintendent's quarters, noted on maps of the academy beginning in the early 1930s, as well as the East Academic Building's 1937 rededication as Jefferson Hall. The honor was short-lived, for a year later academy officials voted to revert to the building's former name, because, they claimed, the new designation "proved very confusing," could "lead to controversy and dissention," and seemed out of step with the generally established practice of naming edifices not for men but for their functions. (Later the academy again renamed the structure, this time in memory of William Bartlett, a long-serving science professor.) During this decade streets were named also after Washington and Thayer, and a few years earlier workmen completed Washington Hall, the building containing the cadet mess, and the Hotel Thayer. Both men retained their more exalted status (and their eponymous buildings), but Jefferson—especially during the Franklin Roosevelt era—at least made inroads.[35]

Thus, by the time of the academy's 150th birthday, Jefferson had regained some of his stature, not only among Americans generally but also within the army. The 1950 announcement of upcoming sesquicentennial exercises by the superintendent, Major General Bryant E. Moore, noted that "Thomas Jefferson, following the advice of George Washington, John Adams, Alexander Hamilton, and others, established a national military academy on the Hudson River at West Point." Two years later, Moore's successor, Major General Frederick A. Irving, remarked at the sesquicentennial convocation that "Jefferson signed the act of Congress which established this institution," because he joined with Hamilton, Knox, and Adams in "realizing the need for a trained source of officers, a corps which would form the nucleus about which a civilian army could be built." As part of its birthday celebration, the academy published an official account marking the occasion. The first chapter, a brief synopsis of West Point's history, began by quoting Jefferson's Military Peace Establishment Act and mentioning that he "signed this legislation on March 16, 1802."[36]

Although the recognition accorded to Jefferson marked a departure from centennial speakers' willful ignorance of his role, its tepid nature still left room for qualification. The official sesquicentennial history, for example, took care to mention that "the Military Academy did not spring into existence with a stroke of the pen. The Act of 1802 simply granted formal recognition to an institution that had been slowly evolving since the first American garrison occupied West Point during the Revolutionary War." Jefferson's advocacy constituted only "the final step" before Thayer's "first step," which was "to reorganize the Corps of Cadets."[37] But did not Jefferson also reorganize West Point? Did he not, in fact, create the academy? Did he, as Moore suggested, base his support for the academy on the recommendations of Federalists—whose ideas he considered subversive to the principles of the American Revolution? Or did he have his own vision for the academy? He signed Congress's bill, as Irving pointed out, but also he pushed for it, as Irving neglected to mention. In all of these accounts, West Pointers pressed Jefferson into the humble and virtually thankless role of successor. Contrary to chronology, they lavished the role of the academy's originator and progenitor on Thayer.

The relatively newfound ability of West Point officials to enunciate Jefferson's name failed not only to alter the basic tenor of public commemorations of the academy's birth but also the substance. The major events of the sesquicentennial included the installation in the Cadet Library of a portrait of Confederate General Robert E. Lee—Jefferson's old adversary—and on March 16 the laying of wreaths by delegations of cadets at the graves of Thayer and Washington, who, despite the fact that he died more than two years before Jefferson established the institution, still received credit as "one of the founders of the Military Academy." The cadet contingent at Mount Vernon had no corollary at Monticello.[38]

Jefferson received less recognition from actual cadets than he did from actors who played ones in Warner Brothers' *The West Point Story*, a 1950 film featuring James Cagney, Virginia Mayo, Doris Day, and Gordon MacRea, who appeared as Cadet Tom Fletcher, a talented singer starring in the academy's annual "100th Night" variety show. Although not an official component of the sesquicentennial celebration, the film focused on the school's origins when, in the opening number of the fictionalized cadet production, Fletcher took the stage and stood before a chorus of classmates. "In the beginning as in all things it was only a dream," he said, "but the dreamers had names: like Washington, Hamilton, Jefferson. They stood on a point of land on the west bank of the Hudson and planned that this fortress that guarded our newborn nation, should become our military academy." In Hollywood's version of history, however, Washington also trumped Jefferson. "The corps was founded," Fletcher continued, "and the father of our country became the father of a legend."[39]

Despite these snubs, the highlight of the sesquicentennial—the May 20 address by President Harry S. Truman—gave to Jefferson more attention than he had received at West Point since the 1820s. Although Truman reiterated the familiar refrain that "twenty years of argument and persuasion" predicated the academy, he chose to focus on the third president. "Listen to this," he commanded. "It was finally started largely because Jefferson took the position that if Congress didn't authorize a military academy, he would set one up himself." When Jefferson "was trying to start it," Truman maintained, some objected because they feared that a strong military would make the nation warlike; others, he said, thought that the academy would prove too expensive. But "these arguments did not prevail against the hardheaded common sense of men like Jefferson."[40]

Truman's avowal of Jefferson's pragmatism and practicality contrasted sharply with the views of the first President Roosevelt, who had officiated at a similar ceremony fifty years earlier. So did nearly concurrent statements by Dwight Eisenhower, Truman's triumphant European-theater World War II commander and Republican successor, who said that he admired Jefferson, because "he understood and feared the implications of the shift we have seen in recent years from local government to Federal government, from freedom to regimentation, from decentralization to centralization." On this crucial point, he confided to a friend, he could not agree more, for "if Federal authority should be extended throughout the country . . . it would eventually stifle the individual freedom that our government was designed to protect and preserve." Douglas MacArthur, Truman's triumphant Pacific-theater World War II commander and fired Korean War point man, struck a similar tone. He informed the Michigan legislature that Democrats had forgotten Jefferson's dictum "that the least government is easily the best government." Several weeks later, during the sesquicentennial year, he asked the Republican National Convention how it could be "that the party of Jefferson and Jackson, which once contributed so magnificently to the building of the Republic, would now sponsor and support" a departure "from our great traditions?"[41]

Although partisan, MacArthur's professed yearning for coalescence around a common set of political beliefs reflected the fleeting spirit of nonpartisanship ascribed to his generation of military officers. It also mirrored, in an only partially distorted manner, the supposed nonpartisanship that animated the so-called "Era of Good Feelings," when Federalists claimed to convert to Republicanism in the years following the War of 1812. This epoch of supposed consensus did not witness an end to political debate, but it did make possible conciliatory gestures. In 1821, for example, many of the same individuals who later that year would ask Jefferson to pose for Sully orchestrated a 200-mile road march by the Corps of Cadets to Boston, where it camped on the Common and then ventured to Bunker Hill, Harvard, and the Quincy, Massachusetts, home of former president John Adams.

According to Josiah Quincy, "the noble corps, numbering more than two hundred students," who by then "were known to be subjected to an intellectual discipline which was quite as severe as their physical drill," paraded seven miles to see the old revolutionary. Quincy's sister, an eyewitness to the event, recorded in her diary that Adams "seemed as much delighted as any one" during the visit. He "beat time to the music" struck up by the West Point band, shook the hand of every cadet, and delivered an address in which he exhorted his young audience to uphold wisdom, benevolence, temperance, and justice, and to avail themselves of "the great Advantages you possess for attaining eminence in Letters and Science as well as Arms." Yet, by far the most important lesson for the cadets, Adams contended, could be learned from the examples of Washington and his "immortal Captains," for their "Glory" came not from conquest but from prudence, restraint, and deference to civilian authority.[42]

Civilian leaders continued to praise Jefferson in the decades after World War II. President John F. Kennedy, for example, described his predecessor as his "hero," one of the "most exceptional men of the 18th century," and one of "our nation's . . . first great scholars." He said at a banquet honoring Nobel Prize winners from North and South America that "this is the most extraordinary collection of talent, of human knowledge, that has ever been gathered together at the White House, with the possible exception of when Thomas Jefferson dined alone." Robert F. Kennedy spotlighted the third president as a man who welcomed the free "exchange of views" between individuals, nations, and cultures.[43]

While Democrats extolled Jefferson as an intellectual, Republicans embraced his ideology. Like Eisenhower and MacArthur before him, Barry Goldwater, the 1964 Republican presidential candidate, claimed Jefferson's mantle. He charged that the Democratic Party was "no longer the party of Jefferson," for it no longer subscribed to "principle and principled liberalism." Instead, he asserted, it stood for "political conformity, social sameness, and regimented rules." That the Arizona senator described Jefferson as his favorite president and named F. A. Hayek, the Nobel Prize–winning free market economist, as his favorite political philosopher, is not surprising. Under his leadership the Cold War Republican Party renewed its commitment, through both foreign and domestic policy, to oppose big government and defend individual freedom. Jefferson, who Franklin Roosevelt had enlisted as a symbol of democracy and egalitarianism to combat Nazis and Republicans, now helped Republicans battle Communists and Democrats. Even Democrat Jimmy Carter admitted that Jeffersonian principles, which included the insistence that people "stop looking to the federal government as a bottomless cornucopia," no longer remained "popular . . . with some members of my party."[44]

Ronald Reagan, who said in his famous campaign speech for Goldwater that Democratic leaders were "taking the party of Jefferson . . . down the road under the banners of Marx, Lenin, and Stalin," in 1987 proclaimed from the steps of the Jefferson Memorial the Republican faith that "economic freedoms" and the political freedoms advocated by Jefferson were "inextricably linked." The fortieth president, who made the same memorial a focus of his inaugural and farewell addresses and quoted the third president in support of everything from deficit reduction and defense spending to prayer in schools, selected the University of Virginia as the setting for his final foreign policy address, a cautious valedictory that stopped short of heralding the end of the "Evil Empire" but predicted that Jefferson's influence, which extended to "every human life ever touched by the daring idea of self-government," was sure to grow.[45]

The Republicanization of Jefferson's image—the emphasis on his support for limited government at home and the expansion of liberty abroad—resonated well within a Cold War context. It also fit perfectly the central themes of the Reagan administration, during which the bulk of the current officer corps came of age and began to undermine the old ideal of an apolitical military. Although during the 1970s more than half of up-and-coming officers described their politics as independent of any specific party, by the late 1990s, only 28 percent made such a claim. Even more striking, those who identified themselves as Republicans constituted 64 percent, a figure eight times larger than the number who called themselves Democrats.[46]

While this phenomenon bodes ill for an all-volunteer military struggling to avoid estrangement from the public it defends (as Jefferson told Washington, "a distinction . . . between the civil and military" classes is best "for the happiness of both to obliterate"), it probably constitutes good news for Jefferson's reputation within the army, which for much of its existence, was led by men who identified the third president with a party that many of them opposed. It also suggests that occasions such as the 2001 Senate confirmation hearing of retired General Colin Powell, Republican president George W. Bush's nominee for secretary of state, may well become more common. Powell, who during the Persian Gulf War commanded all of America's armed forces, described Jefferson as "ahead of the time in which he lived" and himself "as Jefferson's admiring successor" in prepared remarks in which he mentioned Jefferson's name nine times in the first thirteen sentences.[47]

While political developments altered the environment within which military leaders considered Jefferson, so did advances in scholarship. The professionalization of American historians—who now oftentimes possessed advanced degrees and cited and engaged critically their sources—worked to Jefferson's advantage. Since the 1950s, a number of studies, which gave close consideration to Jefferson's role in the creation of the academy, began to push past the old question of whether he played a part in West Point's founding to examine why, as he wrote, he considered it "of major importance."[48]

Their authors' efforts would not be easy, for not only did they have to sift through a dizzying array of documents in which Jefferson's intimations of intent remained frustratingly coy, but also because the climate of opinion at West Point, despite a few breaks in the clouds, continued to chill serious consideration of the academy's Jeffersonian origins. The periodically revised brief history of the academy that appears each year in *Bugle Notes,* the handbook issued to new cadets, contended between 1936 and 1943, for example, that the 1802 law establishing the academy "had no immediate effect." The version that appeared in the mid-1940s contended that "the founder of the Military Academy was George Washington," and between 1949 and 1957 the handbook continued to ignore Jefferson but informed cadets that through the 1802 act "Congress formally established the United States Military Academy."[49]

Against this backdrop, a number of historians began to offer interpretations of Jefferson's reasons for starting the school, however. While some, such as Sidney Forman, Reginald Stuart, and George Pappas, claimed that Jefferson followed the lead of Knox, Hamilton, and Washington and conceived of West Point as a seminary devoted to the art of war, others, such as Stephen Ambrose and Thomas Fleming, argued that Jefferson viewed it as a substitute for his proposed national university, an institution that, had Congress not balked at its creation, would have emphasized science. Still others, such as

Richard Kohn and James Rainey, acknowledged the possibility that Jefferson acted for a variety of reasons.[50]

Perhaps the most influential explanation of Jefferson's intent appeared in the work of Theodore Crackel, who as an army officer served two tours of duty on West Point's history department faculty and then returned as a visiting professor during the bicentennial academic year. Crackel's 1987 *Mr. Jefferson's Army,* which evolved from his doctoral dissertation, constituted the first full treatment of Jefferson's reform of the American military establishment. Building on studies by historians such as Bernard Bailyn, Gordon Wood, Lance Banning, and Drew McCoy—all of whom detected in Jefferson and other members of the Revolutionary generation a "republican" ideology that spurned concentrations of power in the hands of kings, aristocrats, and corrupt office holders as well as the standing armies of professional soldiers, estranged from the populace by experience and economic interest, that they employed—Crackel argued that Jefferson saw a national military school as a mechanism through which the United States Army would "come to reflect the republican society from which it was drawn, and an army whose loyalty to republican principles would be assured."

Since Jefferson saw little distinction between the republicanism of 1776 and the Republicanism that triumphed in the election of 1800, he viewed his hard-line Federalist opponents as apostates of the Revolutionary tradition; that so many of his enemies wore the uniforms of army officers was cause for alarm. Not surprisingly, Crackel contended, Jefferson's 1802 Military Peace Establishment Act not only allowed him to purge the officer corps of the politically suspect but also to use "his new military school" to "train men from the Republican stock of the country for positions of leadership in the new army." As a result, he intended for the academy "to break the upper-class monopoly of education" and clear the way for a military elite characterized not by "the aristocracy of wealth and birth" but by a more natural "aristocracy of virtue and talent."[51]

Crackel's work had an immediate and enduring effect on West Point's sense of self. Although *Bugle Notes,* beginning in 1958, mentioned without explanation that "Jefferson signed" the 1802 law establishing the academy, thirty years later—just months after the publication of *Mr. Jefferson's Army*—a sentence inserted into the *Bugle Notes* history began to inform cadets that "only when Thomas Jefferson became president was it possible to balance the desires for a military academy" expressed by Washington with those of others who wished "to democratize the officer corps." The *Strategic Vision for the United States Military Academy,* issued in 2000 by the superintendent's office, illustrated a brief account of the institution's origins with portraits of Washington and Jefferson and maintained that the third president "envisioned a national military academy as a means to democratize American military leadership and to ensure that it would be more representative of American society." While these official interpretations of Jefferson's rationale played down the partisanship noted by Crackel, their debt to his work was no less clear than the fact the academy's founder, two hundred years after the academy's founding, had been restored to a position of prominence.[52]

The Corps of Cadets' 2001 Acceptance Day parade, which on August 18 marked the formal entrance of the class of 2005 into West Point's "Long Gray Line" of current, former, and future army officers, constituted the official commencement of the academy's bicentennial celebration. For Jefferson's image as the institution's creator, it seemed a propitious moment. Cadet Seth Johnston, a junior from Virginia who narrated the parade for an audience of parents and other well-wishers, read a script prepared by West Point officials that credited Jefferson with establishing "a military academy that could have both military and civilian benefits and broaden the composition of America's military leadership by training and educating representatives from across society." Johnston then quoted Jefferson's Military Peace Establishment Act and noted Jefferson's signing of the law on March 16, 1802. Subsequent bicentennial events would also spotlight Jefferson, including the history department's November conference on "Thomas Jefferson's Military Academy"—during which early drafts of the essays in this volume were presented—and the performance, on April 14, in the Eisenhower Hall ballroom of a period instrument ensemble's interpretation of "Jefferson and Music." Scheduled for the day after the third president's 259th birthday, ticket holders enjoyed not only Handel and Vivaldi but also cake.

By no means, however, did Jefferson's surging prominence guarantee preeminence. Just in time for the bicentennial, the southeastern leg of Jefferson Road—repaved, replanted, and reconsecrated with monuments honoring West Point's honor code, contributions to technology, and fallen alumni—was renamed "Thayer Walk." And although the "Thomas Jefferson's Military Academy" conference, the bulk of which took place in Thayer Hall, focused on Jefferson's establishment of the institution, it also glanced back at calls for an academy during the Revolution and looked forward toward Thayer's superintendency—suggesting that the years between 1802 and 1817 amounted to an understudied, underappreciated period meriting affirmative historical action. Jefferson, confirmed in his rightful role, was no mere token, but the contributions of Washington and Thayer remained crucial benchmarks in West Point's history.

That is, perhaps, as Jefferson would have wished. Throughout the 1790s, one of the favorite rallying cries of the people who in 1800 elected him called on Americans to honor "principles and not men," but later Jefferson seemed to recognize the futility of such exhortations for an increasingly individualistic, democratic nation with a rapidly developing, rapidly expanding political marketplace. The people wanted heroes. If they could not be encouraged to rally around depersonalized ideals—around "principles and not men"—at least they might focus their attention on men of principle. He fell within this category, he thought, and during his retirement worked to ensure that posterity would view him as he viewed himself: fixated not on his own power but instead on the empowerment of others.[53]

Defined in such a way, such a hero would have a healthy influence on cadets at the United States Military Academy—all of whom, as officers, will be entrusted with formidable power themselves. Yet heroes too have power, and Jefferson, like Madison, believed in checks and balances to prevent its abuse. For his own heroes, he selected not one man—as did Hamilton, who Jefferson said lionized Julius Caesar—but a "trinity" consisting of Francis Bacon, Isaac Newton, and John Locke.[54] Will West Point, in its third century, enlarge its pantheon of heroes and make room for Jefferson to stand alongside Washington and Thayer?

Early indications suggest as much. *Assembly,* the magazine published bimonthly by West Point's Association of Graduates, featured in its first 2002 issue a lengthy report, entitled "Thomas Jefferson Returns," of the history department's November 2001 conference. In its next issue, Jefferson returned once more—this time as depicted by Sully in his 1822 portrait, which appeared on the cover. Then, in August, Brigadier General Daniel Kaufman, the academy's dean, announced to West Point faculty that Secretary of the Army Thomas White had approved a plan to designate the proposed new library—to be constructed on the edge of the parade ground between the buildings named for Washington and Thayer—Thomas Jefferson Hall.[55]

What can be predicted with certainty is that West Point's view of its past will reflect the changing present. New people will appropriate Jefferson to support or oppose new issues; the third president's stock will rise and fall at the academy as his popularity fluctuates among the army officer corps and the public it defends. The question will continue to be what always it has been: not whether Jefferson made West Point, but what West Point makes of Jefferson.

Notes

1. Oliver E. Wood, *The West Point Scrap Book: A Collection of Stories, Songs, and Legends of the United States Military Academy* (New York, 1871), 37–38; Robert P. Hay, "The Glorious Departure of the American Patriarchs: Contemporary Reactions to the Deaths of Jefferson and Adams," *Journal of Southern History* 35 (November 1969): 545. Beyond West Point, on 23 October 1826 the adjutant general honored the third president by renaming as the "Jefferson Barracks" Cantonment (John Quincy) Adams, a post near St. Louis. See Henry W. Webb, "The Story of Jefferson Barracks," *New Mexico Historical Review* 21 (July 1946): 190.

2. For the texts, see TJ, Declaration of Independence, (11 June–4 July 1776,) *TJP* 1:417–32; TJ, A Bill for Establishing Religious Freedom, (1777–16 January 1786,) *TJW,* 346–48; TJ, *Notes on the State of Virginia,* ed. William Peden (1787; Chapel Hill, N.C., 1954).

3. For the fullest account of Jefferson's life, see Malone.

4. TJ to Jared Mansfield, 13 February 1821, TJ Papers, Lib. Cong.

5. For the best histories of West Point during the Revolutionary era, see Theodore J. Crackel, *West Point: A Bicentennial History* (Lawrence, Kans., 2002), 5–43; Edgar Denton, III, "The Formative Years of the United States Military Academy, 1775–1833" (Ph.D. diss., Syracuse University, 1964), 1–26. On the contributions of Tousard, see Norman B. Wilkinson, "The Forgotten 'Founder' of West Point," *Military Affairs* 24 (Winter 1960–61): 177–88.

6. Noble E. Cunningham, *The Process of Government under Jefferson* (Princeton, N.J., 1978), 124; Sidney Forman, *West Point: A History of the United States Military Academy* (New York, 1950), 17–19; *The Centennial of the United States Military Academy at West Point, New York: 1802–1902,* 2 vols. (Washington, D.C., 1904), 1:222.

7. Denton, "The Formative Years of the United States Military Academy," 57–59.

8. Jared Mansfield to TJ, 26 January 1821, Jared Mansfield Papers, USMA Lib.; Francis Casimir Kajencki, *Thaddeus Kościuszko: Military Engineer of the American Revolution* (El Paso, Tex., 1998), 67–77, 81–120, 207, 292n18. Jefferson also wears the coat in his 1805 portrait by Rembrandt Peale.

9. So argues Lester A. Webb, *Captain Alden Partridge and the United States Military Academy, 1806–1833* (Northport, Ala., 1965).

10. Daniel Webster, "Notes of Mr. Jefferson's Conversation *1824* at *Monticello,*" (1825), in Charles M. Wiltse and Harold D. Moser, eds., *The Papers of Daniel Webster: Correspondence,* 7 vols. (Hanover, N.H., 1974–86), 1:375–76.

11. Merrill D. Peterson, *The Jefferson Image in the American Mind* (New York, 1960), 20–22, 67–111, 69 (quotation).

12. Ethan Allen Hitchcock, *Fifty Years in Camp and Field,* ed. W. A. Croffut (New York, 1909), 64–67; Andrew Jackson Donelson to Andrew Jackson, 29 November 1818, in Harold D. Moser, et al., eds., *The Papers of Andrew Jackson,* 5 vols. to date (Knoxville, Tenn., 1980–), 4:253–54.

13. On the tension between army officers and Jacksonian politicians, see Samuel P. Huntington, *The Soldier and the State: The Theory and Politics of Civil Military Relations* (Cambridge, Mass., 1957), 204–5, 207, 210–11, 224.

14. Thomas Everett Griess, "Dennis Hart Mahan: West Point Professor and Advocate of Military Professionalism" (Ph.D. diss., Duke University, 1969), 90, 135, 137, 149–51, 156–57, 344–45.

15. Webb, *Captain Alden Partridge and the United States Military Academy,* 133, 186; Winfield Scott, *Memoirs of Lieut.-General Scott, LL.D.,* 2 vols. (New York, 1864), 13, 15, 25, 181–82, 196–203, 260, 264, 273–74; Charles Winslow Elliott, *Winfield Scott: The Soldier and the Man* (New York, 1937), 663, 757, 760–63; Erasmus D. Keyes, *Fifty Years' Observations of Men and Events, Civil and Military* (New York, 1884), 100–102.

16. Douglas Southall Freeman, *R. E. Lee: A Biography,* 4 vols. (New York, 1934–35), 1:117, 72–73, 115; Emory Thomas, *Robert E. Lee: A Biography* (New York, 1995), 79.

17. Henry Lee, *Memoirs of the War in the Southern Department of the United States,* 2 vols. (Philadelphia, 1812), 2:5–15; TJ, Diary of Arnold's Invasion and Notes on Subsequent Events in 1781, (26 July 1816), *TJP* 4:264–65.

18. TJ to Henry Lee IV, 15 May 1826, in Henry Lee, *Memoirs of the War in the Southern Department of the United States* (2nd ed., Washington, D.C., 1827), 207 (the letter is conveniently reprinted in Ford, 10:386–90n); (Henry Lee IV), "Last Scenes *of Mr. Jefferson's Life, &c.,*" *Richmond Examiner,* 27 October 1826.

19. Lee, *Memoirs of the War in the Southern Department of the United States,* 190, 204–8; TJ to Henry Lee IV, 15 May 1826, ibid., 204–5. See also Malone, 6:219–20; Charles Royster, "A Battle of Memoirs: Light-Horse Harry Lee and Thomas Jefferson," *Virginia Cavalcade* 31 (1981): 121–27.

20. TJ to James Monroe, 1 January 1815, in Thomas Jefferson Randolph, ed., *Memoirs, Correspondence, and Private Papers of Thomas Jefferson, Late President of the United States,* 4 vols. (London, 1829), 4:246; TJ to George Washington, 19 June 1796, *TJP* 29:127–28.

21. Freeman, *R. E. Lee,* 1:117, 4:415–19; Henry Lee (IV), *Observations on the Writings of Thomas Jefferson, with Particular Reference to the Attack They Contain on the Memory of the Late General Henry Lee* (New York, 1832); ibid., ed. Charles Carter Lee (2nd ed., Philadelphia, 1839); Henry Lee, *Memoirs of the War in the Southern Department of the United States,* ed. Robert E. Lee (New York, 1869).

22. Stephen A. Ambrose, *Duty, Honor, Country: A History of West Point* (Baltimore, 1966), 167, 170, 172, 180.

23. Harry Williams, "The Attack upon West Point during the Civil War," *Mississippi Valley Historical Review* 25 (March 1939): 491–504, 493, 499 (quotations).

24. Ambrose, *Duty, Honor, Country,* 176–77.

25. *Centennial of the United States Military Academy at West Point, New York,* 1:212, 222; *Bugle Notes,* 97 vols. to date (West Point, N.Y., 1907–), 2:14–15.

26. Sidney Forman, *West Point: A History of the United States Military Academy* (New York, 1950), 18 (quotation).

27. Huntington, *The Soldier and the State,* 259, 270–88.

28. Peterson, *The Jefferson Image in the American Mind,* 333–47.

29. Theodore Roosevelt to William Edward Dodd, 13 February 1912, in Elting E. Morison, ed., *The Letters of Theodore Roosevelt,* 8 vols. (Cambridge, Mass., 1951–54), 7:501; T. Roosevelt to Edward Grey, 22 January 1915, ibid., 8:879; T. Roosevelt to James Bryce, 30 November 1915, ibid., 8:994; T. Roosevelt to Albert Bushnell Hart, 1 June 1915, ibid., 7:927; T. Roosevelt, *Gouverneur Morris* (Boston, 1889), 167, 334–35; T. Roosevelt, *The Naval War of 1812, or the History of the United States Navy During the Last War with Great Britain,* 3rd. edition (New York, 1882), 455.

30. Ibid., 445. For modern analyses of Jefferson's gunboat proposals, see Gene A. Smith, *For the Purposes of Defense: The Politics of the Jeffersonian Gunboat Program* (Newark, Del., 1995) and Spencer Tucker, *The Jeffersonian Gunboat Navy* (Columbia, S.C., 1993).

31. A. T. Mahan, *The Influence of Sea Power upon History, 1660–1783* (Boston, 1890).

32. Alfred Thayer Mahan to the editor of the *New York Sun,* 9 May 1904, in Robert Seager II and Doris D. Maguire, eds., *Letters and Papers of Alfred Thayer Mahan,* 3 vols. (Annapolis, Md., 1975), 3:94; A. T. Mahan to Ellen Evans Mahan, 11 January 1894, ibid., 2:205; A. T. Mahan to E. E. Mahan, 13 November 1894, ibid., 2:361.

33. Peterson, *The Jefferson Image in the American Mind,* 377–79, 423–32.

34. *The Shields, Inscriptions, and Statuettes: Administration Building, United States Military Academy, West Point, N.Y.* (West Point, N.Y., 1911), [2]; Crackel, *West Point,* 169–79.

35. "Main Part of the General Plan of the United States Military Reservation, West Point, New York; Prepared under the Direction of Lt. Col. C. D. Hartman, Q.M.C., Quartermaster" (n.p., [ca. 1933]), Archives and Special Collections, USMA Lib.; "Map No. 3: Outline Map of West Point, N.Y., Showing Main Buildings, Officers Quarters, and Fire Boxes and Fire Districts, [1933]," Buildings and Grounds folders, Archives and Special Collections, USMA Lib.; Headquarters, United States Military Academy, West Point, N.Y., *Weekly Bulletin* 8 (4 October 1937); Memorandum of the Academic Board to the Superintendent, 28 June 1938, in Post Buildings (1920–50) folder, Archives and Special Collections, USMA Lib.; Headquarters, United States Military Academy, West Point, N.Y., *Weekly Bulletin* 8 (18 July 1938).

36. *The Sesquicentennial of the United States Military Academy: An Account of the Observance, January–June, 1952* (West Point, N.Y., 1952), 19, 78, 11.

37. Ibid., 11, 13.

38. Ibid., 38–41, 52.

39. *The West Point Story,* produced by Louis F. Edelman (1950; Burbank, Ca., 1993).

40. *The Sesquicentennial of the United States Military Academy,* 85.

41. Dwight D. Eisenhower to George Arthur Sloan, 29 October 1952, in Alfred D. Chandler Jr., et al., eds., *The Papers of Dwight David Eisenhower,* 21 vols. to date (Baltimore, 1970–), 12:1404; Eisenhower to Everett Edward Hazlett Jr., 20 July 1954, ibid., 14:1198; Douglas MacArthur, Speech to Michigan Legislature, 15 May 1952, in Edward T. Imparato, ed., *General MacArthur: Speeches and Reports, 1908–1964* (Paducah, Ky., 2000), 206; MacArthur, Speech to Republican National Convention, 7 July 1952, ibid., 212.

42. Josiah Quincy, *Figures of the Past from the Leaves of Old Journals* (Boston, 1883), 88–93; John Adams, Address to West Point Cadets, (14) August 1821, USMA Archives.

43. John F. Kennedy, Remarks of Welcome to President Nkrumah of Ghana at the Washington National Airport, 8 March 1961, in Warren R. Reid, ed., *Public Papers of the Presidents of the United States: John F. Kennedy: Containing the Public Messages, Speeches, and Statements of the President: 1961* (Washington, D.C., 1962), 160; Kennedy, Remarks before the National Academy of Sciences, 25 April 1961, ibid., 319; Kennedy, Address at the University of North Carolina upon Receiving an Honorary Degree, 12 October 1961, ibid., 666; Kennedy, Remarks at a Dinner Honoring Nobel Prize Winners of the Western Hemisphere, 29 April 1962, in ibid.: *1962,* 347; Robert F. Kennedy, Speech at the University of Stellenbosch, South Africa, 7 June 1966, in Edwin O. Guthman and C. Richard Allen, eds., *RFK: Collected Speeches* (New York, 1993), 249.

44. Rick Perlstein, *Before the Storm: Barry Goldwater and the Unmaking of the American Consensus* (New York, 2001), 267 (quotation); Lee Edwards, *Goldwater: The Man Who Made a Revolution* (Washington, D.C., 1995), 281; Jimmy Carter, *Keeping Faith: Memoirs of a President* (New York, 1982), 21.

45. Ronald Reagan, Televised Nationwide Address on Behalf of Senator Barry Goldwater, 27 October 1964, *Speaking My Mind: Selected Speeches* (New York, 1989), 33; James Gerstenzang, "Calls 'Economic Freedoms' Proposals 'Shopworn'; Byrd Assails Reagan's Tax Curb Plan," *Los Angeles Times,* 4 July 1987, section 1, page 2; Reagan, Inaugural Address: West Front of the U.S. Capitol, 20 January 1981, *Speaking My Mind,* 65; Reagan, Farewell Address to the Nation: Oval Office, 11 January 1989, ibid., 410; Kiron K. Skinner, et al., eds., *Reagan, in His Own Hand: The Writings of Ronald Reagan that Reveal His Revolutionary Vision for America* (New York, 2001), 9, 14, 232, 359; *Reagan's Final Foreign Policy Address at U.Va.,* videorecording of 16 December 1988 C-SPAN broadcast (Lafayette, Ind., 1999).

46. Peter D. Feaver and Richard H. Kohn, eds., *Soldiers and Civilians: The Civil-Military Gap and American National Security* (Cambridge, Mass., 2001). See also Steven Lee Myers, "When the Military (Ret.) Marches to Its Own Drummer," *New York Times,* 1 October 2000, section 4, page 4.

47. TJ to George Washington, 16 April 1784, *TJP* 7:106–7; Colin L. Powell, "Statement of Secretary of State-Designate Colin L. Powell Prepared for the Confirmation Hearing of the U.S. Senate Committee on Foreign Relations Scheduled for 10:30 a.m., January 17, 2001," available on-line at <http://www.senate.gov/~foreign/testimony/wt_powell_011701.txt>.

48. TJ to Mansfield, 13 February 1821, Jefferson Papers, Lib. Cong. The professionalization of the American historical profession—which began late in the nineteenth century but seems not to have influenced historians of the academy until decades later—is ably surveyed in Peter Novick, *That Noble Dream: The "Objectivity Question" and the American Historical Profession* (New York, 1988).

49. *Bugle Notes* 28 (1936): 13; ibid., 36 (1944): 22; ibid., 41 (1949): 26.

50. Forman, *West Point,* 19; Reginald C. Stuart, *The Half-way Pacifist: Thomas Jefferson's View of War* (Toronto, 1978), 36; George S. Pappas, *To the Point: The United States Military Academy, 1802–1902* (Westport, Conn., 1993); Ambrose, *Duty, Honor, Country,* 18, 19, 21–23; Thomas J. Fleming, *West Point: The Men and Times of the United States Military Academy* (New York, 1969), 16; Richard H. Kohn, *Eagle and Sword: The Federalists and the Creation of the Military Establishment in America, 1783–1802* (New York, 1975), 302–3; James W. Rainey, "Establishing the United States Military Academy: Motives and Objectives of Thomas Jefferson," *Assembly* 59 (May/June 2001): 42–44, 57.

51. Theodore J. Crackel, *Mr. Jefferson's Army: Political and Social Reform of the Military Establishment, 1801–1809* (New York, 1987), 53, 73 (quotations). For an historiographical survey of this ideological interpretation of early America, see Daniel T. Rodgers, "Republicanism: The Career of a Concept," *Journal of American History* 79 (1992): 11–38.

52. *Bugle Notes* 49: 20; ibid., 80: 127; *Strategic Vision for the United States Military Academy—2010* (West Point, N.Y., 2000), 1. Crackel reiterated his interpretation of Jefferson's reasons for establishing the Academy in his *Illustrated History of West Point* (New York, 1991), 71–74, an interpretation retained in the revised, enlarged, annotated, and republished *West Point,* 46–51.

53. Simon P. Newman, "Principles or Men? George Washington and the Political Culture of National Leadership, 1776–1801," *JER* 12 (Winter 1992): 477–507; Robert M. S. McDonald, "Thomas Jefferson and Historical Self-Construction: The Earth Belongs to the Living?" *The Historian* 62 (Winter 1999): 289–310.

54. TJ to Benjamin Rush, 16 January 1811, *TJW,* 1236.

55. "Thomas Jefferson Returns: Bicentennial Conference Remembers USMA's Forgotten Founder," *Assembly* (January/February 2002): 45–47; ibid. (March/April 2002).

AFTERWORD

The Role of Military Virtues in Preserving Our Republican Institutions

JEAN M. YARBROUGH

IN THE BEST OF ALL WORLDS, JEFFERSON ONCE WROTE, AMERICANS would have nothing to do with other nations. If they would just stick to farming and mind their own business, Americans could reap the blessings of liberty and peace. But even as he penned these words, Jefferson recognized that they were nothing more than a dream. Already, Americans of his day had developed "a decided taste for navigation & commerce" that brought them into contact with the wider world. Realistically, he knew this meant that wars would "sometimes"—and maybe even frequently—"be our lot; and all the wise can do, will be to avoid that half of them which would be produced by our own follies, and our own acts of injustice; and to make for the other half the best preparations we can." He clearly foresaw the dangers. American property would be violated on the seas and in foreign ports; her citizens insulted, attacked, and imprisoned. These assaults would have to be met, and met forcibly, because Americans were a "high-spirited" lot, and because not to resist would invite more attacks on American honor. America must develop the capacity to punish those who attack her citizens, because "weakness provokes insult and injury, while a condition to punish it often prevents it."[1]

Strong words these. How did Jefferson propose to back them up? Even before the Revolutionary War had ended, Jefferson warned that "the sea is the field on which we should meet an European enemy."[2] Accordingly, he supported the establishment of a naval force sufficiently powerful to protect

America's coasts and harbors and to repel attacks on her ships at sea. Such attacks were not long in coming. After independence, Great Britain had no desire to protect American ships in the Mediterranean, and they fell prey to attacks by the Barbary pirates. Writing from Paris to John Adams in London, Jefferson recommended decisive action. In contrast to the policy pursued by the European nations, who preferred to pay tribute to these corsairs, Jefferson argued that Americans should obtain peace not by buying it, but through war. In the long run, war would not only be cheaper—republican governments made a virtue of frugality—but, successfully prosecuted, the willingness to fight would also serve the cause of justice and honor.

Fifteen years later, a newly elected President Jefferson would have the opportunity to match his words to his deeds. When these same Barbary powers declared war on the United States in 1801 and demanded tribute in exchange for not attacking American ships, Jefferson stunned the European diplomatic world by sending in the navy and the marines. Cobbling together a "ragtag" army of local insurgents led by ten United States marines, American forces prevailed—as the opening verses of the Marine Corps hymn recollect. By all (save the most partisan) accounts, the peace agreement "established more favorable conditions for the United States than any other nation had ever achieved" up to that point.[3]

Still, as president, Jefferson's overall record on naval power was mixed. Although he was willing to deploy force against what he clearly regarded as a barbaric enemy, he resisted building up the navy to the point where it could repel a more serious threat from the European powers. To do so would sink the country in a sea of debt and taxes. His republican concern with frugality led him—disastrously—to downsize the navy during his presidency, even as he continued to promote international trade. In pursuing so contradictory a policy, he left American citizens and ships vulnerable to foreign attacks and imperiled the very honor and justice that he sought to defend.

Jefferson's ambivalence regarding naval power was nothing compared to his deep and abiding distrust of a standing army. Part of his opposition lay in the conduct of British troops in the years leading up to the Revolution. But even after the Red Coats had been vanquished, Jefferson, faithful to classic Whig doctrine, warned that standing armies were a danger to republican liberty and a nursery for despotism. In Europe, where nobles could buy military commissions, army officers were too closely tied to the aristocracy, and Jefferson feared (wrongly, it turned out) that the well-born army officers who fought for independence might also be tempted to betray the Revolution.[4] He saw conspiracies everywhere. In the "Anas," Jefferson accused two army officers, Friedrich Wilhelm von Steuben and Henry Knox, whom he described as "trained to monarchy by military habits," of encouraging George Washington to assume the crown before the army disbanded. He viewed their proposal to establish the Society of the Cincinnati as a dangerous successor to this scheme and warned that its real purpose was to overthrow republican government at the first opportunity.[5]

Jefferson's distrust of a standing army and its officer corps was greatly exacerbated during the 1790s by Alexander Hamilton's willingness to use the military to suppress what Jefferson regarded as healthy republican dissent. Not only had Hamilton spoken out forcefully in favor of a greatly strengthened national government to put down domestic insurrections in the wake of Shays's Rebellion, but also he helped to put together the overwhelming force used to subdue Pennsylvania farmers in the Whiskey Rebellion of 1794. Worse yet, Hamilton had actually contemplated using the army against Jefferson's Virginia if she proved "refractory" in opposing the Quasi-War against France. Jefferson, by contrast, not only approved of these acts of resistance to government, but also regarded them as marks of civic-spiritedness and sought to encourage more of them. From his perspective, the danger of using the army to "overawe the public sentiment" was real.[6] No wonder he insisted that, until an actual invasion, it was best to rely solely on a militia for internal defense.

Nevertheless, as tensions mounted with France in the late 1790s, and especially after the outbreak of the Quasi-War in 1798, there was a good case to be made for increasing the size of the army and the navy, as well as for establishing a national military academy to train American officers in the arts of war. This was not the first time such a proposal had surfaced. In the early days of the Washington administration, Federalist members of the cabinet, led by Knox, the secretary of war, and backed by Hamilton, the secretary of the treasury, called for the establishment of a national military academy. At that time, Jefferson opposed it, taking shelter behind an impossibly narrow reading of the Constitution. Later, as relations with France deteriorated after the XYZ affair, Hamilton fought to increase the size of the army for possible action in seizing Florida and Louisiana and once again called for the establishment of a national military academy. By contrast, Jefferson remained sympathetic to France and denounced Hamilton's efforts to bolster America's fighting forces as part of a grand and ominous design to reverse the course of republicanism at home and abroad. For Jefferson, the fate of the American republic was inextricably bound up with the French Revolution. To oppose the one was to betray the other.

While Jefferson must be faulted for his judgment regarding the French Revolution, he was hardly alone in fearing that a strengthened military presence loyal to Hamilton was a danger to republican America. Even within his own party, Hamilton was feared and distrusted. John Adams, who was a very different sort of Federalist, worried that Hamilton might turn out to be an "American Bonaparte." Thus, Adams could breathe a sigh of relief when his administration successfully negotiated an end to the Quasi-War with France. Like Jefferson, Adams had a visceral fear of standing armies and was only too glad to thwart Hamilton's military ambitions by defusing political tensions and carrying through on the troop reductions called for by the peace treaty. Hamilton's proposal for a military academy again went nowhere, caught between the sensible recognition that America would need to develop and train a corps of engineers and artillerists and the fearful realization that it was precisely the officer class that had betrayed the original principles of the French Revolution.[7] After the bitterly contested election of 1800, a victorious President Jefferson could breathe another sigh of relief, for he feared (again wrongly) that an army led by Federalist officers might well turn against him in the first election ever to transfer power peacefully from one party to another.[8] Not for nothing in the first inaugural did he slip in a line about "the supremacy of the civil over the military authority."[9]

Thus, it comes as some surprise that only a year after taking office, Jefferson overcame his earlier constitutional scruples and, with the backing of the first Republican majority in Congress, signed into law a bill establishing the national military academy on the grounds of the old garrison at West Point, in Hamilton's New York. And indeed, most Jefferson scholars and military historians have, albeit for different reasons, scarcely mentioned Jefferson's role in establishing West Point.[10] Yet, despite his full-throated fears of the military and its officer corps during the 1790s, Jefferson was not simply the "accidental founder." For in signing the legislation that established West Point, Jefferson intended to republicanize the military and attach it to the preservation of its political institutions. This was no small achievement, especially at a time when Americans were only first establishing the principle that political change could be accomplished by elections, and without resort to the battlefield. Indeed, in what may well be the ultimate irony, West Point may more faithfully embody Jefferson's republican commitment to a natural aristocracy of talent and civic virtue than some of America's premier educational institutions.

How did Jefferson do it? First, the political situation was ripe. With the Federalists driven from the presidency and Congress, and perhaps fatally weakened, Jefferson was reasonably confident that he could control the character and mission of the future academy. For the first time, Republicans would set the agenda for the fledgling academy. Second, the intellectual climate supported it. America had benefited from the assistance of foreign officers, like Friedrich Wilhelm von Steuben, the Marquis de Lafayette, and Thaddeus Kościuszko, who had been trained in the new military academies that were springing up across Europe. As the foremost representative of the American Enlightenment, Jefferson recognized that America could not afford to fall behind in these new military and engineering sciences. He viewed the establishment of a national military academy as one way to promote the spread of scientific knowledge in America. Third, the international situation was propitious. The lull in foreign affairs, combined with the reductions already taking place in the standing army Hamilton had assembled to fight France in America, ensured that the military academy would not assume too prominent a place in society. Fourth, and closely related, the so-called peace dividend allowed him to force the retirement of those senior Federalist officers whom he most distrusted.[11] Whatever Jefferson may have meant when he declared in his first inaugural that "We are all Republicans, we are all Federalists," he most assuredly did *not* mean that officers loyal to Hamilton (and, in his view, secretly favoring aristocracy and monarchy) should remain at the head of the armed forces.[12]

The establishment of West Point solved the problem of from where this new corps of army officers might come. In much the same way that Jefferson would later establish the University of Virginia to weed out "political heresy" and keep alive "the vestal flame" of republicanism, he now saw the advantages of a national military academy that would take promising young men from solid republican homes and modest backgrounds and train them to become the next generation of officers for the army and the militia. Indeed, Jefferson may have viewed the establishment of West Point as an alternative to the dreaded standing army. These professionally trained and politically reliable officers could infuse the republican militias with the discipline and skills necessary to turn them into a formidable fighting force.[13]

Established on March 16, 1802, in the shadow of peace, the mission of the academy took on new urgency with reports the following month that Spain had secretly arranged to cede Louisiana and the Floridas to France (the very contingency Hamilton had feared when he urged a buildup of the regular army during the Quasi-War). Despite his Francophila, it took Jefferson in much the same way. Writing to Robert R. Livingston, the American minister to France, Jefferson warned that the secret treaty "compleatly reverses all the political relations" of the United States. By assuming control over New Orleans, France had, in one move, gone from being America's *"natural friend"* to its "natural and habitual enemy." In language that would rival Hamilton's, Jefferson warned: "The impetuosity of her temper, the energy and restlessness of her character, placed in a point of eternal friction with us, and our character, which though quiet, and loving peace and the pursuit of wealth, is high-minded, despising wealth in competition with insult or injury, enterprising and energetic as any nation on earth, these circumstances render it impossible that France and the United States can continue long friends when they meet in so irritable a position." It was clear what American policy must now be. On the day France takes possession of New Orleans, "we must marry ourselves to the British fleet and nation."[14]

In the *Prince,* Machiavelli writes about the various ways in which leaders can acquire power. Using his categories, it can be said that what Hamilton was prepared to secure by Americans' own arms and virtue, Jefferson was granted by fortune. Napoleon's troops got bogged down in Haiti trying to suppress a slave rebellion and were decimated. With war once again looming in Europe, the French leader offered, quite unexpectedly, to sell not only New Orleans but also the entire Louisiana Territory. Jefferson, despite his constitutional scruples, had the good sense to leap at the opportunity to purchase peace at a few pennies an acre. Though not one of Machiavelli's lions, Jefferson was certainly one of his foxes.

The easing of political tensions between France and the United States after the Louisiana Purchase permitted the Republicans a few more years of peace within which to pursue what Jefferson had described as "a chaste reformation" of the army and its officer corps.[15] Plans to reduce the size of the army could once again be resumed, and West Point could continue the business of training a new corps of republican officers in engineering and artillery. More particularly, Jefferson wished to use the corps for two purposes: first, to survey and fortify seaboard towns and harbors, and second, to map out and explore the West. With the doubling of American territory almost overnight, Jefferson was eager to continue the kind of scientific exploration he had begun with Lewis and Clark. During Jefferson's lifetime, many of America's most distinguished explorers would be graduates of West Point: Auguste Chouteau (class of 1806), Benjamin L. E. Bonneville (class of 1815), George W. Whistler (class of 1819), and William H. Swift (class of 1819). Jared Mansfield, professor of natural philosophy, was appointed surveyor general of the Northwest Territory. Although these expeditions were loosely linked to the national defense, they tended to emphasize the scientific, rather than the military, side of the academy's mission, which suited both Jefferson and the man he appointed superintendent.

Jefferson's choice to lead the academy was Jonathon Williams, a relative of Benjamin Franklin's, and a Federalist. Williams had no military experience, which may be why he was acceptable to congressional Republicans, at least for a time. Like his illustrious forebear, Williams seems to have had certain scientific and philosophic ambitions. In 1802 he established the United States Military Philosophical Society at West Point to disseminate the latest in military science to cadets and interested civilians. Under his leadership, the society flourished, holding meetings at West Point and in other locations. By 1807 its members included some of the most distinguished men in America.

At West Point, however, the society had less of an impact, because the cadets were generally not in a position to benefit from such knowledge. Many arrived at the academy with only a rudimentary understanding of science and mathematics, and instruction in these subjects during Jefferson's administration never went beyond the basics. Moreover, owing to a debilitating combination of congressional frugality and neglect, faculty and resources were minimal for most of Jefferson's presidency. As a result, West Point in the Jefferson years produced very few officers, and most were neither great scientists nor soldiers. But how could they be, Superintendent Williams complained, when the elite Corps of Engineers, consisting of a grand total of sixteen men, was expected both to build seacoast fortifications *and* to "constitute a military academy"?[16] And when Williams himself was seldom there?

Adding to the confusion, graduates of the academy were not required to serve in the regular army, thereby limiting the "chaste reformation" of that institution. True to his republican principles, Jefferson thought these newly commissioned officers could go back to their militia units and direct their training; if war came, they could lead these citizen-soldiers in battle. This, he hoped, would lead to a greater uniformity among the militia units and produce a "spirit of emulation" among the troops. As late as 1806, Jefferson was still confident that the militia could provide for the national defense.

None of this worked out quite as Jefferson had hoped. When war finally did break out in 1812, the academy had graduated only seventy-one cadets, nowhere near the number of officers needed for a wartime army (and far fewer than Jefferson had authorized), and none rose to a high rank.[17] Still, this was nothing compared to the dismal performance of the militias, most of them, of necessity, under civilian command. As Jefferson was finally forced to admit, these citizen-soldiers were far too happy on their farms and resisted long deployments far from them. Only after this stinging defeat did Jefferson belatedly come to appreciate the role West Point could play in training a republican officer corps to lead regular troops in defending American justice and honor.

This account of West Point's founding, rooted in the controversies between Federalists and Republicans over standing armies and militias, science and soldiering, has much to do with the mission of the academy today. The legacies of that struggle remain very much alive; reflecting on them may help citizens to appreciate more fully the place of the military virtues within their broader civilian and republican culture. Consider the academy's strikingly Jeffersonian statement of its historic purpose, taken from the brochure outlining its strategic vision for 2010. According to the Office of Policy, Planning, and Analysis, the purposes of the academy are first "to provide the Army with officer-leaders of character," and second "to serve as one of the important links between the officer corps and society." Taken together, they seek to minimize the inevitable tensions between the civilian and military cultures—though these tensions raise different problems at different times.

Two hundred years ago, Jefferson worried about recruiting an officer corps exclusively from the ranks of the well born and well bred. He feared that these men, inflamed by aristocratic notions of honor and sympathetic to monarchy, might be tempted to betray the democratic republic to advance their own ambitions. He tried to force them out of the regular army and to replace them with those natural *aristoi* whose loyalty and honor he could count on.

Today, the problem is almost the reverse: the great danger to the preservation of the America's republican institutions comes not from its military academies, which are far more representative of the United States and far more likely to embrace its virtues, but from the fashionable anti-Americanism that thrives in the rarefied atmosphere of America's elite colleges and universities. Yet this is where the sons and daughters of the nation's political and cultural ruling class wish to be educated. It is the rare eighteen-year-old from America's so-called aristocracy who considers applying to the service academies. As Gore Vidal, who was himself born in the cadet hospital at West Point, observes, "In this century our nobles have not encouraged their sons to go to West Point."[18] Of course, the service academies suffer no shortage of talent; they are filled with Jefferson's natural aristocrats, along with the children of former graduates and military officers.

But the "trust fund babies" and children of America's civilian elites are elsewhere. Citizens of the Republic don't have to force their most privileged sons and daughters out of the officer corps, for these young people wouldn't be caught dead in it. These students—also idealistic and eager to serve their country—enroll in law schools and public policy programs. They seek careers in Washington, where they can "make a difference." Just as they did not consider the service academies when they were looking at colleges, they do not consider military service after graduation. The world of America's elite colleges and universities and the world of its military academies run along parallel tracks, destined never to meet.

It is only because the present Bush administration has drawn so many of its top officials from the ranks of the forgotten 1950s generation that this problem has temporarily been overcome. Recall, however, the Clinton administration, where neither the president nor his secretary of defense (a Bowdoin graduate who dropped out of ROTC—the Reserve Officers' Training Corps), nor his secretary of state, had ever served in the military. As former Secretary of the Navy James Webb has noted, "the greatest lingering effect of the Vietnam era on our society is that, by default, it brought a new notion: that military service during time of war is not a prerequisite for moral authority or even respect." This is dangerous, because it erects too solid a wall between America's military and civilian cultures and makes the virtues of each seem foreign to the other. On the first day of the Iraq War, a poll of Harvard students revealed that fewer than 22 percent would have "ever consider[ed] volunteering to serve" in the effort to oust Saddam Hussein. Meanwhile, exactly 100 percent of West Point cadets had already volunteered to serve wherever their commander in chief directed. Even more of the brightest young men and women need to think about military service and officer training. As things stand now, it is the children of the most privileged who are largely AWOL.[19]

Of course, to achieve this kind of cultural cross-fertilization between the civilian and military worlds, Americans will need to think about more than just the role of West Point and the service academies. Not everyone is cut out to live the life of a combat officer. This is especially true in the kind of commercial republic the framers established. America is neither Sparta nor Rome. But it would be a good thing for both the military and the broader civilian society if more of the nation's young people had at least some minimal experience of the demands and rigors of military life, and some firsthand appreciation of its distinctive virtues.

One way to achieve this is to join in the growing chorus of voices calling for the return of ROTC to America's elite campuses, from which they were ingloriously evicted during the tumultuous Vietnam years. Indeed, at the beginning of the 1990s, these institutions would not even permit military recruiters on campus, arguing that the Clinton administration's policy of "don't ask, don't tell" violated their moral commitment not to discriminate against anyone on the basis of sexual preference. Interested students had to meet with recruiters at designated off-campus sites. Beginning in 1994, Congress began to fight back, informing these institutions that they must either permit recruiters on campus or risk losing their federal funds. But these institutions have done so only grudgingly, and have made sure that students understand that they in no way approve of these visits. This is the climate in which the current debate over ROTC is taking place. At the moment, among the Ivies, only Cornell has ROTC units of all three service branches on campus. Princeton offers only Army ROTC; Penn, Navy ROTC; Harvard and Yale, along with Columbia and Brown, offer programs with exercises conducted at other institutions, imposing considerable burdens on the students enrolled in these programs. The so-called conservative Ivy, Dartmouth, offers an Army ROTC program, off-campus and an hour away. If anything, the situation is even worse at the top liberal arts colleges, where there are not only no ROTC programs, but there are not even debates about whether to bring them back.

What the presence of ROTC programs on college and university campuses did was to help bridge the gap between the military and civilian worlds, much as Jefferson thought the militia might do. (In fact, here too, ROTC seems another reversal of what Jefferson intended. Rather than West Point graduates returning to lead their militia units, civilian-educated officers serve limited tours of duty in the active army.) Of course, there are the inevitable tensions between the graduates of the academies and the officers coming out of the

ROTC programs, between the combat professionals and those fulfilling their short-term military obligations, but on the whole, this kind of leavening is good for the officer corps—and good for the country. Some of this cross-fertilization is still going on, of course, but without the participation of political and cultural elites. Before the "embedding" of reporters with coalition forces during the Iraq War, it was nearly impossible to imagine respected journalists or media personalities under the age of sixty having had sustained contact with the armed forces. Reporters had little understanding of and sympathy for the military and its virtues.

Yet, even if the present war on terrorism puts an end to the debilitating "Vietnam syndrome" that has gripped America's educated classes and opinion makers since the 1970s, the United States will never overcome completely the tension between the civilian and military cultures. Here again, the situation seems to be the reverse of the problem Jefferson faced. He worried about a military culture that did not reflect the values and virtues of the larger republican society. Of course, there are critics of the military who believe that this is still the problem. A more plausible view, however, is that the United States military has been pushed too hard—often by politicians with no military experience—to reflect the values of the broader civilian culture. As one critic observes, whenever people talk about the need to close the gap between the civilian and military cultures, what they mean is that the military must give way.

In one sense this is right and proper, for military authority is constitutionally subordinate to civilian authority. But in another sense, it is wrong and dangerous, because it imperils the distinct mission of the armed forces. "The military cannot and should not try to mirror exactly the principles of democratic society," I have written elsewhere. "The military is not a 'civic instrument' that reflects social progress. Nor is it a social welfare agency. The relationship between the military and civilian spheres is more complicated. Although the military defends the principles of democratic society, it cannot fully embody them." Its end is victory, not liberty; its virtues are courage, loyalty, and obedience, not justice and tolerance; its structure is hierarchical, not pluralistic and open-ended. "In short," as I have noted, "although the military defends democratic principles and is [inevitably] shaped by the regime of which it is a part, it is not, and should not try to be a microcosm of the larger society."[20] And if this is true when the civilian culture is strong and healthy, it is even more so when the larger culture has grown soft and corrupt. To try to bring the military into closer alignment with such a culture is especially corrosive, because it undermines the distinctive virtues of military life while exposing it to all the vices of civilian life. Specifically, the more West Point seeks to emulate the ethos of these institutions, the more it will wind up with the same problems: cheating, drugs, sex scandals, and the like.

At the most theoretical level, this requires a recognition that the service academies and leading colleges and universities will nurture and develop different parts of the human soul. West Point will speak to the spirited part of the soul—the part that is roused by anger and righteous indignation to fight for the higher principles to which America is dedicated. It will elevate honor and subordinate self-interest, even the interest in self-preservation. What spiritedness seeks to preserve is not the life of the individual soldier, but a way of life; in accepting their duty, soldiers reach back to the sacrifices of warriors gone before: "The Long Gray Line." Spiritedness operates in the grand tragic-heroic mode.

In theory, America's liberal arts colleges and universities seek to encourage the love of knowledge, wisdom, and beauty for their own sakes. At their best, they seek to awaken the deepest longings of the soul, though in practice these days they usually succeed only in stimulating the desires of the body. When genuine liberal learning takes place, it calls forth a certain playfulness that is more closely akin to comedy. Often, however, it operates at the level of farce.

At a more practical level, this means that the kind of education West Point cadets receive should differ from that of America's leading liberal arts colleges and universities. To be sure, there is a place for the humanities and fine arts at West Point—but these subjects should be taught in such a way as to reinforce the kind of heroic character and military virtues the academy wishes to promote. It must strive to reinforce a *shared* understanding of duty, honor, and country among its students, and to bind the present corps of cadets back to the principles and ideals of previous generations. To be sure, civilian and military instructors should also encourage a spirit of critical inquiry, but the last thing West Point needs is to become infected with the kind of relativism and soft nihilism that plagues elite colleges and universities in the United States.

The heart of the West Point education must focus on those subjects that bear most directly on its central mission, which is to prepare its officers for leadership. From the beginning, this has meant an emphasis on math and science, on the one hand, and the combat arts on the other. Within the military world, a great battle rages over what should be the proper mix in identifying and promoting the next generation of officers. On the one side are those who argue that technological competence, academic performance, and managerial skills are the most reliable indicators of who will make the best leaders. They assume that future wars will be fought with high-tech weapons and that traditional combat skills will play a smaller role. Not surprisingly, this side tends to get a more respectful hearing in times of peace. On the other side are those who argue that it is often the mediocre student, or going back further in history, the untutored aristocrat, who turns out to be the warrior who shapes the course of history. As Victor Davis Hanson notes, "Stonewall" Jackson and William Tecumsah Sherman were two such American generals. Both were graduates of West Point. Lord Salisbury wryly observes that after England abolished the sale of military commissions and replaced it with a system of competitive examinations, neither Marlborough nor Wellington would have made the grade. Lord Wellington, who clearly was no neutral, thought it was a choice between the clerks and the warriors. Gilbert and Sullivan also take a shot at British military reforms in their patter song, "The Modern Major General."

The tension between the scientific and the warrior spirit goes back to the days of Jefferson. However it is resolved, West Point can never be just another college. Its mission, in the words of Douglas MacArthur, "remains fixed, determined, inviolable—it is to win our wars." So, in addition to the regular complement of academic courses, cadets must also learn about "rifle marksmanship, road marches, tactical training and other military skills." Says one recent administrator, "West Point is not going to school to be a physics major; it's learning to drive a tank." Inevitably, this education produces a different kind of character, albeit one which is vital to the preservation of America's republican way of life.

Perhaps no one has written more perceptively on these differences than Patrick C. Hoy, an academy graduate who has taught English at both West Point and Harvard. While teaching at West Point, he frequently lamented that the students had no time to think, to wrap their minds around a problem, and forge perhaps a more creative response. Students' lives at the academy are highly regimented, and there never seems to be time for the kind of "woolgathering" that seems to characterize the most highly creative minds outside its walls. Cadets learn early on to suppress individualism, to act and think in teams. What matter most are discipline and cooperation, not individual freedom. "A lone rifleman does not wage war and win." At Harvard, the students are quirkier, no doubt about it, and likely more brilliant in late night bull sessions. But then, they don't have to worry about early-morning reveille. The downside, observes Hoy, is that Harvard students never seem to get beyond their own thoughts and needs; what is missing is any notion of community, any sense of subordinating oneself to a common good. There duty, honor, and country are in short supply.[21]

Can anything be done to bring these two worlds together? It is understandable—and altogether in the Jeffersonian spirit—that we should try to resolve these tensions: To find the charmed third way between those like Hamilton, who would prepare the Republic for war, and Jefferson, who feared and distrusted military power. To discover the thread that will lead Americans out of the maze of civil-military relations. To produce warriors who are open to the call of truth and beauty. To identify officers who possess superior technological and managerial skills, but who are also brilliant leaders of troops. To foster the individualism of Harvard and the community of West Point. Yet these tensions are rooted not only in America's history, they are part of human nature. Some things shall *not* be overcome.

Dealing with matters of life and death, with honor, duty, and courage, military men and women may grasp this more instinctively than civilians do. In the coming months and years, graduates of Jefferson's military academy will continue to be called upon to protect their nation from a new and more deadly round of barbaric assaults. And in what may be the ultimate Jeffersonian irony, it may well be the military officers—along with their civilian counterparts—who lead Americans back to the republican virtues of patriotism, courage, and steadfastness. Because these are the virtues West Point has always sought to instill in its cadets, the days ahead, whatever the hardships, will be better days for them. And as Jefferson, too, came to understand, they will be better days for America because of them.

Notes

1. TJ to G. K. van Hogendorp, 13 October 1785, *TJP* 8:633; TJ, *Notes on the State of Virginia,* ed. William Peden (Chapel Hill, N.C., 1954), 175; TJ to John Jay, 23 August 1785, *TJP* 8:427.

2. TJ, *Notes on Virginia,* 175.

3. Robert M. S. McDonald, "Partisan Views of Jefferson's Pact for a Pacific Mediterranean," *The Consortium on Revolutionary Europe, 1750–1850: Selected Papers, 1996* 26 (1996): 168.

4. Stephen Ambrose, *Duty, Honor, Country: A History of West Point* (Baltimore, 1966), 1–3.

5. TJ, "Anas," 4 February 1818, *TJW*, 663–64.

6. TJ to Elbridge Gerry, 26 January 1799, *TJP* 30:646.

7. Ambrose, *Duty, Honor, Country*, chapter 1. Hamilton, furious at being deprived of the chance to go to war against France, supported Charles C. Pinckney in the upcoming election. His immoderation helped split the Federalist party and set it on the road to extinction. See the fine discussion in Karl-Friedrich Walling, *Republican Empire: Alexander Hamilton on War and Free Government* (Lawrence, Kans., 1999), chapter 10.

8. TJ to Nathaniel Niles, 22 March 1801, in Ford, 8:24.

9. TJ, First Inaugural Address, 4 March 1801, *TJW*, 495.

10. The Jeffersonians seem to be at a loss for how to explain Jefferson's action, and so say nothing, while the military historians generally attribute its founding to the stillborn proposals of Hamilton, Knox, and Washington a decade earlier.

11. Theodore J. Crackel, *Mr. Jefferson's Army: Political and Social Reform of the Military Establishment, 1801–1809* (New York, 1987), especially chapters 2 and 3.

12. TJ, First Inaugural Address, 4 March 1801, *TJW*, 493.

13. Ambrose attributes this argument to Hamilton, but it applies with equal, if not greater, force to Jefferson. See Ambrose, *Duty, Honor, Country*, 13.

14. TJ to Robert R. Livingston, 18 April 1802, *TJW*, 1105.

15. TJ to Nathaniel Macon, 14 May 1801, in L&B, 10:261.

16. Ambrose, *Duty, Honor, Country*, 22.

17. Ibid., 43.

18. Bill Kauffman, "The West Point Story," *The American Enterprise* (July–August 1999), 29.

19. James H. Webb Jr., "Military Leadership in a Changing Society," Naval War College Conference on Ethics, 16 November 1998, available at http://www.hq.navy.mil/n3n5/mlcs.htm; "Crimson Poll: Harvard Students, Nation Diverge," *Harvard Crimson*, 31 March 2003.

20. Jean Yarbrough, "The Feminist Mistake," *Policy Review* (Summer 1985): 48–52.

21. Patrick C. Hoy II, "Scholars and Soldiers," *Sewanee Review* 103 (Winter 1995): 60–76.

Contributors

Theodore J. Crackel is Professor and Editor in Chief of *The Papers of George Washington* at the University of Virginia. He was Visiting Professor of History at the United States Military Academy in 2001–2002. His books include *Mr. Jefferson's Army: Political and Social Reform of the Military Establishment, 1801–1809* (1987) and *West Point: A Bicentennial History* (2002).

Don Higginbotham, Dowd Professor of History at the University of North Carolina at Chapel Hill, is a former Visiting Professor at West Point. He is the author or editor of three books on George Washington, including *George Washington Reconsidered* (2001).

David N. Mayer is Professor of Law and History at Capital University in Columbus, Ohio, where he teaches courses in English and American legal and constitutional history, jurisprudence, and intellectual property law. He is the author of *The Constitutional Thought of Thomas Jefferson* (1994) and several articles in law reviews as well as history and political science journals.

Christine Coalwell McDonald, former Research Associate at Monticello's International Center for Jefferson Studies, is Chair of the Departments of History and Social Studies at the Storm King School in Cornwall-on-Hudson, New York.

Robert M. S. McDonald, Associate Professor of History at the United States Military Academy, has published several articles and essays and is working on a book to be titled *Confounding Father: Thomas Jefferson and the Politics of Personality.*

PETER S. ONUF is the Thomas Jefferson Foundation Professor of History at the University of Virginia. His most recent publications include *Jefferson's Empire: The Language of American Nationhood* (2000) and (with Leonard Sadosky) *Jeffersonian America* (2001).

ELIZABETH D. SAMET, Associate Professor of English at the United States Military Academy, is working on a book about the poetries of war. She is the author of *Willing Obedience: Citizens, Soldiers, and the Progress of Consent in America, 1776–1898* (2004).

JENNINGS L. WAGONER JR., Professor of the History of Education at the Curry School of Education, University of Virginia, is past President of the History of Education Society and author of *Jefferson and Education* (2004) and (with Wayne Urban) *American Education: A History* (3rd edition, 2004) as well as numerous articles and essays.

SAMUEL J. WATSON is an Assistant Professor of History at the United States Military Academy. His books on Winfield Scott and the Army officer corps in the borderlands of the early republic will be published in 2005.

JEAN M. YARBROUGH is Gary M. Pendy Sr. Professor of Social Sciences and Professor of Government at Bowdoin College. She is the author of *American Virtues: Thomas Jefferson on the Character of a Free People* (1998) as well as numerous articles and essays.

Index

Jeffersonian America

Jan Ellen Lewis and Peter S. Onuf, editors
Sally Hemings and Thomas Jefferson: History, Memory, and Civic Culture

Peter S. Onuf
Jefferson's Empire: The Language of American Nationhood

Catherine Allgor
Parlor Politics: In Which the Ladies of Washington Help Build a City and a Government

Jeffrey L. Pasley
"The Tyranny of Printers": Newspaper Politics in the Early American Republic

Herbert E. Sloan
Principle and Interest: Thomas Jefferson and the Problem of Debt (reprint)

James Horn, Jan Ellen Lewis, and Peter S. Onuf, editors
The Revolution of 1800: Democracy, Race, and the New Republic

Phillip Hamilton
The Making and Unmaking of a Revolutionary Family: The Tuckers of Virginia, 1752–1830

Robert M. S. McDonald, editor
Thomas Jefferson's Military Academy: Founding West Point